THE
AMERICAN
CENSUS

MARGO J.
ANDERSON

The
American
Census:
A
Social
History

YALE UNIVERSITY PRESS
NEW HAVEN AND LONDON

Published with assistance from the Louis Stern Memorial Fund.

Designed by Nancy Ovedovitz and set in Baskerville type with Gill Sans by Keystone Typesetting Company, Orwigsburg, Pennsylvania. Printed in the United States of America by Braun-Brumfield, Inc., Ann Arbor, Michigan.

Library of Congress Cataloging-in-Publication Data

Anderson, Margo J., 1945–
  The American census: A social history.
  Bibliography: p.
  Includes index.
  1. United States—Census—History.   2. United States—Popula-
tion—History.   3. United States—Statistical services—History.
I. Title.
HA37.U55A53 1988   304.6'0973   87-29828
ISBN 0–300–04014–8 (cloth)
        0–300–04709–6 (pbk.)

The paper in this book meets the guidelines for permanence and durability of the Committee on Production Guidelines for Book Longevity of the Council of Library Resources.

10   9   8   7   6   5   4   3   2

To Steve

CONTENTS

ILLUSTRATIONS

ACKNOWLEDGMENTS

This census history grew out of my earlier work on the development of census occupational statistics and the origins of modern social science. Like other American social historians, I had used the decennial census to probe questions about the nature and growth of American society. As I did so, I recognized that the earlier generations of Americans who took the census had debated many of the same questions that interested me. They framed the census inquiries and organized the data that they published in ways that mirrored their notions of contemporary social problems. I also discovered that the census frequently became entangled in the larger political controversies of the nation—for example, in the sectional disputes of the 1840s and 1850s, several wars, Reconstruction, or the role of the new welfare state during the 1930s. The more I discovered, the more I recognized that a history of the development of the American population census is a crucial aspect in the study of the intellectual, political and social development of the nation. This book is the result.

Support from several institutions have permitted me to research and write the book. In 1980 I received a Summer Stipend and in 1982 a Fellowship for Independent Study and Research from the National Endowment for the Humanities to conduct much of the archival research. In 1983 I received a Graduate School Summer Award from the University of Wisconsin—Milwaukee. The Urban Research Center at UWM helped with word processing and xeroxing. UWM Photo Services prepared figures and photographs. In 1985–86, I was Flora Stone Mather Visiting Professor in the History Department at Case Western Reserve University. Case Western Reserve provided me with crucial time and facilities to finish the manuscript draft. Thanks go to Carolyn Elliott, Carl Ubbelohde, and David Van Tassel especially.

The archival materials necessary to piece together this census history were scattered among many collections. The major sources are available in the Washington, D.C., area at the National Archives, the

Library of Congress, and in the Census Bureau Library in Suitland, Maryland. Many people helped me ferret out the material, but archivist Jerry Hess at the National Archives deserves special mention. He provided critical help in the collections of the Census Bureau and other related federal agencies. The private papers of key twentieth century statisticians were located in the Herbert Hoover, Franklin Delano Roosevelt, and Harry Truman Presidential Libraries. Other key sets of papers and documents were in the Library of Congress.

Over the years a number of colleagues, professional statisticians and friends have read and critiqued pieces of the manuscript, introduced me to new contact people, or listened to the arguments as they developed. Among those who deserve thanks now are Frederick Bohme, Carolee Bush, Lynda Carlson, James Cassedy, Constance Citro, Harvey Choldin, Theodore Clemence, Patricia Cohen, James Cronin, Robert Davis, Victor Greene, Michael Grossberg, David Hammack, Morris Hansen, Daniel Melnick, Steve Meyer, Walter Nugent, Dave Pemberton, Terry Radtke, William Seltzer, Carole Shammas, Simon Szreter, Conrad Taeuber, Daniel Walkowitz, and Deborah White. Members of the Caucus for Women in Statistics introduced me to the world of the American Statistical Association. I am of course responsible for the work as it stands.

ABBREVIATIONS

ACLS	American Council of Learned Societies
ACSL	Advisory Committee to the Secretary of Labor
AEA	American Economic Association
ASA	American Statistical Association
CGLS	Committee on Government Labor Statistics
COGSIS	Committee on Government Statistics and Information Services
CWA	Civil Works Administration
DAB	*Dictionary of American Biography*
GAO	Government Accounting Office
GPO	Government Printing Office
HHPL	Herbert Hoover Presidential Library, West Branch, Iowa
JASA	*Journal of the American Statistical Association*
LC	Library of Congress, Washington, D.C.
NA	National Archives, Washington, D.C.
NIRA	National Industry Recovery Act
PECE	President's Emergency Committee for Employment
POUR	President's Organization on Unemployment Relief
RG	Record Group

Introduction

During a congressional committee hearing in the late 1960s, as a Census Bureau official told it, a congressman was questioning statisticians from the bureau about the projected scope and costs of the 1970 census. The tenor of his questions was highly critical. Why did the bureau need to ask so many questions? Did not the projected questions constitute an invasion of individual privacy by the government? And why did the census cost so much?

Bureau officials responded patiently to each question, although it was clear that the congressman was unconvinced. Why did the federal government have to get so involved in collecting statistics in the first place, the congressman asked. After all, he continued, whenever he needed statistical information, he just went and looked it up in an almanac.[1]

Census officials told this story to illustrate the enormous ignorance they felt they faced when they tried to explain to the general public what they did, why they did it, and how important their work was. Census data are taken for granted. They seem to most of us given, obvious, uncontroversial—part of the background information we all absorb in our everyday lives. It does not occur to us to question where the almanac gets its information. And yet the census officials knew that taking the decennial census—or many of our other modern statistical surveys—is an enormous organizational, intellectual, and financial exercise. On one level it is the simplest of efforts—a counting of noses, a headcount—necessary for the apportionment of the Congress and state legislatures. On another, it is a most complex exercise, involving the collection of many bits of information on—among other things—families, households, housing, consumer pat-

1. William Petersen related this story in "The Protection of Privacy and the United States Census," in *Censuses, Surveys, and Privacy,* ed. Martin Bulmer (London: Macmillan, 1979), p. 273.

terns, work, mobility, race, and ethnicity. All this information is published, analyzed, and used to describe and monitor the social and economic condition of the population.

Every ten years the United States Bureau of the Census conducts a population census. Currently all residents receive a form in the mail or a visit from a census enumerator. Most receive a short form with a few basic questions about themselves and their households: name, age, sex, marital status, racial or ethnic background, and relationship to the household head. The remaining 20 percent make up a larger sample survey and receive a longer form with dozens of questions about such issues as their style of life, work, income, housing, or education level. The person fills out the form and either mails it to a local temporary census office or returns it to the enumerator. The form is checked at the local level for mistakes or omissions and corrected if necessary. Then it is sent on to the Census Bureau to be checked again and entered into a computer. Census statisticians and technicians tabulate and cross-tabulate the millions of records and publish the census results for the nation, states, and local areas.

The data is perhaps some of the most reliable information the nation has. Every ten years we take a census, so every ten years we know "the respective numbers" of the population. We can look back to old censuses; we know exactly when the next one will occur. The census is deeply embedded in American political life through myriad apportionment mechanisms; it is also a crucial marker for American history. We date the end of the frontier from the 1890 census, the creation of the urban nation at the 1920 census. We use it to project the population into the future—what will the population be in ten years, a generation, a century?

Here follows the story of the decennial population census—how and why we have taken the census, and what its relevance has been in American history. The story is necessarily a long one; it spans two centuries of American life and the wars, economic changes, and social movements that have occurred in that time. The story is continuous, since the census has been taken, tabulated, published, and interpreted at decennial intervals since 1790. It is both a demographic and an institutional history—a history of the development of the American population and a study of the key statisticians, economists, politicians, and intellectuals who ran the Census Office and the Census Bureau. These men—and until quite recently they were overwhelmingly men—made the decisions about what questions to ask, how to tabulate the answers, what to publish in those weighty volumes. They put an irrevocable stamp on what we know about the American people at any time.

This study encompasses a broad sweep through American history. I have quite consciously chosen to take this broad perspective in order to trace the recurring themes that have surrounded the census. There is, I would suggest, a highly complex and continuous "politics of population" in the United States, and the census is an apportionment tool for managing the controversies. Issues of race and region, growth and decline, equity and justice have been fought in census politics over the centuries, although because decades may pass between flare-ups of particular issues, the participants are often unaware of relevant earlier debates. A goal of this study, then, is to bring the earlier debates to light and to place them in their appropriate historical context.[2]

By the same token, however, I have had to sacrifice some detail in the discussion of census history to prevent the book from growing to unmanageable length. In particular, I have chosen not to treat the administrative or technical history of particular censuses systematically since much of this history is available elsewhere. The bibliographic essay at the end of the book directs the reader to some of these sources. The reader may also consult the Appendix for basic population and apportionment data and for summary statistics on census staffing and costs. I have also chosen to focus exclusively on the decennial population census and thus to discuss other census efforts—economic censuses, vital statistics, current surveys, and so forth—only as they affect the decennial population census. Such decisions flow from my basic view of the census as an apportionment mechanism.

This story is thus part social history, part intellectual and political history, part a description of the remarkable changes that have taken place in the United States in the past two hundred years and part a commentary on how Americans have interpreted those changes and integrated the growing regions and population groups into American society. And remarkable the changes have been. The United States, as census takers have always known, has had one of the fastest growing and most heterogeneous populations in the world. From a mere 3.9 million people spread up and down the eastern seaboard in 1790, Americans spread across, conquered, or overran the entire continent by 1890. There were almost 63 million of us by then. Having filled up the continent, we proceeded to build great cities, fill them to bursting, and then spread suburbs and metropolitan areas and exurbs over the land. There are now over 240 million of us. In the nineteenth century, the United States had one of the fastest growth rates of any nation in the world; it stood as living proof of Malthus's predictions of relentless population growth.

But the growth told only part of the story. In addition to phenomenal growth, extraordinary economic change occurred. Like most of mankind, Americans were primarily farmers until about a century ago. That phenomenal growth in the nineteenth century was fueled by land-hungry settlers bringing new areas under cultivation. But about a century ago

2. William Petersen, *The Politics of Population* (Garden City, N.Y.: Doubleday, 1964).

farming ceased to be the major economic enterprise for most people in the advanced nations. The Industrial Revolution had taken hold. Noticeable first in England in the late eighteenth century, the changes in manufacturing and transportation spread throughout the world in the nineteenth century. Railroads replaced rivers and canals as the dominant inland transportation system. The factory system replaced craft and home production. The United States began its industrial transformation as it was still conquering the West. The two processes fueled each other and led to faster and more dramatic population growth in certain areas. Chicago, a marshy settlement of 4,500 souls when Boston was already two centuries old, outgrew Philadelphia by 1890 and had a population of over 1 million people.

And where did all these people come from? Who made up this remarkable and fortunate population that conquered a continent and built the richest country in the world in the course of a little over a century? Hector St. Jean de Crevecoeur posed the question two centuries ago, and it has been asked and answered repeatedly since—often with reference to information from the census. For the very volatility of the population has meant that Crevecoeur's question is not easy to answer. The simple answer is that the United States has had both high fertility rates and a large immigration of people for much of its history. Yet the population is also extremely heterogeneous, racially and ethnically diverse, and highly mobile. That heterogeneity and diversity, as American history reminds us, has both built the nation and periodically ripped it apart in civil war and social conflict. The question of who are "true Americans" has always been problematic. Americans have argued, struggled, and died for their vision of the "American way of life," to include or exclude various people from the American polity and American dream.

In other words, the counting of the population and the measurement of the population's growth and spread has also entailed its classification into its heterogeneous groups and the comparison of the demographic "progress" of the groups with one another. Is the West growing faster than the East? Are the cities growing at the expense of the countryside? Do immigrants have larger families than native-born Americans? Is the Sunbelt overtaking the Snowbelt? These questions, though they seem to lead to objective answers, are politically charged and controversial. Their answers contain implications for social, economic, and political power.

Census statisticians have been the messengers with the decennial news about the trajectory of the population. They, sometimes in consultation with, sometimes in opposition to, the nation's political leaders, have determined the categories and classifications used to interpret population change. In turn, they have created and shaped the very concepts we use to understand social change. They have provided the basal readings, the baseline measures, the figures for the almanacs and the categories we think in. And they have done so quite consciously, debating whether to change their methods of measuring or categorizing throughout our history.

In short, this history is also an attempt to explain just what census officials and statisticians did and do and why it is important to American social policy. In this sense the history of the census also provides an answer to the congressman who did not understand why the government needed to collect all that information. It belongs to a broader set of studies on the history and politics of statistics and the social sciences. Most of this literature is cited at relevant points throughout the book, but a few preliminary points can be made here.

As a number of authors have recently shown, statistics, or the systematic collection and analysis of quantitative information about a population—human or otherwise—is a relatively recent form of research knowledge. Histories, chronicles, tales, and records date back thousands of years, but the science of statistics dates only from the seventeenth century at the earliest. The great breakthroughs in data collection and analysis date from the nineteenth and twentieth centuries. The United States was the first nation in the world to institute a regular census of population, for example.[3]

The quantitative knowledge we have about populations from earlier periods has generally been reconstructed from records and materials kept for other reasons. For example, parish registers of births, deaths, and marriages were kept to keep track of the spiritual lives of the church members—not to allow statisticians to calculate fertility or mortality rates.

Thus, it is to the nineteenth and twentieth centuries that one must look

3. See, e.g., James H. Cassedy, *Demography in Early America: Beginnings of the Statistical Mind, 1600–1800* (Cambridge, Mass.: Harvard University Press, 1969); Cassedy, *American Medicine and Statistical Thinking, 1800–1860* (Cambridge, Mass.: Harvard University Press, 1984); Patricia Cline Cohen, *A Calculating People: The Spread of Numeracy in Early America* (Chicago: University of Chicago Press, 1982); Michael J. Cullen, *The Statistical Movement in Early Victorian Britain* (New York: Barnes & Noble, 1975); Ian Hacking, *The Emergence of Probability: A Philosophical Study of Ideas about Probability, Induction and Statistical Inference* (New York: Cambridge University Press, 1984); David V. Glass, *Numbering the People: The Eighteenth Century Population Controversy and the Development of the Census and Vital Statistics in Britain* (New York: D. C. Heath, 1973); Stephen Jay Gould, *The Mismeasure of Man* (New York: Norton, 1981); Theodore M. Porter, *The Rise of Statistical Thinking, 1820–1900* (Princeton, N.J.: Princeton University Press, 1986); Stephen M. Stigler, *The History of Statistics: The Measurement of Uncertainty before 1900* (Cambridge, Mass.: Harvard University Press, 1986); Donald MacKenzie, *Statistics in Britain, 1865–1930: The Social Construction of Scientific Knowledge* (Edinburgh: Edinburgh University Press, 1981); Simon Szreter, "The Genesis of the Registrar-General's Social Classification of Occupations," *British Journal of Sociology* 35 (1984): 522–46; Desley Deacon, "Political Arithmetic: The Nineteenth Century Australian Census and the Construction of the Dependent Woman," *Signs* 11, no. 1 (1985): 27–47; and D. B. Owen, ed., *On the History of Statistics and Probability: Proceedings of a Symposium on the American Mathematical Heritage* (New York: M. Dekker, 1976).

for the ideas that informed the numbers to be collected and analyzed. By and large, these numbers pertained to the nature of the state: hence the origin of the word *statistics*. Such new knowledge of the population was a function of the economic and population growth and the industrial development of the period. Mathematically, statistics is the inverse of gaming theory or gambling—the theory of probability. The card player wants to beat the "odds," or the average; the statistician wants to know the average. The mathematical foundation of the science of statistics, therefore, dates from the late medieval or early modern period. But *statists* or *statisticians* did not systematically apply those mathematical theories to the analysis of human populations or social and economic change until the nineteenth century. The body of rules for data collection, the various methods for the determination of "the average," and the analysis or correlates of a phenomenon have all been developed in the nineteenth and early twentieth centuries. Sampling theory and inductive statistics date from the early to mid-twentieth century. The first statistical societies—particularly the Royal Statistical Society and the American Statistical Association—were founded in the first half of the nineteenth century. The first American college textbooks on statistics date from the 1880s and 1890s.[4]

In short, the American census was itself a pioneering institution in the creation of modern social science. Its origins, as we shall see, are rooted in the efforts of the revolutionary leaders to develop a new series of governing instruments suitable for their experiment in republicanism. And its development and "progress" since is part and parcel of the broader political and social history of the United States. It is to this story that we now turn.

4. For the broader context in which statistical knowledge developed, see Paul Starr, "The Sociology of Official Statistics," in *The Politics of Numbers*, ed. Paul Starr and William Alonzo (New York: Russell Sage, 1987). The growth of American learned societies and higher education is described in Alexandra Oleson and Sanborn Brown, eds., *The Pursuit of Knowledge in the Early Republic* (Baltimore: Johns Hopkins University Press, 1976), and Oleson and John Voss, eds., *The Organization of Knowledge in Modern America, 1860–1920* (Baltimore: Johns Hopkins University Press, 1979). The first statistics text was Richmond Mayo Smith's *Science of Statistics*, part 1: *Statistics and Sociology*, and part 2: *Statistics and Economics* (New York: Macmillan, 1895, 1899), first published in 1888 by the AEA.

ONE || The Census and the New Nation:
Apportionment, Congress, and
the Progress of the United States

*The most decisive mark of the prosperity of any country is the
increase of the number of inhabitants.*
— *Adam Smith,* The Wealth of Nations *(1776)*

*To apportion, is to distribute by right measure; to set off in just
parts; to assign in due and proper proportion.*
— *Daniel Webster, Senate speech, 1832*

Two hundred years ago, in May 1787, delegates from the
original thirteen American states convened in Philadelphia
to discuss amendments to the Articles of Confederation.
National government under the articles had been cumbersome and unsatisfactory for some time, and the Philadelphia
Convention was one of several efforts to strengthen the
powers of Congress and to resolve some of the many issues
of finance, trade, and sovereignty that had plagued the infant United States since independence. Nevertheless, the
charge to the delegates was perhaps both modest and somewhat imprecise: to revise the Articles of Confederation. Few
observers expected the results that were published when the
convention adjourned in the late summer of 1787: namely, a
completely new, theoretically complex, and breathtakingly
innovative national governmental structure to be presented
to the states for ratification.

Ever since that summer, political commentators and historians have analyzed and debated, praised or condemned,
and wondered over the document that the framers produced. It is still the fundamental basis of the American gov-

7

ernment; it has been amended surprisingly little since. The Constitution of 1787 created executive, legislative, and judicial branches of government. It created a bicameral legislature to accommodate the conflicting pressures between those who wanted representation by states and those who wanted direct popular representation in Congress. It mandated that the president be elected nationally but indirectly through the mechanism of the electoral college. A national judiciary would oversee conflicts rooted in the federal character of the American republic—for example, between the national government and the states, among the states themselves, or between citizens of different states, A complex set of checks and balances among the elements of the new government guarded liberty and protected the states and individual citizens from infringements of power by the new, more powerful national government. Clearly, the proposed Constitution was a far more ambitious document than had been contemplated in the months before the convention.[1]

Nevertheless, as historians have shown, the drafters of the Constitution necessarily drew on the experience—and in particular the frustrations—of the Confederation era to guide their deliberations and goals. They knew that national government under the articles had continually stumbled over the same set of issues. Whether during the War for Independence or during the quieter years after 1783, Congress had had trouble raising revenue. Theoretically it had the authority to force the states to provide funds for the national government, but the state legislatures always seemed to be able to find some reason to object to, to minimize, or to postpone the tax. Similarly, sectional issues between north and south seemed to underlie much of the wrangling in Congress; the continuation of the institution of slavery was the most obvious sore point. Third, small states and large states looked on one another jealously. The large resented the equal voting authority of the small in Congress; the small feared the bullying of the large. States with claims to western lands feuded with those that had no such future bounty. States that needed access to the Mississippi River for trade worried that national diplomatic efforts might not protect their interests.[2]

In short, because of the different historic traditions among the former colonies and the varied bases of their economies and social forms, the infant United States faced a series of extraordinarily difficult questions about the proper apportionment of power and representation among the states, among the citizens of the various states, and between the national

1. See, e.g., Gordon Wood, *The Creation of the American Republic, 1776–1787* (Chapel Hill, N.C.: University of North Carolina Press, 1969), and Bernard Bailyn, *The Origin of American Politics* (New York: Vintage Books, 1967).

2. Merrill Jensen, *The New Nation: A History of the United States during the Confederation, 1781–1789* (New York: Knopf, 1950); Jack N. Rakove, *The Beginnings of National Politics: An Interpretive History of the Continental Congress* (New York: Knopf, 1979).

government and the individual citizen or state. And because much of the land area of the infant nation had not yet been settled, the framers had to determine how to incorporate both new people and new states into the United States and how to accommodate the relative shifting of power and resources within the nation in the future.

The creation of a periodic national census to measure the relative strength of the population in different parts of the country was one of the mechanisms the framers used to address these problems. It seems to us, as twentieth-century Americans, one of the least controversial innovations of the Constitution, though the United States was the first nation in the world to institute such a census and to use it as an apportionment mechanism. Even in 1787, the new national census was not terribly controversial. Compared with the huge and contentious literature—both contemporary and historical—about other elements of the Constitution, the debates on the census clause were quite tame. Nevertheless, the relevant sections of Article 1, Sections 2 and 9, introduced a fundamental new tool of representative government, and it deserves examination in its own right.

Article I of the Constitution defined the legislative branch of the federal government. Section 1 created the bicameral Congress. The Senate was composed of two representatives for each state; the House of Representatives was elected by the people. Section 2 detailed the composition of the House. Paragraph 3 of Section 2 defined the method for apportioning members of the House of Representatives among the states:

> Representatives and direct Taxes shall be apportioned among the several States which may be included within this Union, according to their respective Numbers, which shall be determined by adding to the whole Number of free Persons, including those bound to Service for a Term of Years, and excluding Indians not taxed, three fifths of all other Persons.

The paragraph continued by describing how the census itself was to be conducted:

> The actual Enumeration shall be made within three Years after the first Meeting of the Congress of the United States, and within every subsequent Term of ten Years, in such Manner as they shall by Law direct.

Since the new national government would convene before the first census was taken, the paragraph continued by defining the temporary House apportionment for the first Congress.

Paragraph 4 of Article 1, Section 9, contained the other relevant mention of the new census:

> No Capitation, or other direct, Tax shall be laid, unless in Proportion to the Census or Enumeration herein before directed to be taken.

With these simple paragraphs, the framers laid the groundwork for the apportionment system and, relatedly, the federal statistical system. Several questions surrounded the new apportionment tool. One fear revolved around worries that the old biblical taboo on censuses would make people reluctant to be counted and that the census would not work. Lacking direct evidence of such reluctance, though, the delegates decided to worry about that problem only if it arose. Far more important were the supposed advantages to be gained from the coupling of the apportionment of taxation and representation through a census. Such a coupling was one of the classic checks and balances of the Constitution. Large states would receive more House representation but would pay more taxes. And the coupling would guard against fraud in taking the census. Areas that might wish to overestimate their population to gain representation would pay the penalty of raising their tax burden. Likewise, areas that tried to evade taxes through undercounting their population in the census would also lose representation in Congress. The census was intended to solve the intractable problem of defining the basis for representation and taxation—by balancing the gains from representation against the penalties of taxation for a state or local area.[3]

But this well-known characteristic of the new census mechanism was just the most obvious aspect of the innovation. Much more in the census clauses both at the time and in the long run has proved more important. First, and most obviously, the census was to be taken by the federal government itself. Federal officials would count the population, despite the fact that most government functions that reached down to the local level remained reserved to the states. It is fairly clear that the framers made this exception, since Congress had the authority to determine its own rules and membership and determining the apportionment base logically flowed from the authority of Congress. Further, the Continental Congress had years of experience of asking the states to take censuses for apportionment purposes and had found either that states did not comply or that their methods were not uniform. Nevertheless, as we shall see, it was not easy for the federal government—in the absence of a developed system of federal officials on the local level—to take a national census. The Constitutional imperative was so strong that the framers were willing to wrestle with the logistics of the problem.

3. James H. Cassedy, *Demography in Early America: Beginnings of the Statistical Mind, 1600–1800* (Cambridge, Mass.: Harvard University Press, 1969); James Madison, *Journal of the Federal Convention*, ed. E. H. Scott (Chicago: Albert Scott, 1893); E. R. A. Seligman, *The Income Tax: A Study of the History, Theory and Practice of Income Taxation at Home and Abroad* (1914; reprint, New York: Augustus M. Kelley, 1970), pp. 548–55. For the biblical allusion, see 2 Sam. 24 and 1 Chron. 21. As punishment for the "sin of David" for "numbering" Israel, the Lord sent a "pestilence upon Israel." See Patricia Cline Cohen, *A Calculating People: The Spread of Numeracy in Early America* (Chicago: University of Chicago Press, 1982), pp. 35, 39.

Second, the framers and Americans generally were already aware of the problem of rapid and differential population growth among the various subdivisions of the country and its impact on problems of representation. Again, much of the contemporary and historical debate about representation in the new nation revolved around the theories of virtual and actual representation, representation by orders or corporate units, and the nature of sovereignty. But another aspect of this discussion concerned the problem of growth itself and the trajectory of the American population over time. By the late eighteenth century, Americans were well aware that their population was growing dramatically. We know now that the colonial population grew from about 250,000 in 1700 to 2.8 million in 1780. Benjamin Franklin at midcentury had predicted that the population would double every generation. Revolutionary war propaganda used demographic data to show that the infant United States had a large and growing population and could withstand war with England for many years. At the time, by contrast, English commentators feared that their population was either stationary or declining. And during the war years the colonies had made repeated estimates of their populations to determine their war readiness, tax capacity, and so on.[4]

In short, the framers knew that they had to build into the new federal Constitution a method for periodic reassessment of the basis for political representation and taxation and hence for shifting power and resources among the constituent elements of the polity. Just as regular and periodic elections would provide smooth mechanisms for adjusting the shifting political power within the nation, so too would the periodic census and reapportionments adjust the power and burdens among the people. And, like other constitutional mechanisms, the census would operate according to its own decennial rhythm—somewhat divorced from the other electoral mechanisms. Every twenty years a census coincided with a presidential election. Congressional elections would occur in the same year as a census once every ten years.

Third, and relatedly, the Constitution made population the measure of power and tax capacity. Again, Americans furiously debated both the appropriate basis for legislative representation and taxation and the more practical question of how to calculate it. Broadly speaking, during the Philadelphia Convention the delegates suggested that taxes be apportioned on the basis of wealth; political representation derived from population. But again, the experience of the revolutionary era indicated that

4. Cassedy, *Demography in Early America*, pp. 180–205; Wood, *Creation of the American Republic*, pp. 162–96, 593–615; Walter Nugent, *Structures of American Social History* (Bloomington, Ind.: Indiana University Press, 1981); David V. Glass, *Numbering the People: The Eighteenth Century Population Controversy and the Development of Census and Vital Statistics in Britain* (New York: D. C. Heath, 1973).

the issue was more complex than it seemed on the surface. For example, Article 8 of the Articles of Confederation had mandated that "All charges of war and all other expenses" for the United States were to be paid for by the states "in proportion to the value of all land within each State, granted to or surveyed for any person." A land census was supposed to determine the exact figures. Congress, however, never managed to implement either this article or the land censuses.

Problems arose at several points. First, measuring wealth was not easy. If land were the measure, how did one accommodate improved versus unimproved or fertile versus barren land? What about mercantile wealth? Further, and more crucially, how did one evaluate property in slaves? Southern states did not count their slaves for legislative apportionment, but to exclude slaves from apportionments for taxes would necessarily give the slave-holding states an undue advantage. Thus the delegates revived an expedient method proposed in 1783 as a replacement for the ineffective Article 8 of the Confederation: slaves would be counted as three-fifths of a free person. Population, which everyone admitted was more easily measured and was highly correlated with wealth in any case, thus became the apportionment base for both representation and taxation. James Madison and Alexander Hamilton readily admitted in the *Federalist Papers* that this apportionment rule had "imperfections." They conceded that the numeric calculation of a slave as three-fifths of a free person was clearly arbitrary; they also admitted that no cogent theoretical justification existed for including slaves in the legislative apportionment base. Nevertheless, they argued that although the "reasoning" defending the rule "may appear to be a little strained in some points," overall "it is evidently the least objectionable among the practicable rules." In short, some rule had to be found. An imperfect rule on which everyone might compromise was better than no rule.[5]

Finally, the particular definition of the apportionment rule—requiring the separate determination of the free, slave, and Indian populations by states—built into the census a tradition of differentiating these three great elements of the population. Henceforth national policy would be conceived in relation to these categories; as we shall see, later differentiation of the elements of the population would be conceived with reference to these initial distinctions. An ongoing discussion of the meaning of

5. Rakove, *Beginnings of National Politics*, p. 320; Alexander Hamilton, John Jay, and James Madison, *The Federalist*, no. 54 (New York: Random House Modern Library, 1937), pp. 354–58. See also Michael V. McKay, "Constitutional Implications of a Population Undercount: Making Sense of the Census Clause," *Georgetown Law Journal* 69 (1981): 1427–63, and Theodore G. Clemence, "Historical Perspectives on the Decennial Census," *Government Information Quarterly* 2, no. 4 (1985): 355–68.

differential population growth among the races, states, and regions was thus written into the political fabric of the new nation.

Once the Constitution was ratified, the new governmental machinery had to be set in motion. Americans learned about how their new census and apportionment mechanisms, like the other new instrumentalities, actually functioned as the years went on. Between 1790 and 1840, six censuses were taken, and Congress was reapportioned after each. Congress levied direct taxes apportioned among the states in 1798 and during the War of 1812. Over the years, Congress and the American public experimented with and debated the virtues of their efforts at census taking and apportionment and slowly accumulated a body of knowledge about how the system worked. From today's perspective, the first six censuses exhibited basic common features; they deserve to be analyzed as a set.

The first censuses were administered by either the president or the Department of State; no census office in a modern sense existed. Since the federal government was so small, men at the top of the government hierarchy handled the details of the census and apportionment process. George Washington, Thomas Jefferson, Alexander Hamilton, John Quincy Adams, and Martin Van Buren, to name the most prominent, worried over the census. The questions raised by the census and apportionment process were very much on the minds of America's most distinguished political leaders. Third, the census unit to be counted was the household. The census taker asked, "how many males," "how many females," and so on, were in a particular household. No individual level information was collected; the head of the household's name was listed for organizational purposes only. Finally, the census was fundamentally subordinated to the apportionment process. The data were collected and published almost exactly the way they arrived from the United States marshals in the field. By the second year after the census date, the whole effort ended for the decade.

Within this basic framework, though, incremental changes did take place. Thus the whole early process of census taking and apportionment needs to be explored to understand the issues that shaped its development.

One of the first tasks of the new government was to conduct the census. In early 1790, Congress debated a bill for taking the census. They decided that the United States marshals would be in charge of the field enumeration; the marshals in turn would appoint assistants (about 650 in all) to travel the country and collect the information. The census date was set for August 1790; the marshals had nine months to complete the count. Once the assistants had completed their work they were supposed to post a copy of the schedules they had used in two public places to make sure that they were accurate. The assistants would turn over their work to the U.S. marshals; the marshals would file the assistants' returns with the clerks of the federal district courts. The marshals in turn would add up the totals from all of their assistants and would report "the aggregate amount of each description of persons within their respective districts" to the president.[6]

Congress also discussed whether the census should collect any information beyond a mere headcount necessary for apportionment. James Madison proposed a rather elaborate schedule to categorize the population by age, sex, race, and occupation. He suggested that the census could be used to explore the potential military strength of the nation (men of draft age) and the range of the economy as well as the distribution of the population. He was successful in convincing Congress to request information about some basic distinctions of race, sex, and age, but the Senate deleted the census of occupations, because, Madison wrote to Jefferson, they considered it "a waste of trouble and supplying materials for idle people to make a book."[7]

Thus the 1790 census limited its inquiries to six: each household reported the name of the head of the family, the number of free white males over sixteen and under sixteen, the number of free white females, the number of other free persons, and the number of slaves. The census law made no provision for any kind of central office to process the statistics. The law did not call for a formal report or publication of the data, although a fifty-six-page report was eventually published. The president merely totaled the headcounts and reported them to Congress. The assistant marshals were free to collect the information as they chose. Neither Congress nor the president thought to print and mail out special census forms; nor did they specify any size or type of paper. (Not until 1830 would the federal government print the census forms and mail them to the enumerators.)

In retrospect, it is perhaps just as well that Madison's more ambitious census plans were not implemented. Given the novelty of the task it was undertaking, the federal government could ill afford to fail in its first effort to count the population. As it was, the field enumeration took eighteen months to complete, and George Washington suspected that the reported total of 3.9 million people was too low. But the data did come in and were acceptable enough to allow Congress to undertake its first census apportionment.[8]

6. Carroll Wright and William C. Hunt, *History and Growth of the United States Census* (Washington, D.C.: GPO, 1900), pp. 13–15.

7. Cassedy, *Demography in Early America*, p. 216.

8. Ibid., p. 219.

In October 1791, Washington reported the results of the census to Congress, and Congress began consideration of an apportionment bill. Congress and the American people now discovered a new set of problems with the census apportionment clause. The Constitution had set a minimum proportion of population to House members. There was to be no more than one representative for each thirty thousand of the "representative population"—that is, free persons and three-fifths of the slave population. But the Constitution was silent on both the particular method of apportionment and the total size of the House. Further, Congress readily discovered that although it was possible to apportion tax liabilities precisely it was not possible to apportion 4.2 or 3.7 or 5.1 congressmen to a state. As Michel Balinski and H. Peyton Young have so aptly described in their book, *Fair Representation,* "a perfectly fair division" of representatives "is impossible to achieve owing to the indivisibility of seats." "Finding the best compromise," they have pointed out, "forms a fascinating historical and scientific tale."[9]

That tale began with Congress's efforts to draft a satisfactory apportionment bill in 1791. Congress first discovered that the constitutional apportionment discriminated against certain states. Rhode Island, North Carolina, Virginia, Massachusetts, and New York had received less than a fair share of House representation; the other states had received more than their fair share. One solution was to enlarge the House so that the overrepresented states would lose relative, but not absolute, numbers of representatives. The Jeffersonians also argued that a bigger House would be more democratic. The House of Representatives thus drafted an apportionment bill setting one representative for each 30,000 people; they produced an apportionment of 112 seats. Delaware received one seat; Virginia, at the opposite end of the spectrum, twenty-one. The Senate objected to this bill and drafted one with a divisor of 33,000 and a House size of 105. Congress deadlocked as members realized that different divisors affected the representation of the various states differently. Dropping or rounding the fractions from the quotients also affected the apportionment results.

As the winter wore on, the controversy deepened, and Congress wrestled with the complexities of the mathematics and the politics of the situation. Alexander Hamilton added a further complication by suggesting that both House and Senate bills were flawed because the House size should be determined before the proportional representation of each state was determined. He showed that, for example, if Congress first determined to set the size of the House at 112 and then attempted to

9. Balinski and Young, *Fair Representation: Meeting the Ideal of One Man, One Vote* (New Haven and London: Yale University Press, 1982), p. ix.

apportion each state's share of the whole, Virginia's delegation would shrink from 21 to 19.531. How could such anomalies be allowed?

By the early spring of 1792, the situation was reaching crisis proportions. The supposedly simple, automatic, and reasonable new method of census apportionment was proving to be extremely troublesome to implement. And, as Patricia Cline Cohen has shown in her study of "numeracy" in early America, the arithmetic skills of the American population in the 1790s were not terribly well developed. Thus Congress stumbled not only on the political problems of shifting power from one state or region to another but also on the pure mathematical problems of devising an elegant and fair apportionment method. Calculating alternative apportionments with different divisors and different House sizes was an extremely tedious business, as was exploring the biases that emerged from one or another method. That Congress debated these issues intensely for months is an indication of the problem's severity.[10]

Nevertheless, by March 1792, President Washington and Congress had learned a few things from their first effort at apportionment. They knew that some methods gave consistently better results for small states, others for large. They began to articulate a standard of commonsense fairness: if shifting the method slightly resulted in dramatic changes in a state's quota, then the method was unfair. They also knew that they had to compromise ultimately and pass a bill. In late March, Congress passed a bill to give the House a size of 120 with an apportionment that used Hamilton's method. Southerners saw in this bill a sectional affront to the South. Washington solicited advice from his cabinet, and, predictably, Hamilton supported the bill, while Jefferson opposed it and suggested a different method. Washington vetoed the bill in early April—using the presidential veto for the first time. Congress failed to override the veto and passed a "Jeffersonian" apportionment in mid-April 1792. The size of the House was set at 105; the divisor for apportioning seats was set at 33,000.[11]

By mid-1792 then, the infant United States had completed its first exercise in census taking and congressional apportionment. The government had learned a great deal about the difficulties of taking a census, the value of the data thus produced, and the complexities presented by the apportionment system. If the new constitutional mechanism for adjusting the relative strength of the various constituencies in the United States had

10. Ibid., pp. 10–22; Cohen, *A Calculating People.*
11. Using Jefferson's method, one set the size of the House and chose a divisor so that the whole numbers of the quotients added to the House size. Each state received its whole number quotient; fractional remainders were dropped. Using Hamilton's method, one set the size of the House, divided to find each state's quota, and gave each state the whole number of the quota. If the numbers did not add up to the required House size, the additional seats were assigned to the states with the largest remainders.

proved to be less objective and more cumbersome than it might have seemed at first blush, it nevertheless did the job. The president did count the population; the Congress did reapportion itself. The new government had passed a critical test.

During the 1790s, officials in the new government also implemented the tax system. The touchy subjects of taxation and finance pitted Hamiltonians and Jeffersonians on opposite sides of a broadening philosophical divide. As many historians have documented, the two factions began to articulate dramatically different notions of the nature and role of the new government. The Hamiltonians were generally more willing to consider taxes to guarantee the stability of the new government. Jeffersonians were more concerned with the relative burdens that taxation laid on the population. Within this general context, Congress had to define the types and amount of taxes for the new nation. Tariffs or customs duties were initially used to fund the federal government. These were found to be very efficient in raising revenue and were generally accepted as fair to all elements of the population. Excise taxes, most notably on whiskey, but also on other such items as snuff, sugar, and carriages, were less satisfactory. The whiskey tax excited full-scale rebellion in western Pennsylvania; other excises and duties tended to encourage tax evasion. By the middle of the decade, the Treasury Department and Congress also began to debate the use of an apportioned direct tax. In 1798 the Adams administration levied the first such tax for an assessment of two million dollars. The tax was levied on land, dwelling houses, and slaves and was apportioned among the states. The justification for the tax was twofold: new revenue was needed, and Congress wanted to broaden the government's revenue base. The tax proved cumbersome to collect. The census had no land assessment information, and the Treasury Department had to use state assessments. The federal government also had no mechanism for determining either the number or the valuation of houses. By 1801 only 80 percent of the tax had been collected. After the 1800 election, President Jefferson did not attempt to revive the tax.[12]

As would occur for much of the next fifty years, once the census was taken and Congress was reapportioned, federal officials and the broader American public paid little attention to the issues of census taking and apportionment until the time for the next census rolled around. Some farsighted thinkers took the census data and wove it into discussions of the nature of the new nation. Tench Coxe, assistant secretary of the Treasury, used the 1790 census results to refute Lord Sheffield's *Observations on the Commerce of the American States*. Sheffield had predicted that the

12. Sidney Ratner, *Taxation and Democracy in America* (1942; reprint, New York: John Wiley & Sons, 1967); Davis R. Dewey, *Financial History of the United States* (New York: Longmans, Green, 1924), pp. 97–117.

United States population would stop growing and there might even be a pattern of emigration from the former colonies. Coxe showed Sheffield's data to be wrong and predicted continued rapid demographic and economic growth for the nation. Similarly, such men as Benjamin Rush, Thomas Jefferson, Jeremy Belknap, and Jedidiah Morse used census data in their essays and histories of their states. Overall, though, in the early years of the republic, there were no efforts to create a permanent federal statistical agency or institution to take the census or interpret its results.[13]

In early 1800, Congress passed a law to take the second census. The law was very similar to the 1790 act. Again, the United States marshals and their assistants were designated as the census field force; the returns were again to be collected, corrected, and totaled by the marshals. The assistants had nine months to collect the data; the marshals were to transmit the aggregate responses to the secretary of State by September 1801. Secretary of State James Madison totaled the data for the nation and reported it to Congress and the president. The House of Representatives published the entire census results in a large folio volume of seventy-four pages. The American population in 1800 came to 5.3 million people.[14]

The census of 1800 incorporated several refinements in the data collection efforts. Minor civil divisions were listed at the top of the schedules. The free white population was differentiated into males and females under 10, 10 and under 16, 16 and under 26, 26 and under 45, and 45 and up. The Indian, slave, and free black populations were listed by total number only. Memorials from Thomas Jefferson speaking for the American Philosophical Society and Timothy Dwight speaking for the Connecticut Academy of Arts and Sciences requested that much more information be collected in the census. Both men wanted occupational or economic data to be collected and asked that the census distinguish the native-born and immigrant populations. They requested finer age distinctions and information on the marital status of the population. Again, Congress ignored such appeals.

Congress was reapportioned after the second census using the same method as in 1790. A divisor of 33,000 distributed 142 seats among seventeen states. Delaware, again the smallest state, received one representative; Virginia, still the largest, received twenty-two representatives.

The census of 1810 employed much the same procedures for census taking and Congressional apportionment. Congress tried unsuccessfully to shorten the time of the census from nine months to five. It specified that federal marshals divide their districts into enumeration areas based on local geography and civil boundaries; marshals were to assign their assistants to particular counties or minor civil divisions; the assistants

13. Cassedy, *Demography in Early America*, pp. 220*ff*.
14. Wright and Hunt, *History and Growth*, pp. 17–20.

were to be residents of their census area. Congress further specified that the assistants actually visit the households to collect data. The 1810 census counted 7.2 million people. The results were printed in an 180-page volume published in 1811. Congress was reapportioned using a divisor of 35,000; the House size came to 186.[15]

Congress also authorized a census of manufactures in 1810. The United States had been struggling to avoid being dragged into the Napoleonic Wars for a decade, yet the need to export agricultural products and import manufactured goods had necessarily entangled the United States in the naval incursions of Britain and France. Jefferson had tried to embargo American exports; policymakers called for the development of American manufactures. The first manufacturing census was designed to find out just what Americans did produce. Secretary of the Treasury Tench Coxe oversaw this effort, and the data were published in a 233-page report in 1813.

While the results of this effort were sufficient to inspire pride in American growth and development, from the perspective of the history of census taking the first manufacturing census was a very sobering experience. Coxe readily admitted that he had to cope with "*numerous* and *very considerable* imperfections and omissions in returns from cities, towns, villages, townships, hundreds, counties, and, to valuable articles and branches, from States." The assistant marshals simply did not collect all the data; it was not easy to decide whether home manufacturing should be classified as "agricultural" production or as manufacturing. Ambitious future census efforts would be evaluated with this experience in mind.[16]

The increase in tensions surrounding the Napoleonic Wars and the coming of the War of 1812 also prompted Congress to reinstitute direct taxes. In 1813 Congress levied a $3-million direct tax on land, houses, and slaves and apportioned it among the states. The law was quite similar to the 1798 effort and was again part of a series of new taxes designed to finance the war and diversify the federal tax system. The tax was made annual and raised to $6 million in 1814. In 1815 the provision for an annual tax was repealed, and the levy was reduced to $3 million. Again federal officials found the tax difficult to assess and collect. By 1817, $10.4 million of the $12 million had been collected. These laws also contained a novel provision that allowed a discount of 10 to 15 percent for a state that paid its apportionment into the federal Treasury by a certain date. Thus although the tax was technically a federal levy against individuals and was collected by federal internal revenue agents, it also resembled the old requisitions made by Congress against the states during the Confederation era. During the 1810s, therefore, some states paid the tax; in others

15. Ibid., pp. 20–25.
16. Ibid., emphasis in original.

federal officials collected it from individuals. But because the measure was a war tax and not generally thought to be a permanent feature of the federal internal revenue system, this somewhat contradictory mechanism for raising revenue was little discussed.[17]

As the War of 1812 ended, the United States had taken three censuses, had reapportioned Congress successfully, had twice instituted direct taxes based on census apportionments, and had experimented with more elaborate census efforts. In the 1810s, several interested observers pondered the meaning of these quantitative explorations and began to codify a set of conclusions about American population and economic growth, data collection, and the trajectory of American society. With the evidence from the decennial censuses to support such thinking, Americans were truly becoming, as Cohen has put it, "a calculating people."

Several facets of the census and apportionment experience prompted these efforts. First, by 1810, scholars and writers were beginning to recognize that voluntary private efforts to collect statistical data were largely unsuccessful. Men such as Jeremy Belknap and David Ramsey had tried to travel their states to collect statistical data or to collect information by circular letter from key local leaders. But if letters were not answered, or local correspondents made mistakes or did not understand what was asked for, such voluntary efforts led to a hodgepodge of indigestible information. The results were often published anyway, but, like the 1810 manufacturing census, they were known to be defective. The census experience showed that building even a temporary field enumeration system required the force of law, a schedule for doing the work, adequate payment for work done, oaths of office, checking for errors, and penalties for noncompliance.[18]

The census experience also showed that questions had to be simple and inquiries few in number if results were to be reliable. Even then, officials from George Washington on doubted the accuracy of the results. But they decided that if the data were good enough for the purpose of political apportionment, the census was successful. Any changes in census questions or calls for additional data would be evaluated in terms of the potential loss in accuracy and timeliness of the basic apportionment data. The use of census-based apportionments for direct taxation was more problematic, but officials decided that the problem was with the tax, not with the census apportionment process.

Third, by 1810 the periodic character of the census provided some basic checks on error. By 1810 Americans could create a population table

17. Dewey, *Financial History*, pp. 138–41, 219; Charles Franklin Dunbar, "The Direct Tax of 1861," *Quarterly Journal of Economics* 3 (1889): 436–61.
18. Cassedy, *Demography in Early America*, pp. 152–53.

by states and calculate growth rates from 1790 to 1800 and from 1800 to 1810. They could compare changes in the population of minor civil divisions between censuses and decide if the numbers met commonsense tests of adequacy. And they could predict future population trends on the basis of the past; if current patterns held, they could determine the population in 1820, 1830, and so forth.

Such exercises in data analysis became increasingly common and of interest to Americans in the 1810s, as they discovered some rather remarkable characteristics about their new nation. In particular, the first three censuses showed that the United States population was growing at the rate of about 35 percent a decade. When Americans compared the results of their census with those of the new English censuses of 1801 and 1811, they realized that they were fast overtaking their former ruler in population. England and Wales had a combined population of about 12 million in 1811; the American population was 7.2 million. (The American population would outstrip England's by 1840.)[19]

Demographic comparisons promoted national pride and prompted further efforts at understanding the demographic realities of the new nation. They reinforced the assumptions of the framers of the Constitution and earlier colonial thinkers that rapid population growth and change was a continuing feature of American society. And they led to efforts to examine the patterns of population growth and change in particular states and regions and among the various racial and ethnic groups counted in the census.

In 1818, Adam Seybert, a member of the House of Representatives from Pennsylvania, published an eight-hundred-page volume that summarized most of the statistical data that had been collected by the federal government since 1789 as well as some state and local data. Entitled *Statistical Annals: Embracing Views of the Population, Commerce, Navigation, Fisheries, Public Lands, Post-Office Establishment, Revenues, Mint, Military and Naval Establishments, Expenditures, Public Debt and Sinking Fund, of the United States of America Founded on Official Documents,* the work demonstrated both the extraordinary pride that early Americans had in their new republic and a fascination with the new science of "political arithmetic." Seybert devoted his first chapter to an exploration of the data from the population census, noting approvingly the postulate of Adam Smith: "The most decisive mark of the prosperity of any country is the increase of the number of inhabitants." He calculated population growth rates for states, whites, nonwhites, and slaves. He noted that the free white population

19. For the history of censuses and their meaning in England, see Glass, *Numbering the People*; Richard Lawton, ed., *The Census and Social Structure: An Interpretive Guide to Nineteenth Century Censuses for England and Wales* (London: F. Cass, 1978); and Michael J. Cullen, *The Statistical Movement in Early Victorian Britain: Foundations of Empirical Social Research* (New York: Barnes & Noble, 1975).

grew faster than the slave. He speculated on the size of the immigrant population. He provided a summary table of congressional apportionments at all three censuses that allowed the reader to see the relative shifts in the size of the congressional delegations of the various states.[20]

Seybert's work was the first of a genre that chronicled the growth and shifts in the American population. After each census, a new set of publications could be expected, bringing the data up to date, tracing new trends, assessing the possibilities for the future. By the 1840s, as the high growth rates and overall prosperity of the nation continued, George Tucker, former member of Congress from Virginia and professor of moral philosophy at the University of Virginia, explained to his readers in the beginning of his study, *Progress of the Population of the United States in Population and Wealth in Fifty Years,* why he was "desirous of further gratifying the curiosity he had always felt on the subject of the census of the United States." He traced the history of the census clause and apportionment in the Constitution and noted that by the nineteenth century, the census "was soon found to have substantial merits of its own." This "authentic document" was "invaluable to the philosopher and political economist, as well as to the statesman and legislator." "As the numbers of a people are at once the source and the index of its wealth," he continued, "these enumerations enable its statesmen to see whether national prosperity is advancing, stationary, or retrograde. They can compare one period with another, as well as different parts of the country with each other." Thus "speculations in political philosophy of great moment and interest may be made to rest on the unerring logic of numbers."[21]

In short, in the early nineteenth century, Americans began to realize that they were living in one of the most demographically dynamic nations in human history. We know now that the remarkable rates of population growth (30 to 35 percent per decade) continued until the Civil War. We also know that the United States has consistently displayed rapid settlement patterns, sharp demographic transitions, and major migrations, all in the context of a racially and ethnically diverse population. Accordingly, the census and the apportionments derived from census data play a crucial role in American political and social life. It is the census that triggers increased (or decreased) power or resources for a geographic region, and thus it is the census that has been used to illustrate the virtues or vices of particular regions, peoples, or ways of life in America.

It is no accident that the first authors of the interpretive analyses and compendia of census data were congressmen. By 1820 the patterns of

20. Seybert, *Statistical Annals* (1818; reprint, New York: Augustus Kelley, 1970), esp. pp. 3–4.
21. Tucker, *Progress of the Population of the United States in Population and Wealth in Fifty Years* (1843; reprint, New York: Augustus Kelley, 1964), pp. 1, 13–14.

differential population growth and change had begun to affect the political system. The original thirteen states were losing political power to the western states. More critically, the relative equilibrium between northern and southern states—and hence free and slave states—was being disrupted by more rapid growth in the free states. From the 1820s on, debates about the census and the congressional apportionments derived from it became increasingly contentious as Americans sought to understand and control their dynamic social and political order.

The census legislation of 1820 differed little from that of 1810. The overall character of the questions was the same as in 1810; the effort at a manufacturing census was repeated—with equally unsatisfactory results. Nevertheless, the obvious value of even partial data prompted Congress to ask Secretary of State John Quincy Adams to try to collect more information. In 1820 the census classified the slave and free black population by sex and age for the first time. In 1810 the enumerator filled two columns per family with information on the nonwhite population; in 1820 he had to fill out eight. The census also finally began to collect crude occupational information and information on the unnaturalized foreign population; the enumerators were instructed to list the number of persons engaged in agriculture, in commerce and in manufactures (including slaves), and the number of unnaturalized foreigners in each household.

As in the past, the results of the census were tallied and tabulated in the field. The secretary of State published a 160-page report of the population data and a 100-page report of the manufacturing data. By 1820 the census reports were in great demand. The printing appropriation contained instructions to send copies to federal officials, state governors, congressmen, and all colleges and universities in the country.[22]

The congressional apportionment of 1820 again used Jefferson's method. Twenty-four states divided 213 seats. New York received 34 seats, while Delaware and the new states of Mississippi, Illinois, and Missouri received 1 each. Connecticut, Delaware, Vermont, and Virginia, four of the oldest states, saw the size of their congressional delegations shrink absolutely for the first time. The overall decennial population growth was 33 percent, but growth in the West was 108 percent. Clearly, dramatic changes were taking place in the balance of forces in the new nation.

The framers had of course hoped that the new nation would grow westward and plant communities and new states on the other side of the Appalachians. The Northwest Ordinance and the constitutional accommodations for the admission of new states to the Union on the basis of equality with the original thirteen demonstrate clearly that new admis-

22. Wright and Hunt, *History and Growth*, pp. 25–27.

sions were planned. Kentucky and Tennessee were admitted to the Union in the 1790s, Ohio in 1803. Nevertheless, the Louisiana Purchase and the acquisition of Florida in 1819 changed the character of the process fundamentally. Only five states were to be carved out of the Northwest Territory, and only four more out of the remaining 1783 territorial claims. Thus the original thirteen would still dominate. After the Louisiana Purchase, such an orderly plan for the trajectory of power disappeared. In the 1810s, five states were admitted to the Union. The West would eventually dominate the East. After 1840, western senators outnumbered those from the original thirteen colonies. After 1860, western members also dominated the House.

There was a good deal of debate about the meaning of this rapid westward movement and its implications for the republic, but by and large Easterners did not feel threatened by the changes. Residents of the states that had made up the original thirteen colonies took comfort from the fact that the new western states were peopled by their own sons and daughters. Citizens on the frontier were likely to hold most of the same political, religious, and cultural beliefs as those who stayed in the East. No major East-West social conflict threatened to disrupt the Union and make the differential population growth rates problematic.[23]

More ominously, the census of 1820 revealed that population growth was more rapid in the free states than in the slave states. Since the House apportionments rewarded the most rapidly growing states with more seats in Congress, Southerners began to worry about their ability to carry their positions in the national government in the future. In 1790 and 1800, the slave states represented 46 percent of the seats in the House and between 47 and 50 percent in the Senate. In 1810 the House share dropped to 44 percent, while the Senate share remained at 50 percent. After the 1820 census, the House share dropped to 42 percent and, as we shall see, continued to drop in future censuses. Maintaining equality with the free states in the Senate and thus carefully regulating the admission of new states to maintain southern power became a fundamental tenet of southern politics. As Southerner George Tucker put it:

> The dangers threatened by this gross inequality of power [in the House], and the changes which its distribution is ever undergoing, are effectually guarded against by the senate, a co-ordinate branch of the legislature, in which every State has two members. By this provision, the smaller States are protected from the possible abuse of the power possessed by the larger; and the community from those sudden changes of public policy, which might be apprehended from the changes in the relative weight of the States after each census.[24]

23. Nugent, *Structures*; Robert Wiebe, *The Opening of American Society* (New York: Random House, 1985).
24. Tucker, *Progress*, p. 124.

In short, by the 1820s, differential population growth was becoming a "problem" to be managed, one that would increasingly affect national politics and drive further legislative efforts at census taking and apportionment.

In 1830 Congress abandoned the manufacturing census but refined the population census. Congress requested rudimentary information on the number and race of deaf, dumb, and blind persons in each family. The secretary of State printed the schedules for the first time and transmitted them to the field to assure uniformity. A temporary office staff of forty-three in Washington, D.C., attempted to standardize the compilations of the marshals for the final printed volume. Francis Walker, census superintendent in the late nineteenth century, however, found the 1830 effort "absolutely valueless" because the clerks missed mistakes or made new ones in their efforts at correction. It would be many decades before the federal government, as well as private statisticians, codified rules for correcting and evaluating the census schedules.[25]

Congress changed the census date from August 1 to June 1. The enumerators were to take the census in six months, but Congress later had to extend the deadline until August 1831. Throughout the nineteenth century the U.S. population was extremely difficult to count not only because it was primarily rural and spread over a huge area but also because decent local transportation often did not exist. The correspondence between officials in Washington, D.C., the federal marshals, and the enumerators is filled with tales of woe about reaching remote communities. Secretary of State Martin Van Buren published a 163-page report on the population; three thousand copies were printed. For the first time the government also included comparative data from previous censuses.

The apportionment process after the census of 1830 was particularly contentious. As Balinski and Young have shown, Jefferson's apportionment method is biased against the smaller states because it drops remainders. By 1830, the New England states were particularly sensitive to their loss of power in the House. James K. Polk, a Westerner and a follower of Andrew Jackson, sponsored the House apportionment bill. John Quincy Adams, former president and the secretary of State who had overseen the 1820 census, now a Massachusetts representative and Jackson's political nemesis, objected strenuously. Adams in the House and Daniel Webster in the Senate embarked on a new effort to change the apportionment method. Congress wrangled with the problem for the first four months of 1832. Webster devised a new method and spoke eloquently on the theory and practice of apportionment. But Polk forces had the votes, and the 1830 apportionment bill again used Jefferson's method. Twenty-four states divided 240 House seats; the total population of

25. Wright and Hunt, *History of the Census*, pp. 28–32.

the United States stood at almost 12.9 million. Delaware received one seat; New York, the largest state, received forty.

In the late 1830s, Congress also used a census apportionment to disburse federal revenue to the states. After the War of 1812, the federal government had returned to the tariff as its principal revenue generator. Between the late 1810s and the Civil War, the federal government had sufficient revenue from the tariff and secondarily land sales that it found no need to institute direct or other onerous taxes. In 1837, Congress found itself with such an embarrassment of riches in the federal Treasury that it authorized the distribution of surplus revenue to the states on the basis of an apportionment quota that summed a state's House and Senate members. About $28 million was distributed. Like the direct taxes levied earlier in the century, this disbursement did not set a precedent for a new fiscal relationship between the states and the national government. The loss of revenue after the Panic of 1837 effectively ended the experiment and rendered the distribution an anomaly in the financial history of the country.[26]

In 1840 the census was enlarged again. Congress requested new information on revolutionary war pensioners, schools and colleges, literacy, occupations, idiocy, and insanity, as well as commerce and industry. Secretary of State John Forsyth appointed William Weaver, a Virginian with "a rather spotty record in government service" and little or no experience in statistics, to be the clerk to oversee the census. Weaver placed most of the questions on one two-sided schedule; he thus required the enumerator to fill in eighty columns of answers for each household. The enumerators had to total the columns for their districts. The marshals then totaled the columns from their enumerators and sent the results to Washington, D.C. Congress again authorized a small clerical staff in Washington to "correct" the returns; they ordered the publication of ten thousand copies of the census and a compendium.[27]

In 1840 the population of the United States reached 17 million; the decennial growth rate was 33 percent. Again the growth rates in the western states frequently amounted to 100 percent. Since 1820, the states of Missouri, Maine, Arkansas, and Michigan had been admitted to the Union. Without a substantial increase in the size of the House, the slower-growing states would again lose House representation.

The process of drafting an apportionment bill began as usual in early 1842 with a House bill that used Jefferson's method. The states jockeyed for position by suggesting divisors that would benefit one party or region

26. Dewey, *Financial History*, pp. 219*ff.*

27. Wright and Hunt, *History and Growth*, pp. 32–39; the quote about Weaver is from Cohen, *A Calculating People*, p. 185.

over another, and a bill enlarging the size of the House passed as usual. In the Senate, however, there was sentiment to stop the growth in the size of the House. Senators argued that 200 was the ideal House size and that sooner or later a cap would have to be set and maintained. They also suggested that the framers of the Constitution expected the House to have around 200 members. They further objected to Jefferson's method of apportionment and substituted Webster's method, which required that Congress choose the House size, determine each state's proportion of the House, and then find a divisor that would come closest to this proportion. In 1840, therefore, the Senate proposed a House size of 223, and the House reluctantly concurred. This apportionment cut Virginia's and New York's delegations by 6 members each, North Carolina's and Pennsylvania's by 4 each. The western states were the chief beneficiaries.[28]

In this same 1840 apportionment, Congress also passed the first legislation to regulate the House districting process. The Constitution was silent on how House members were to be elected within the states once the apportionment allocated their numbers. There is fairly good evidence that the framers intended the states to organize the House seats by equally sized districts, but until 1842 Congressmen in some states were elected at large or from multimember districts. After the 1842 legislation, representatives were to be "elected by districts composed of contiguous territory equal in number to the Representatives to which said states may be entitled, no one district electing more than one Representative." This language remained in apportionment legislation for the next eighty years.[29]

The 1840 census and apportionment process thus marked something

28. Balinski and Young, *Fair Representation,* pp. 31–35. In Balinski and Young's language, Webster's method required one to "choose the size of the house to be apportioned. Find a divisor x so that the whole numbers nearest to the quotients of the states sum to the required total. Give to each state its whole number" (p. 32). They argue that this method is ultimately the fairest one for apportioning the House, even though it has not been used since 1940; see chap. 6, below. Webster's method grants states with remainders over 0.5 an additional House member. In 1789 Congress submitted an amendment to the states that would have set the relationship between the size of Congress and the ratio of representation. The article, never ratified, required that once the House size reached 200, the minimum ratio of representation would be 50,000. Beyond that, Congress did not project. Donald O. Dewey, *Union and Liberty: A Documentary History of American Constitutionalism* (New York: McGraw-Hill, 1969), pp. 56–57.

29. Congressional Quarterly, "History of Reapportionment and Redistricting," in *Guide to U.S. Elections* (Washington, D.C.: Congressional Quarterly, 1975), pp. 519–41, quotation on p. 526. Under the Constitution, the state legislatures draw the House districts. Drawing the districts to maximize a party or factional advantage is a time-honored tradition. It may be done by electing at large, by creating multimember districts (the methods outlawed by the 1842 legislation) or by the more accepted method of gerrymandering—that is, drawing district boundaries in such a way as to guarantee one party dominance of the district. Gerrymandering is only now under scrutiny in the courts (Davis v. Bandemer, 106 S. Ct. 2797 [1986]) for its impact on representation. See chap. 6 and Conclusion, below.

of a milestone. The scope of the census enlarged dramatically, the apportionment method changed for the first time since 1790, the size of the House stabilized, and the apportionment legislation added districting language. Essentially, the original thirteen states conceded that they could not stop the fundamental shift of political power westward. Webster's new apportionment method was not biased toward the larger states as was Jefferson's. The small, older states and the small, newer, but growing states could see a common advantage in changing methods.

After a half-century of census taking, then, the nation had accumulated a major body of experience in census taking and apportionment. While that expertise may look rudimentary to twentieth-century Americans, it represented a considerable development in building a science of statistics and the mathematical theory of political apportionment. In the days before computers, calculators, or even adding machines, compiling census data and calculating apportionment quotas was extraordinarily tedious and difficult. It was also fast becoming the province of a few experts who understood the mathematics and administrative intricacies of the process. The apportionment debates of 1842 reveal, for example, that most congressmen had little idea of what all the numbers meant. On one day in that debate the House voted on fifty-nine divisors for an apportionment. Clearly, most members voted according to their perception of local political advantage, not of the theory of apportionment. For the sake of orderly constitutional change, they were willing to be convinced by the most influential experts and vote a reapportionment.[30]

But what if the census and apportionment process had technical problems congruent with established political divisions in the society? What if the census and the apportionment process became overly politicized and no longer seemed fair, orderly, accurate, or credible to a portion of the American public? This danger always lurked behind census and apportionment debates because taking the census was a complex process that few Americans understood. And, as in an election, the losers in a reapportionment have to accept the results.

Such a situation developed in the months after the 1842 apportionment as interested readers pored over the 1840 census results. The 1830s saw a flowering of interest in what one might call social statistics—perhaps best symbolized by the founding of the American Statistical Association in Boston in 1839. Newspapers and magazines carried the usual articles on what the new census data showed: where the population was growing, what the age, sex, and racial distributions were, and so forth. Most results were interesting but uncontroversial. The literate public was especially interested in the results of the new inquiries on the economy, idiocy and insanity, marital status, and so on. As the articles began to

30. Balinski and Young, *Fair Representation*, p. 34.

appear, several authors noticed that the new data seemed to show a surprisingly high rate of insanity among the free black population. In the North, 1 in every 162 blacks was insane or an idiot; in the South, the ratio was 1 in 1,558. (The rate for whites was about 1 in 970.) Southerners gleefully concluded that the census showed that slaves went insane when freed: "The free negroes of the northern states are the most vicious persons on this continent, perhaps on the earth," reported the *Southern Literary Messenger*. Northerners responded that something must be wrong with the census data and set about to find the errors.[31]

For the next two and a half years, government officials, slavery defenders, antislavery activists, and the infant statistical community battled over the data. Massachusetts intellectual and early leader of the new American Statistical Association Edward Jarvis examined the results in detail to look for the mistakes; John Quincy Adams vainly tried to create an effective investigating committee in Congress to search out and correct the errors. But John C. Calhoun, by then secretary of State, found the data too useful to discredit, so he appointed William Weaver, the man first responsible for the errors, to report to Congress on the census. Weaver of course defended his actions as census clerk, and the 1840 census data remained as printed.

The historical concensus is that the data were wrong. Cohen has written the definitive explanation of how the errors crept into the reports. The unwieldy 80-column schedule made it easy to enter answers in the wrong spaces—particularly to list elderly whites, who were, as Cohen puts it, "considered idiots in the common parlance" in the "colored" column, because the word *colored* was not prominently displayed (see fig. 1). Since the small census staff had no formal procedures for cross-checking and cross-validating the answers, they did not discover the anomalous entries of, say, idiotic blacks in households with no black members. In the South, small numbers of "idiotic" whites listed as blacks would not show up because the black population was so large; in the North, however, the black population was so small that any such consistent error would inflate the insanity rate alarmingly.[32]

As Cohen showed, though, those involved in this dispute could not admit this explanation. The politics of slavery led Calhoun to defend the census against all complaints. Jarvis and Adams first saw the work of the "slave oligarchy" in the mistaken data. When Jarvis discovered that the errors were in the manuscript schedules as well as in the printed data, he "was content to resort to a random-error argument, resulting from multiple copies and fluttering eyes." Jarvis, probably one of the most sophisti-

---

31. My account is taken from Cohen, *A Calculating People*, pp. 175–204, quotation on p. 195.

32. Ibid., pp. 203–4.

CENSUS OF 1840.

CENSUS OF 1840—Continued.

NUMBER OF PERSONS EMPLOYED IN—
- Mining.
- Agriculture.
- Commerce.
- Manufactures and trades.
- Navigation of the ocean.
- Navigation of canals, lakes, and rivers.
- Learned professions and engineers.

Number of pensioners for revolutionary or military services.

DEAF AND DUMB, BLIND, AND INSANE WHITE PERSONS.

DEAF AND DUMB.
- Under 14.
- 14 and under 25.
- 25 and upwards.

Blind.

INSANE AND IDIOTS.
- At public charge.
- At private charge.

DEAF, DUMB, BLIND, AND INSANE COLORED PERSONS.

DEAF, DUMB, AND BLIND.
- Deaf and dumb.
- Blind.

INSANE AND IDIOTS.
- At private charge.
- At public charge.

SCHOOLS, &c.
- Universities or colleges.
- Number of students.
- Academies and grammar schools.
- Number of scholars.
- Primary and common schools.
- Number of scholars.
- Number of scholars at public charge.
- Number of white persons over 20 years of age who cannot read and write.

Name of county.

Name of ward, town, township, parish, precinct, hundred, or district.

FREE WHITE PERSONS.

MALES.
- Under 5.
- 5 and under 10.
- 10 and under 15.
- 15 and under 20.
- 20 and under 30.
- 30 and under 40.
- 40 and under 50.
- 50 and under 60.
- 60 and under 70.
- 70 and under 80.
- 80 and under 90.
- 90 and under 100.
- 100 and upwards.

FEMALES.
- Under 5.
- 5 and under 10.
- 10 and under 15.
- 15 and under 20.
- 20 and under 30.
- 30 and under 40.
- 40 and under 50.
- 50 and under 60.
- 60 and under 70.
- 70 and under 80.
- 80 and under 90.
- 90 and under 100.
- 100 and upwards.

FREE COLORED PERSONS.

MALES.
- Under 10.
- 10 and under 24.
- 24 and under 36.
- 36 and under 55.
- 55 and under 100.
- 100 and upwards.

FEMALES.
- Under 10.
- 10 and under 24.
- 24 and under 36.
- 36 and under 55.
- 55 and under 100.
- 100 and upwards.

SLAVES.

MALES.
- Under 10.
- 10 and under 24.
- 24 and under 36.
- 36 and under 55.
- 55 and under 100.
- 100 and upwards.

FEMALES.
- Under 10.
- 10 and under 24.
- 24 and under 36.
- 36 and under 55.
- 55 and under 100.
- 100 and upwards.

Total.

---

1. Census of 1840. This copy of the questions from the 1840 Census illustrates how difficult it was for the assistant marshal to fill it out correctly. The assistant marshal entered tallies on each line for each family and could easily lose his place as he moved across the page.

cated statisticians of his day, did not see that systematic errors could result from the design of the schedule.

Thus, by the census of 1840, Congress and the Americans interested in statistical descriptions of the "progress of the United States in population and wealth" had learned that the numbers could also be less precise, accurate, and informative than they seemed at first glance. Congress had learned in its first effort at apportionment that there existed several, equally valid—or at least equally defensible—mathematical ways to apportion Congress. In 1840 Americans learned that the census itself could produce incorrect, and politically explosive, results. This experience, and the growing interest in the implications of American social and economic expansion, prompted further thinking about the census and the apportionment process. By the late 1840s a small but influential group of intellectuals, including Jarvis, pressed for major reform of the census machinery. As Carroll Wright and William C. Hunt noted later in the century, "The census of 1840 brought to a close . . . the first period of census taking in this country." This novel innovation of the Constitution had served the country well. But, like other pieces of the American constitutional system, it was about to confront the impending crises of sectionalism and the future of the Union.[33]

33. Wright and Hunt, *History and Growth*, p. 38.

| Sectional Crisis and
Census Reform in the 1850s

This [census] bill—a sort of interlude in the great context of the day—contains nothing of the tragic interest that surrounds the question that has so long claimed the attention of this body, the dissolution of the Union. *It regards the Union as it is, and I trust it will be for ages to come. In place of regarding it in fragments, weakened and distracted, its object is to ascertain its strength and resources, in its unity and beauty.*
—Congressman James Thompson (Democrat–Pennsylvania),
Speech, House of Representatives, 1850

The history of the middle decades of the nineteenth century appropriately tends to focus on the growing sectional conflict between North and South and the coming of the Civil War. This period witnessed, in John C. Calhoun's words, "the cords which bind these states together in one common Union" break apart.[1] Much of the political history of the period emphasizes the growing fractiousness of congressional debate, the paralysis of congressional policy-making, the disintegration of the Whig party, the realignment of the Democrats, and the birth of the Republican party. Further, because we know that the question of slavery did ultimately lead to the break-up of the Union and to Civil War, much biography has focused on those leaders who recognized the dangers inherent in the situation and tried, from whatever standpoint, to solve the problem. We

1. For Calhoun's speech, see *Congressional Globe*, 31st Cong., 1st sess., 1850, pp. 451–55.

focus on the Clays, Calhouns, Lincolns, or Douglases because they saw the depth of the crisis and tried to cope with it.

Nevertheless, the attention to these issues should not distract us from understanding other aspects of the political and social history of the 1850s—in particular why the various compromises, truces, and resolutions of the sectional conflicts proved so unstable. The compromises were ultimately based on an understanding of a balance of power and compromise of interest between North and South, and this balance required a rough equality of resources, population, and wealth between the sections. It was precisely the dynamism of the growth in population, wealth, and resources in the nation that disrupted the balance and led each section to see the other gaining an unfair advantage and jeopardizing the Union.

Such questions of foreign policy as further acquisitions of territory brought Congress and the presidents back to the issues of the extension of slavery and sectionalism. Questions of railroad development and the settlement of the vast lands of the West created crises over slavery extension. And debates over whether the states or the federal government should foster economic development and internal improvements alternately aroused fears of disunion or federal encroachment on local rights. In other words, in the 1850s Americans came to realize that the population growth and territorial expansion that they thought of as part of their "manifest destiny" and as evidence of the vitality of their republican form of government could also undermine the Union.

At the same time, Americans called for new institutions to support a more complex and integrated economy. Among these were government institutions to monitor, analyze, and organize that development. In the 1830s and 1840s, the infant statistical community had begun to press for the creation of a more professional national statistical system. Like Madison, Jefferson, and Hamilton before them, men like Edward Jarvis or George Tucker saw the decennial census as the centerpiece of any new effort. In this view, the census could be much more than an accounting of the population for apportionment. It could monitor the process of growth and development in a variety of ways and thus could serve, in Tucker's words, the "philosopher," "political economist," "statesman and legislator."

In the 1850s, amid acrimonious battles between North and South, Congress grappled with reforming the census. Congress made major innovations in the national statistical system—that is, created a complex new structure for taking the decennial census—during the contentious debates over the Compromise of 1850. Powerful underlying nationalizing and centralizing tendencies characterized the period—despite the centrifugal forces. Congress redirected the census from its traditional role as an apportionment instrument and added major new scientific functions to the decennial effort. In so doing, Congress opened a new phase in the statistical history of the country.

In the lame duck session of Congress in the winter of 1848–49, the Senate Select Committee on the Census reported a bill for taking the 1850 census. Modeled quite closely on the 1840 census law, the bill (S. 353) reached the floor on February 26, the last week of the session. It did not fare well. On March 1, two days before adjournment, Whig senator Joseph R. Underwood of Kentucky brought the bill up "for the last time." Sensing that the Senate did not intend to pass the measure, Underwood made one last plea for passage. He pointed that the census required much preparatory work: forms printed, assistant marshals appointed through-out the country, the machinery of census taking organized. He noted that the previous census bill had passed in the session before the census year, in 1839, and pointed out that Congress would be out of session from March until December 1849. To lay the matter over to the Thirty-first Congress would leave too little time to organize the census.

His fellow senators were unconvinced. Two lines of thought character-

2. Joseph Camp Griffith Kennedy, superintendent
of the Census Office, 1850 and 1860.

ized the opposition to the bill. On one hand, states' rights advocates such as Democrat John C. Calhoun of South Carolina thought that the bill overstretched the power of the central government. It was "an illustration of the tendency of the action of this government towards a concentration of power." Statistics of agriculture, commerce, or manufactures such as were envisioned in the bill, he felt, should be collected either by the states or by local agricultural or voluntary associations. On the other, Whig senator John Davis of Massachusetts objected to Underwood's bill because it did not go far enough in correcting the problems of the 1840 census and in extending the statistical efforts of the national government. Davis proposed an amendment to create a Census Board composed of the secretaries of State and Interior and the postmaster general to "prepare a bill which the statistics of the country will require, and report that bill to Congress at the commencement of the next session." Senator Robert M. T. Hunter of Virginia endorsed Davis's proposal, arguing that "it will give us time to mature a bill." He further encouraged such a plan since it was "especially . . . important for the American statesman to obtain a full and accurate view of all the parts of that vast society whose machinery he directs. He should have all possible facilities for studying our progress, and tracing the connection between cause and effect."

That day the matter was tabled. On Saturday, March 3, the last day of the session, Davis's amendment passed, creating the Census Board with an appropriation of ten thousand dollars and the authorization to appoint a secretary to organize the board's efforts. Two months later, in May 1849, Whig president Zachary Taylor appointed Joseph C. G. Kennedy, a thirty-six-year-old Pennsylvanian, to the position of secretary (fig. 2).[2]

We now know that the creation of the Census Board and the appointment of Kennedy as its secretary marked a major change in American census taking. The 1850 census was more extensive in scope and more scientific in form and procedure than earlier censuses, and Kennedy was to oversee the administration of the census for most of the next sixteen years. For the first time the federal government marshaled scientific and financial resources to discuss what should be asked on the census, how the information should be collected, and how it might be reported afterwards. Traditionally Congress had legislated not only the general outline of the census but the actual form of the questions on the schedules. Congress had determined that the canvass would be a household count and what primitive age, sex, color, or civil condition classifications would be made. The secretary of State had merely sent the instructions to the

2. For Senator Underwood's bill, see *House and Senate Bills and Joint Resolutions*, 30th Cong., 2d sess., 1849, S. 353; for the report on the bill, see "On the 7th Census, or Enumeration of the People," *Senate Report* 323, 30th Cong., 2d sess., 1849 (Serial 535); for the Mar. 1, 1849, debate, see *Congressional Globe*, 30th Cong., 2d sess., 1849, 20:626–29.

marshals, did minimal checking of the totals, and arranged for printing and publication of the compilations. The tabulation of the figures for towns and minor civil divisions had been done at the local level by the assistants to the U.S. marshals. The clerks in the Census Office had merely checked for clerical errors in the totals that they received.[3]

The imminent change in census procedure was not immediately obvious. Taylor's appointment of Kennedy followed in the time-honored tradition of offering such administrative positions to loyal political supporters. Kennedy's only qualification for the job was the ardent effort he made for Taylor in the fall 1848 election in Meadville, Pennsylvania. Kennedy was a relatively well off farmer from a "good" family who had dabbled in newspaper work. Like William Weaver before him, no evidence suggests that he showed any interest in statistics or federal social research before his arrival in Washington in the spring of 1849.[4]

Kennedy began his new career as census clerk by soliciting information on the form of the schedules. He discovered a small lobby of scholars and statisticians who had very definite opinions on the form of the 1850 census and who proceeded to press for a radical revision of existing procedures. These men had concluded that the problems of the 1840 census derived from its cumbersome schedule and decentralized tabulation procedures. They proposed that the unit of analysis for the population census be the individual, not the family or household, and that complete data be collected on every individual in the country. They further proposed that this data be tabulated and analyzed by the Census Office in Washington rather than by the local enumerators in the field. In the fall of 1849, the Census Board asked Lemuel Shattuck of the American Statistical Association and Archibald Russell of the American Geographical and Statistical Society to come to Washington to help Kennedy draw up the schedules. They did so, and the process of census taking was changed forever. Shattuck, Russell, and Kennedy restructured the census

3. For a discussion of census procedures before 1850, see Patricia Cline Cohen, *A Calculating People: The Spread of Numeracy in Early America* (Chicago: University of Chicago Press, 1982), pp. 175–204; Carroll Wright and William C. Hunt, *History and Growth of the United States Census* (Washington, D.C.: GPO, 1900), pp. 12–39; and Robert C. Davis, "The Beginnings of American Social Research," in *Nineteenth-Century American Science: A Reappraisal*, ed. George Daniels (Evanston, Ill.: Northwestern University Press, 1972), pp. 152–78.

4. Biographical information on Joseph C. G. Kennedy is scattered; I have pieced together much of his life history from his official and personal correspondence, which was very broad. He left no unified collection of papers. For his early life, see *DAB*, 5:335–36; Paul J. Fitzpatrick, "Leading American Statisticians in the Nineteenth Century II," *JASA* 53 (September 1958): 692–94; and Hollis Kellogg, *Life of the Venerable John Fox of Meadville, Pa.* (Meadville, Pa.: n.p., 1921), pp. 40–44 (chapter entitled, "I hire out on the farm of Joseph C. G. Kennedy," 1846–49). Other materials are in the archives of the Pelletier Library at Allegheny College, Kennedy's alma mater, in Meadville, Pa. A small file of his papers are in the Walter Willcox Collection, Library of Congress.

schedules to collect individual-level data. These schedules in turn guaranteed the creation of a large statistical office in Washington to tabulate and publish the results of the new inquiries.[5]

When Congress returned in December 1849 it found that the Census Board and its secretary had indeed been busy. John M. Clayton, Reverdy Johnson, and Jacob Collamer reported to the president on December 1, 1849, that they had "prepared and ordered to be printed such forms and schedules as seemed necessary, under the law, for a correct enumeration of the inhabitants of the United States, and to obtain full information concerning the industrial resources and the pursuits, education, and condition of the people." Kennedy, Shattuck, and Russell had categorized the inquiries asked on previous censuses and had constructed six schedules to encompass different aspects of the census. They expected each schedule to be simple enough for the assistant marshal to record the data accurately. Schedule 1 was for the free population; it contained thirteen questions. These included the person's name, address, age, sex, color, occupation, and place of birth. The schedule also asked whether the person had been married or had attended school within the year, whether the individual was deaf and dumb, blind, insane, idiotic, a pauper, or a convict, whether the person was illiterate if over age twenty, and the amount of real estate owned by the person. Schedule 2 was for the slave population. It requested the name of the slaveowner, the name, age, sex, color, and place of birth of the slave, and whether the slave was deaf and dumb, blind, insane, idiotic, or a fugitive. It also contained inquiries on the number of children each woman had borne and whether the children were alive. Schedule 3, for persons who had died in the previous year, asked questions similar to those on the population schedules. Schedules 4 and 5 requested information on agriculture and manufacturing by farm or establishment, respectively. Schedule 6 asked the assistant marshal to provide a broad description of "social statistics" for his subdivision, including information on taxes collected, schools, newspapers, pauperism and crime, wages, religion, and libraries. Although each schedule was simple enough, the aggregate with their separate instructions would obviously increase the work of the assistant marshals considerably.[6]

---

5. Jesse Chickering and Nahum Capen had provided recommendations on the 1850 census in 1849. See "Letters Addressed to the Hon. John Davis Concerning the Census . . . ," S. Misc. Doc. 64, 30th Cong., 2d sess., 1849 (Serial 533). Edward Jarvis also sent a plan to Joseph C. G. Kennedy on taking the 1850 census; see Gerald Grob, *Edward Jarvis and the Medical World of Nineteenth-Century America* (Knoxville, Tenn.: University of Tennessee Press, 1978), p. 142. For Shattuck's and Russell's contribution, see Davis, "Beginnings of Social Research," pp. 164–65. Josiah Nott, a Mobile physician, had recommendations for the slave schedule; see *Congressional Globe*, 31st Cong., 1st sess., 1850, 21, pt. 1:677.

6. "Report of the Census Board," 31st Cong., 1st sess., 1849, S. Ex. Doc. 1 (Serial 549), p. 851.

The Senate and the House received the report of the Census Board as part of the president's message but apparently did not understand that the board had prepared the schedules. After waiting impatiently for three weeks for the House to elect a Speaker (it could not conduct business in the interim), the Senate created its own Select Committee on the Census and began the process of drafting a census bill. In January, Kennedy supplied the Senate Select Committee with copies of the schedules the board had prepared. At this point a grand misunderstanding developed between the Senate Select Committee, Kennedy, and the Census Board over the division of authority in planning for the census. The board had already gone ahead with a printing order since it understood its charge to be to prepare the schedules. The senators, on the other hand, conceived the process of drafting a census bill as including both writing the enabling legislation and drafting the schedules. Thus the Senate began its efforts by amending the schedules prepared by the board, even though Kennedy had already sent the schedules to the printer. In late January the Senate Select Committee reported the census bill to the full Senate with new schedules. In early February the board realized that the Senate intended to exercise its prerogative to amend the tables and "directed the printer to suspend operations." Heated debate broke out on the Senate floor about the executive's usurpation of the functions of the legislative branch. The census bill was off to a controversial start. For the next four months, the census bill worked its way through Congress amid the sectional crisis and debates over the Compromise of 1850. On May 23, some eight days before the actual count was to begin, the 1850 census bill became law.[7]

Its tortured legislative history reveals much about the nature of the state and society in the mid-nineteenth century. The members of the Thirty-first Congress who debated the census bill and the Great Compromise were keenly aware of the potential power of the statistics they were about to mandate. Thus the issues of union or disunion, slavery, the proper scope of federal power, the appropriate trajectory for future population and economic growth, and the balance of power between North and South influenced the type of questions asked on the census, the structure of the bureaucracy set up to administer the census, and the character of the reports published from the data.

In the Senate, the census bill had to vie for attention with Clay's

---

7. The Thirty-first Congress got off to a bad start because neither party had sufficient support to elect a Speaker of the House, and the Senate could not begin business until the House was organized. See David Potter, *The Impending Crisis, 1848–1861* (New York: Harper & Row, 1976), pp. 90*ff.*, and *Congressional Globe*, 31st Cong., 1st sess., 1849, pp. 1–66. For the history of the Senate bill and the misunderstanding between Kennedy and the Senate, see *Congressional Globe*, pp. 75, 96, 232–33, 282–92; "Report of the Census Board," 31st Cong., 1st sess., S. Ex. Doc. 38, 1850 (Serial 558). For the original Senate bill (S. 76), see *House and Senate Bills and Joint Resolutions*, 31st Cong., 1st sess., 1850.

| SCHEDULE 2.—Slave Inhabitants in | | | | | | in the County of | | | | | State | | |

3. Schedule 2, Slave Inhabitants, 1850. The 1850 slave schedule was shorter than the schedule for the free population (see fig. 6). It contained a column for the name of the slaveowner; each slave was identified by number only.

compromise measures and the floor debates on them. After a day of debate in early February over the prerogatives of Congress to determine who would get the printing contracts, the bill languished for over a month. In mid-March it was again brought to the floor but again became bogged down in discussions of printing and the propriety of the Census Board's actions. Meanwhile, Kennedy was getting increasingly nervous about the preliminary preparations for setting up the field administration. By early January he assumed that he would continue to administer the census after the passage of the final bill, and he wrote to the secretary of the Interior asking for the authority to contact the U.S. marshals in the "most distant" part of the country. In the House in early March, Democrat James Thompson of Pennsylvania began an independent process of drafting a bill and referred the matter to the House Judiciary Committee. On April 8, Thompson reported a bill on the House floor. Still no definite action took place.[8]

Finally, on April 9 and 10, the Senate debated, amended, and passed a bill. During that debate, the second schedule (fig. 3), that for enumerating the slave population, became the target for the opposition to the bill as a whole. In previous censuses the assistant marshals had asked questions of the household head. How many free white males or females in a particular age cohort lived in the household? How many free black males or females? How many slaves? How many pensioners? The new schedules would ask questions about the characteristics of every individual in the

8. *Congressional Globe*, 31st Cong., 1st sess., 1850, pp. 282–92, 502, 540–43, 547–48, 565–70, 604, for the Senate's progress on the bill. For efforts to draft a bill in the House, see ibid., pp. 473, 653. For Kennedy's efforts to make preliminary efforts to take the census, see Joseph C. G. Kennedy to Thomas Ewing, Jan. 9, 14, 25, 1850, Records of the Secretary of the Interior, Entry 280, RG 48, NA.

country—even the slaves. The new schedules thus expanded the potential detail tremendously and made it possible—as social scientists and historians have proved—to analyze the character and trajectory of the population in extraordinary ways. And since Congress was also debating the future of slavery at the same time, it was obvious to both sides that increased data on slaves would increase analyses that compared the situation of the black and white populations in the United States. Few southern Democrats wanted new federal investigations into the "peculiar institution."

As recommended by the Census Board, the schedule could be used to show not only that slaves were "owned" but also that they had family ties. The data produced in the schedules would allow the researcher to chart the migration patterns of slaves. The new schedule asked not only for the name of the slaveowner, as in previous counts, but also for the name of each slave and an individual accounting of the slave's age, sex, color, and place of birth. It further required of all female slaves the number of children they had borne and the number of those known to be alive or dead. Finally, it asked whether the slave was "deaf and dumb, blind, insane, or idiotic," and his or her "degree of removal from pure white and black races." Southern concern with this schedule was immediate. Democrat Andrew Butler from South Carolina moved to delete the names of the slaves and list them merely by number; the amendment passed. Democrat William King of Alabama moved to delete the question on the place of birth of slaves; it was agreed to. King then moved to delete the question about the number of children born to female slaves, somewhat disingenuously defending his proposal on the grounds that these questions were too complex for a census enumeration and would jeopardize the overall accuracy of the count. At this point, Davis of Massachusetts and Underwood of Kentucky, defenders of the bill, came to the floor to oppose further changes. Both argued that important social and political judgments about the relative fecundity and longevity of the white and black races could be made from the data. Underwood pointed out that it was a southern physician, Josiah Nott, who had recommended the schedule form and had requested the data for life insurance tables.[9]

Davis and Underwood's arguments merely exacerbated the general mood and encouraged other senators to malign the entire proposal for expanding the scope of the census. By the time Whig William Seward of New York spoke in favor of the original schedule, tensions had reached a high level. Seward drew out the explosive implications in the questions and noted that he saw these data as a means for finding out "how rapid"

9. For Josiah Nott's racial theories and his interest in the census, see Reginald Horsman, *Dr. Nott of Mobile: Southerner, Physician, and Racial Theorist* (New Orleans, La.: Louisiana State University Press, 1987).

the "progress" of the African race was in this country; he sardonically concluded that such "improvement" "constitutes, the only excuse, as I understand, that we have for holding them in servitude."

Southern reaction was sharp. King accused Seward of stirring up sectional prejudice and "ministering to that miserable fanatical spirit" that would split the Union. Debate continued, and King's amendment to delete the question on children born to female slaves passed. Opponents of a broadened census, smelling an opportunity, then moved to delete the other questions and return to the form used in the 1840 census. On a series of votes, this proposal failed, though the question on mixed blood was deleted. In so doing, the Senate had shown its willingness to bow to proslavery sentiments and to restrict severely the amount of information collected on the slave population. Nevertheless, the basic expanded schedule remained, and the most conservative efforts to turn back to the mode of census taking in 1840 failed.[10]

The following day, the Senate considered and passed the rest of the bill. On April 11 the bill reached the House and was sent to the Judiciary Committee. It was reported back on April 22 with amendments and was scheduled for debate. On April 24 James Thompson of the Judiciary Committee opened the debate with an impassioned plea for early passage and a call for members to see the census as a unifying force for a nation in crisis:

> I may be allowed in the outset to remark, that this bill—a sort of interlude in the great contest of the day—contains nothing of the tragic interest that surrounds the question that has so long claimed the attention of this body, the *dissolution of the Union.* It regards the Union as it is, and I trust it will be for ages to come. In place of regarding it in fragments, weakened and distracted, its object is to ascertain its strength and resources, in its unity and beauty.

Nevertheless, Thompson's hope was only partially fulfilled. Daily debate on the bill continued for two weeks. The House touched on the same issues of sectionalism, slavery, and the proper reach of the federal government in economic and social matters that had concerned the Senate. Opposition to the bill was led by Alexander Stephens of Georgia on the grounds that the Constitution did not justify the proposed expansion of the role of the federal government in the collection of statistics.

The House, though, was not terribly sympathetic to Stephens's views and in fact added provisions that strengthened the federal statistical apparatus and lent permanence to the system embodied in the bill. From the House Judiciary Committee came an amendment, probably written by Joseph Kennedy, to create a superintendent of the census at a salary of $2,500 a year. From the floor, Whig Samuel Vinton of Ohio amended the

10. *Congressional Globe,* 31st Cong., 1st sess., 1850, pp. 671–80, 687–94.

bill to make it permanent—that is, to enable future censuses to be taken according to the 1850 law unless Congress legislated otherwise. Finally, Vinton proposed a permanent and automatic method of apportionment of Congress. He pointed out that, in the current crisis over the future of slavery, Congress could ill afford to engage in another debilitating apportionment fight. He thus suggested that the apportionment method and House size be set before the census was taken. When the numbers were in, the Interior Department would calculate the apportionment and send the information to Congress and the state legislatures. After much wrangling, House members agreed and set the size at 233. An apportionment system, which came to be known as the Vinton method but which was actually Alexander Hamilton's method, was approved. The House thus acknowledged the demographic realities evident in the previous thirty years. Representation was shifting to the West; the South was losing relative standing in relationship to the North.[11]

On May 8 the amended bill passed the House. For the next two weeks, the bill returned to the Senate, went to conference, and was passed. Kennedy became census superintendent, and the 1850 census began.

During the summer of 1850 Kennedy organized the Census Office, sent out sets of the six schedules to the forty-five marshals, rented quarters for the clerical staff, and waited for the returns to come in. The primary office work involved packing and sending the schedules, instructions, and oaths. Kennedy employed about twenty people, mostly packers who organized and mailed the one hundred tons of forms to the marshals. On August 29 the first returns arrived back in Washington; the deadline for the arrival of the rest was the beginning of October. The assistants to the U.S. marshals who actually went door to door and took the census were to receive half their pay when they began their task and the remainder when the job was done, received in Washington, and checked for errors and omissions.

By the end of November, when Kennedy filed his annual report, 967 of the 3,231 assistant marshals (30 percent) had returned the schedules. Kennedy began to increase the clerical staff to tabulate and "condense" the returns. By the end of the year 35 to 40 clerks were working at tallying by hand the information on the schedules into summary form.[12] The rest

11. Ibid., pp. 808–14, 820–23, 830, 836–42, 855–63, 874–83, 895–98, 904–9, 910–14, 923–30, 939–40. Thompson's remarks are on p. 809. Opponents to the Thompson bill introduced a substitute on April 22 (John Miller [D–Ohio] amendment), which returned to the form of the 1840 census legislation. Miller's bill suggested an individual-level schedule but asked only for the name, age, sex, and color of free persons, and for slaves, the name of the slave-owner, number of slaves owned, and ages, sex, and color. Authority to administer the census was to be returned to the Department of State.

12. Census Office, "Payroll for Census Office Employees, 1850–55," no. 9, Records of the Bureau of the Census, RG 29, NA; "Annual Report of the Superintendent of the Census," Nov. 30, 1850, 31st Cong., 2d sess., S. Ex. Doc. 1 (Serial 587); Wright and Hunt, *History and Growth*, pp. 47–48.

of the returns dribbled in. By July 1851 Kennedy had received all of the schedules except for some in Mississippi and Indiana and a large portion of those from newly acquired territory in Texas, California, and Utah. The "Census Office" itself spread to four buildings in downtown Washington. By the end of December 1851 its office staff of 174 represented 10 percent of the federal work force in Washington.[13]

During 1851 both Kennedy and Congress began to understand some of the implications of the new system of census taking. Hand tallying the numerous columns of numbers from the census schedules had always been a tedious business, but before 1850 most of the figuring had been done by the assistant marshals before they sent their work to Washington. The Census Office in Washington had relied on the temporary clerical aid of the several thousand assistant marshals and had only checked for mistakes and further aggregated the data.

The new legislation, though, directed the marshals merely to take the census and then to deliver the raw schedules to Washington for tallying. There, the census clerical staff transferred the information on the schedules to tally sheets and totaled and classified the population. The published 1850 census volume provided examples of six "condensing forms" used to classify the free population by age, sex, color, occupation, nativity, and physical or mental disability (see fig. 4). Each time a form was used, the schedules had to be handled. The results of these initial tabulations for local areas and counties then had to be further aggregated into larger and larger geographic units. If data were missing on the schedules, the clerks had to decide whether to interpolate the information, write to the assistant marshal and ask for the missing information, or simply omit it. On open-ended questions, such as for the classification of the labor force into occupational categories, rules had to be devised for handling double answers, vague answers, and obviously incorrect answers. As far as we know, none of these logistical and procedural problems had been anticipated by either Congress or the officers of the Interior Department.[14] In fact, there is evidence to suggest just the opposite. In the congressional debates of the Thirty-first Congress, one of the objections made to collecting individual-level data was that it would be too much to publish. Several senators thus did not even understand that there was to be a tabulation process that would "condense" or, as we would say, "cross-tabulate," the

13. Superintendent to the Secretary of the Interior, June 21, 1851, Correspondence of the Secretary of the Interior, entry 280, RG 48, NA. See letters in the "1851 letters" package on the location of the Census Office staff. See also "Report of the Secretary of the Interior," Aug. 25, 1852, 32d Cong., 1st sess., S. Ex. Doc. 111 (Serial 621), pp. 3–7. For an estimate of the total federal work force in the early 1850s, see Bureau of the Census, *Historical Statistics of the United States*, pt. 2 (Washington, D.C.: GPO, 1975), p. 1103.

14. Census Office, *Seventh Census of the United States: 1850* (Washington, D.C.: Robert Armstrong, 1853), pp. 13–14. For a discussion of the problems of hand tabulating the census, see Margo Anderson Conk, "Labor Statistics in the American and English Census: Making Some Individual Comparisons," *Journal of Social History* 16 (Summer 1983): 83–102.

1. CLASSIFICATION OF FREE INHABITANTS IN THE COUNTY OF ————.

	Whites.	Colored.	Total.			White.		Colored.		Native.		Foreign.	
				Born in State		M.	F.	M.	F.	M.	F.	M.	F.
Under 1 .... Male				Born in Maine									
Female				Born in New Hampshire									
				&c., &c.									
1 and under 5 .... Male				Born in England									
Female				Born in Ireland	At school								
				Born in Scotland	Adults who cannot read and write								
&c., &c.				Born in France	Paupers								
				&c., &c.	Convicts								
				Married in year									

2. CLASSIFICATION IN THE STATE OF ————.   3. CLASSIFICATION—Continued.

Counties.	WHITES.								COLORED.								TOTAL WHITE.		TOTAL FREE COLORED.		Aggregate.

(tables 2 and 3 are extensive multi-column census breakdowns with headers: Under 1., 1 and under 5., And so on, for all ages; Under 1.; Aggregate; Attending School — White, Free colored; Native, Foreign, Total; Adults who cannot read & write—[Same div'ns as attending school.]; Paupers—[Same divis.]; Convicts.—[Same divis.]; Married in the year; Slaves—Under 1., And same divisions as free population.)

4. EDUCATION.   5. OCCUPATIONS.

COLLEGES. — County; Assistant marshal; Number; Teachers; Pupils; Endowment—amount received annually; Raised by taxation; From public funds; From other sources; Total income.

PUBLIC SCHOOLS. [Same divisions as Colleges.]

ACADEMIES AND OTHER SCHOOLS. [Same divisions.]

LIBRARIES. — Public; Private; Total. Number; Volumes; [Same div'ns.]; [Same div'ns.]

5. OCCUPATIONS.
Actors ....
Agents ....
Apothecaries ....
&c., &c. ....
Bakers ....
Other occupations ....
And so on, for about 450 different pursuits.

6. DEAF AND DUMB, BLIND, INSANE, AND IDIOTIC.

DEAF AND DUMB WHITES.					DEAF AND DUMB COLORED.	WHO CANNOT READ AND WRITE.							PLACE OF BIRTH.						
Under 10.	10 and under 30.	30 and under 70.	70 and upwards.	Total.	[Same divisions as whites.]	Whites.				Colored.		Aggregate.	In State.	United States.	Foreign.	Unknown.	Having occupation.	No occupation.	Blind, insane, idiotic.
						20 and under 30.		30 and above.		Total whites.	[Same div'ns.]								
						M.	F.	M.	F.										

* The divisions for blind omitted the occupation and distinction of age and color of those who cannot read and write, simply noting the fact of such incapacity. For the insane and idiotic the divisions were the same as for the blind, except that the fact of reading and writing is not noted, and the ages are taken as under 10, 10 and 20, 20 and 40, 40 and 60, 60 and 80, 80 and over, for both colors.

7. NATIVITIES.   8. CHURCHES IN THE COUNTY, &c.

COUNTIES.	BORN IN STATE.	BORN IN UNITED STATES.				FOREIGN BORN.			Aggregate.
		Maine.	New Hampshire.	And so on, for all States.	Total.	England.	And so on, for all foreign States.	Total.	

8. CHURCHES IN THE COUNTY, &c.

Churches.	Number of churches.	Aggregate accommodations.	Value of church property.
Baptist			
Christian			
And so on, for every known sect and division of sect.			

9. MEDICAL STATISTICS.   10. DEATHS.

CAUSES OF DEATH.	MORTALITY OF FIRST YEAR.				1 year and under 2.	2 and under 5.	5 and under 10.	And so on, as in printed classified ages.
	First half.		Second half.					
	M.	F.	M.	F.				
Abscess								
Accident, not specified								
Accident, by fire								
&c., &c.								
Cancer								
And so on, for all known diseases classified.								

10. DEATHS.

	Whites.	Total whites.	Colored, free.	Total colored, free.	Total.
Under 1 .... Male					
Female ...					
1 and under 5 ... Male					
Female ...					
And so on, for classified ages to 100 and upwards.					

4. Blank Forms Used in the Census Office for Condensing Information, 1850. This form illustrates how the Census Office hand-tabulated the data from 1850 to 1880.

raw data. In other words, contemporaries did not clearly distinguish the phases of census taking into data collection, data tabulation and analysis, and the presentation of results. And, before the federal census of 1850, the only well-known individual census was Lemuel Shattuck's 1845 census of Boston. That census was the model for the 1850 effort. Nevertheless, the procedures that were adequate to count a concentrated, urban population of 100,000 were far from adequate to count a national, primarily frontier and rural, population of 23 million.[15]

In short, the census office of 1850 was almost overwhelmed by the magnitude and complexity of its task. Adding to its difficulties were the highly politicized atmosphere of Washington, the tensions generated by the disintegration of the party system and the sectional crisis, and the rather flamboyant character and sharp practices of Joseph Kennedy. In calmer times, Kennedy and the Census Office would have come under partisan scrutiny and perhaps attack for a "bloated" staff and slow progress in completing the census. In the early 1850s, though, there was little hope that they would receive a dispassionate evaluation. No one had any standard by which to judge the relative efficiency or competence of the processing of the census. Thus Congress and the press either vilified Kennedy as a crook and incompetent who had used his office to line his own pockets or praised him as a hard-working and hard-pressed bureaucrat who struggled to create both a new method of social investigation and a document that would illustrate the "unity and beauty" of America. As in most controversies of this kind, there was some truth to both positions.

When the Thirty-second Congress convened in December 1851, the members expected the results of the census for apportionment. Given the experience of previous censuses, they also expected some indication as to when the final census volumes would appear and the census apparatus would again be mothballed for the decade. They were quickly disabused of their optimism on both counts. From President Millard Fillmore's state of the Union message and from the annual reports of the secretary of the Interior and Kennedy, they learned that the population had again grown by 36 percent to 23 million. They also learned, however, that some of the census returns from California had been burned. Arrangements had been made to retake the census, but there was no indication when the results would reach Washington. The new automatic reapportionment could not proceed.[16]

15. *Congressional Globe*, 31st Cong., 1st sess., 1850, pp. 672–73; Paul J. Fitzpatrick, "Leading American Statisticians in the Nineteenth Century," *JASA* 52 (September 1957): 301–21.

16. "Annual Report of the Superintendent of Census," Dec. 1, 1851, *Congressional Globe*, 32d Cong., 1st sess., Appendix, pp. 73–82. For the report of the secretary of the Interior, see ibid., p. 13.

Kennedy submitted the probable apportionment of Congress in his December 1851 report. He estimated that the population of California was 165,000, though he had returns for only 92,000. The returns from San Francisco, Santa Clara, and Contra Costa counties were missing. He proposed that California receive two representatives.[17] Discussions had gone on from May 1851 through the winter about the need to retake the California census. In January 1852 Kennedy wrote to the secretary of the Interior suggesting that reapportionment proceed without the missing California returns.[18] He explained that granting California a second seat would have the effect of denying a sixth house seat to South Carolina. The Democratic Congress was not pleased with these figures, since a second seat for California would probably add a Whig to the House, while a sixth seat for South Carolina would add a Democrat. Congress wrangled over the reapportionment through the summer of 1852 and finally solved the problem by setting the size of the House at 234, thus giving both California and South Carolina an additional seat. The controversy again underscored the problems with the new census. Given the distances to be traveled and the frontier character of much of the country, though, it is surprising that Kennedy managed to avoid other instances of lost returns. Mail from California went by sea; letters took three months to reach Washington.[19]

Fillmore also informed Congress that he had sent Kennedy to Europe during the summer of 1851 to explore the possibility of organizing an international statistical congress and to examine the census methods of other nations. Kennedy had visited England, France, Belgium, Austria, and Prussia, had met with the most eminent statisticians of the day, including Adolphe Quetelet, William Farr, and Charles Babbage, and had studied the progress of the English and French censuses while they were being taken. The first International Statistical Congress met in 1853, and Kennedy remained an important American correspondent to it for the next twenty years.[20]

17. For the correspondence between Kennedy and the local enumerators in California, see "1851 letters," Correspondence of the Secretary of the Interior, entry 280, RG 48, NA.

18. In February, Interior Secretary Alexander Stuart reported an apportionment to Congress (32d Cong., 1st sess., 1852, S. Ex. Doc. 36).

19. For the debates in Congress on the reapportionment, see *Congressional Globe*, 32d Cong., 1st sess., 1852, pp. 968–76, 1007–15, 1051, 1161–62, 1177, 1187, 1792, 1888, 1933. The missing schedules never materialized. In January 1853 Congress authorized the Census Office to append the 1852 California State Census totals to the federal data in the published census volume. The state census showed a population of 255,000, though the data still contained many inconsistencies. See Census Office, *Seventh Census*, pp. xx, 965–85. For a discussion of the problems with censuses in California in this period, see Peter Decker, *Fortunes and Failures: White-Collar Mobility in Nineteenth-Century San Francisco* (Cambridge, Mass.: Harvard University Press, 1978), pp. 265*ff*.

20. For the importance of Kennedy's efforts in organizing the International Statistical

The members further learned that the size of the Census Office had grown from roughly 70 to over 170 between the time the Thirty-first Congress had adjourned and the Thirty-second had convened. And they learned that Kennedy had prepared a sample of the proposed census volume. He had compiled the data for the state of Maryland and had included information on geography and history, as well as the statistical results of the census.

Congress took up the question of publishing the census in the form of a joint resolution to offer the printing contract for the main volume to Donelson and Armstrong, the printers of the local Democratic party newspaper, the *Union*. The Democrats controlled both houses of Congress, and it was their prerogative to offer the contract to a printer favorable to their political views, even though the Whigs controlled the executive branch. Whigs in both houses naturally opposed the resolution, arguing that the printing contract should be handled by the Interior Department—that is, by the Whigs—and that it should be given to the low bidder.[21]

The debate raged on acrimoniously from January to March with no resolution. On March 9, the Senate set up a select committee to determine both the type of material that they wanted to include in the published census volume and how the printing would be handled. The committee reported back on June 28, charging that much of the material in Kennedy's sample census volume on Maryland was "unfit for publication," "a mass of useless and erroneous matter" filled with "errors and deficiencies." The committee recommended that the proposed statistics compiled by Kennedy be reduced by "four-fifths" to provide only the data whose accuracy could be guaranteed. The committee further documented which of the sections and tabular statements it believed to be "not only useless but injurious" and thus not to be authorized by Congress.[22]

In particular, the committee considered the statistics of mortality and manufactures to be filled with errors. These data were only published much later in the decade—the mortality data in 1855 and the manufacturing data in 1859. The committee recommended deletion of some twenty pages of historical and geological sketches about each state that Kennedy had included with the census data. And they objected to the introduction of any interpretive material into the body of the census volume beyond that necessary as "remarks . . . explanatory merely of the

Congress, see *DAB*, 5:335. For the diary of his trip and his notes on his discussions with the major statisticians in Europe, see the Kennedy file in the Walter Willcox Collection, LC, and his correspondence with the Secretary of the Interior, entry 280, 1851 file, RG 48, NA.

21. *Congressional Globe*, 32d Cong., 1st sess., pp. 21, 34, 104, 155–57, 203–7, 245–51, 259–66, 471–77.

22. Ibid., pp. 694, 702; "Plan for Publication of Returns of Census," 32d Cong., 1st sess., 1852, S. Rept. 276 (Serial 631), pp. 1, 2, 10.

tables." Specifically, they objected to Kennedy's "opinion" that "it does not appear [from the census data] that the introduction of the African race among the body of the population had any marked effect upon its progress." As in 1842, the census was again becoming entangled in the debates about the future of black Americans and the institution of slavery.[23]

Needless to say, the Senate report was a devastating indictment of the census, Kennedy, and the results of the new statistical efforts. And it prompted even more scrutiny of the Census Office to find out what had gone wrong and what might be done to rectify the situation and salvage the enormous expenditure of time and money. At the time, the Senate Committee was unsure where the problems lay. They identified three areas for further investigation: (1) "the short period allowed for the performance of the service"; (2) "want of capacity"; and (3) "negligence on the part of the subordinate agents."[24]

For the rest of the summer, the Democratic-controlled Senate continued to investigate the functioning of the Census Office. Congress was reapportioned, but only by adding one House member to make up for the probable missing population from California. At the same time, the two political parties selected candidates for the upcoming presidential election, and it became obvious that the Whig party was collapsing from the internal strains of the antislavery issue. Winfield Scott, the Whig nominee and the protégé of the Seward faction, was "soft" on the question of the finality of the Compromise of 1850 and thus unacceptable to the southern wing of the party. By the fall, such key southern Whigs as Alexander Stephens and Robert Toombs had abandoned the party. The Democrats nominated Franklin Pierce and pulled together for the sake of patronage and the spoils of office. The Census Office, as a major Whig enterprise, thus came under increasing attack.[25]

In August, the Senate requested information on the financial affairs of the office and publicized the fact that Joseph Kennedy owned two of the four buildings used for the Census Office. Suspicions were immediately aroused that he had overcharged the government for rent. The Senate also questioned whether Kennedy had overcharged the government for expenses for his European trip. And they wanted to know whether he had

23. "Plan for Publication," p. 2. For the proposed volume, see Census Office, 7th Census, 1850, *History and Statistics of . . . Maryland* (Washington, D.C.: Gideon & Co., 1852).

24. "Plan for Publication," p. 1. The final resolution authorizing publication of the quarto volume of the census was not passed in the first session. On the last day of the second session, Mar. 3, 1853, publication was finally authorized, essentially according to the guidelines laid out in the June 28 Senate report.

25. David Potter, *Impending Crisis,* pp. 225–66. For the apportionment history, see n. 9, above, and Michel L. Balinski and H. Peyton Young, *Fair Representation: Meeting the Ideal of One Man, One Vote* (New Haven and London: Yale University Press, 1982), pp. 36–37.

been drawing excess salary, since he claimed to be both secretary to the old Census Board and census superintendent. The 1850 law authorized $3,000 for the secretary's position and $2,500 for the superintendent's. Kennedy attempted to draw $3,000, though in Congress he was accused of drawing $5,500.[26]

Finally, Congress wanted to know why it was taking so long to "condense" the data; their inclination, given Kennedy's personal conduct and the heightened political climate, was to charge the office with incompetency and delay. One hundred and forty years later, it is very difficult to determine just how much truth there was to the charges of inefficiency and graft in the office, though some points can be made.

First, it is fairly obvious that the 1850 Census Office was probably the largest centralized clerical operation of the federal government at the time. It was also a new operation; office routines and work and production methods had not yet been developed. Nor were there relevant organizational efforts in the private sector that Kennedy could copy. The factory system was still in its infancy in the United States; "mass production" methods for white-collar, highly skilled, mathematical work would not be developed for another half-century. As Alfred Chandler has pointed out, railroads and wholesale and retail trade companies were all still relatively simple operations—with little understanding of what he called the efficiencies to be gained by rapid "throughput."

Yet the problems encountered during the processing of the census were quite akin to those faced by the entrepreneurs who developed the new factory system. The hand tallying of the census required precise, accurate, but highly repetitive, notations on the condensing forms. These forms then had to be checked for errors and further aggregated. Since the work could not be considered "complete" until all the elements of a tabulation—that is, all the counties, towns, states, and so on—had been completed, the process was plagued with bottlenecks. Further, since the raw schedules contained information that had to be combined in several ways, the process of handling the schedules and tallying had to be repeated over and over again. Again, the "flow" of materials and production through the system had severe problems. Finally, though the work itself was highly routinized, it was also highly skilled, since the clerks did have to make discretionary decisions about missing or contradictory information. And they had to have good work habits. It would not do to try

26. "Statement of Certain Expenditures for and on account of Seventh Census," 32d Cong., 1st sess., 1852, S. Ex. Doc. 111 (Serial 621); *Congressional Globe*, 32d Cong., 1st sess., 1852, pp. 1973, 2055–64, 2139–40, 2232. There is some evidence that Kennedy overcharged the government on rent for the "8th St. Office," as it was called. A letter of Dec. 30, 1853, from the former owner to the chief clerk of the Interior Department estimated that $1,000 per year would have been a fair rent. Kennedy had received $1,750 per year. See Correspondence of the Secretary of the Interior, entry 280, RG 48, NA.

to harass them and speed them up, since accuracy and precision would be sacrificed.[27]

There is much evidence to document these difficulties in processing the 1850 census, though none of the individuals involved analyzed the system as we have just done. Rather, Kennedy and the office staff experimented as they went along, sometimes finding solutions to their problems, sometimes not. For example, it was not until December 1850, six months after the count began, that Kennedy established a large office with twenty rooms to house the staff. Even this office was too small, and additional quarters had to be found. The clerical staff itself grew slowly; only in the third quarter of 1851, after Kennedy returned from his tour of European census offices, did the Washington office staff soar to 170 people. And the Interior secretary's annual report of December 1851 attests to the concerns the officials had with accuracy and the skill of the clerks. The secretary was well aware that only about 20 people were involved in the processing of the 1840 census. In defense of his current "extravagance," he wrote that during his administration "no pains have been spared to secure perspicuity of arrangement and accuracy of execution in the census." Such "perfect work" "required that all the calculations and classifications should be made by responsible clerks in office, instead of being confided to females and other persons having no interest on the subject, as has been done on former occasions." "Responsible clerks" were men; they cost one thousand dollars per year to employ.[28]

Finally, no census staff in later decades ever returned to the pre-1850 shoestring operation. Kennedy returned to supervise the 1860 census and employed roughly the same number of clerks that he had in 1850. Francis Amasa Walker, superintendent of the 1870 and 1880 censuses, found it necessary to expand the clerical staff in Washington in quantum jumps. The 1870 census, taken under the same legislative mandate as

27. For the difficulties of processing the census by hand, see Margo Anderson Conk, "Accuracy, Efficiency and Bias: The Interpretations of Women's Work in the U.S. Census of Occupations, 1890–1940," *Historical Methods* 14 (Spring 1981): 65–72, and Conk, "Labor Statistics." For discussions of the organizational difficulties of large factories or bureaucracies, see Alfred Chandler, *The Visible Hand: The Managerial Revolution in American Business* (Cambridge, Mass.: Harvard University Press, 1977), and Daniel Nelson, *Managers and Workers: Origins of the New Factory System in the United States, 1880–1920* (Madison, Wis.: University of Wisconsin Press, 1972). Bruce Laurie and Mark Schmitz have calculated the distribution of workers in manufacturing firms in Philadelphia in 1850. They show that almost 57% of the manufacturing workers in Philadelphia worked in firms with 50 or fewer employees. Philadelphia, the second largest city in the country, was the most diversified manufacturing city of its day (Laurie and Schmitz, "Manufacture and Productivity: The Making of an Industrial Base, Philadelphia, 1850–1880," in *Philadelphia: Work, Space, Family, and Group Experience in the Nineteenth Century*, ed. Theodore Hershberg [New York: Oxford University Press, 1981], p. 50).

28. *Congressional Globe*, 32d Cong., 1st sess., 1851, Appendix, p. 13.

those of 1850 and 1860, though with a larger total population, employed a peak office staff of 450. In 1880 the office staff reached almost 1,500.[29]

In short, it is unlikely that the contemporary charges of total incompetence and corruption in the processing of the 1850 census were true. It is doubtful that there then existed anywhere in the country the requisite knowledge, administrative skill, or will to run a census office that would have lived up to Senate standards. On the other hand, it was Kennedy's misfortune to be the incumbent administrator when the tabulation "crisis" came to light. Not surprisingly, when Franklin Pierce won the presidency in November and the Democrats came to town looking for patronage jobs, Kennedy found himself out of a job.

Kennedy was replaced by James D. B. DeBow, a renowned statistician in his own right and editor of *DeBow's Review,* the major commercial magazine of the South. DeBow took over in March 1853. He immediately "reorganized" the Census Office, dismissed fifty-five clerks, and set about preparing the final tables for the printer. On June 15, he sent the first material to the printer; in early November the one-thousand-page quarto volume of the census appeared in published form in time for the meeting of Congress. In his introductory and explanatory material on the statistics, DeBow implied that he had compiled most of the material. The "former superintendent" was not identified in the volume, and DeBow was of course willing to take credit for what was a quite impressive volume. Again, though, by comparing the material that Kennedy had already published in his annual reports and the final volume, it is fairly clear that DeBow's office had merely finished what was already an almost completed volume. To give one example, DeBow claimed that he had prepared the occupation tables for a number of states—including Maryland—between March and June of 1853. However, Kennedy's sample volume of the statistics of Maryland, published in 1852, contained occupation statistics for Maryland. DeBow's tables listed 6 percent fewer workers than did Kennedy's, and the classification differed slightly. It is doubtful, however, that DeBow did more than edit the work done by Kennedy's staff.[30]

29. Wright and Hunt, *History and Growth,* pp. 51, 56, 67.

30. For DeBow's career, see Ottis Clark Skipper, "J. D. B. DeBow and the Seventh Census," *Louisiana Historical Quarterly* 22 (April 1939): 479–91, and Skipper, *J. D. B. DeBow: Magazinist of the Old South* (Athens, Ga.: University of Georgia Press, 1958). DeBow and Kennedy had corresponded before 1853 and had been on friendly terms. DeBow had referred to Kennedy as the "able Superintendent of the Census Department" in an article in *DeBow's Review,* and Kennedy had furnished DeBow with unpublished census data for the *Review* ("J. D. B. DeBow and the Seventh Census," p. 483). Their relations cooled when DeBow became census superintendent. Kennedy stayed in Washington, and the Census Office was, of course, housed in a building owned by Kennedy until the end of 1853. Kennedy charged DeBow with stealing his personal papers and books—especially correspondence and volumes received from European statistical offices. He also charged that the

DeBow, though, was much better connected politically than Kennedy was, and thus the historical record has credited DeBow with the accomplishments of the 1850 census. And because DeBow had good relations with Congress, he was able to convince Congress to appropriate funds for further analysis and publication of census data. In January 1854, Congress authorized the publication of a "new and condensed edition" of the census, what has come to be called the *Compendium*. DeBow and a small staff of fifteen to twenty worked on this volume; it appeared in September 1854. By this time, DeBow had also become concerned about the problems of data processing and recommended the establishment of a permanent statistical office to take the census and to publish other demographic and economic studies in the intercensal period.

At the end of 1854, DeBow prepared to close the Census Office since no further work needed to be completed. Two months later he reopened it; Congress had authorized an additional census volume on the statistics of mortality. This volume was prepared with the help of Dr. Edward Jarvis of Massachusetts and was published in 1855. In November 1855 the office was finally disbanded, almost six and a half years after Joseph Kennedy had come to town to prepare the 1850 census schedules.[31]

In the contentious years of the mid-1850s, the debates about census policy ended. Congress was reapportioned; the published census volumes were distributed around the country. In the face of the battles over the Kansas-Nebraska Act and Bleeding Kansas, it looked for a time as if the census might even be the instrument with which all Americans might contemplate, in James Thompson's phrase, "the Union as it is . . . in its unity and beauty." After all the furor, the work had been begun by a northern Whig and completed by a southern Democrat. James DeBow's name on the published volumes did much to soothe Southern fears that the census would become an instrument of abolitionists and antislavery advocates. Congress was extremely generous in its orders for the final volumes—in terms both of the volume of statistics finally published and of the number of copies distributed. The 1840 census had been printed in folio form; Kennedy had earlier noted that this practice made it almost impossible to use, carry, or store. When he visited European statistical

Eighth Street Building was not properly repaired and cleaned when it was vacated in November 1853. See 1853–55 letters, Correspondence of the Secretary of the Interior, entry 280, RG 48, NA.

31. See Census Office, *Statistical View of the United States, Being a Compendium of the Seventh Census* (Washington, D.C.: A. O. P. Nicholson, 1854); Census Office, *Mortality Statistics of the Seventh Census of the United States* (Washington, D.C.: A. O. P. Nicholson, 1855). Jarvis's role is detailed in Grob, *Edward Jarvis,* pp. 137–54.

offices, he found the 1840 census volumes under the bookcases gathering dust.[32]

In contrast, the 1850 census was printed in quarto or octavo form. Congress ordered hundreds of thousands of copies of the various reports—especially of the smaller octavo volumes. Most notably, Congress published 320,000 copies of the *Compendium*, more than one for every hundred inhabitants. Harriet Beecher Stowe's *Uncle Tom's Cabin*, by comparison, sold 300,000 copies during its first year in print. And, though the Census Office was attacked for taking too long to publish the reports and for wasting the taxpayer's money, it was not accused of producing biased or blatantly incorrect statistics in an effort to promote the interests of one section or another, as had occurred in 1840. Neither Kennedy nor DeBow used his position as the government's chief statistician to promote a particular sectional perspective in the official reports. In fact, they tended to promote a rather intense nationalism that reflected pride in the strong growth and territorial expansion of the country as a whole. As a result, this first major expansion of the American census and creation of a large-scale statistical office in Washington proved successful.[33]

Nevertheless, the sectional debates were much too intense to allow the 1850 census statistics to stand merely as evidence for national growth and development. Although the census contained little evidence on slavery per se—only eight relatively innocuous questions on a separate schedule—census users somehow wanted to tease out of the statistics sectional comparisons that could vindicate or condemn the "peculiar institution." Neither abolitionists nor fire-eaters could easily conclude much to serve their purposes from the information on the age, sex, or geographic distribution of the slave population, but that did not stop them from trying. The late 1850s were filled with statistical defenses of and attacks on slavery. Interestingly, the statistics did little to convince either side to change their positions since both sides argued that their opponents misused the data. In fact, both sides did misuse the data. Moreover, in some cases, later generations of historians and social commentators have tended to repeat the arguments with little critical evaluation of the validity and reliability of the statistical evidence.

The most notable example of this form of argument was Hinton Helper's *Impending Crisis of the South*, published in 1857. Helper rearranged the reported aggregate census statistics for the slave and free states to show that the North surpassed the South in agricultural produc-

32. Kennedy to Stuart, July 1851, Records of the 1850 Census, Office of the Secretary of the Interior Department, entry 280, RG 48, NA.

33. Skipper, *J. D. B. DeBow*, p. 77; cf. Frank Luther Mott, *Golden Multitudes: The Story of Best Sellers in the United States* (New York: Macmillan, 1947), pp. 114–22.

tivity, wealth, commerce, and social progress. The North produced more hay and livestock, manufactured more, had more canals and railroads, libraries, schools, churches, and newspapers. Helper compiled over fifty tables of data comparing the free and slave states, and in every one the free states dominated. His explanation of "why the North has surpassed the South" was simple: "Slavery!" "Slavery" had driven ambitious, energetic whites out of the region, had "sunk a large majority of our people [that is, whites] in galling poverty and ignorance," and had "rendered a small minority conceited and tyrannical." Nonslaveholding whites would be advised to ally with northern abolitionists to end slavery and establish a new South on free labor principles.[34]

Proslavery advocates responded to these statistical attacks on their economy and institutions by pointing out that the same census data could be used to condemn the North—most notably in its treatment of wage laborers. Employing the conservative arguments made most famous by Sen. James Hammond of South Carolina in his "King Cotton" speech, proslavery advocates argued that all societies had to have a menial laboring class—what Hammond called the "mudsill of society." Since civilized society could not exist without a "class to do the menial duties, to perform the drudgery of life," the only important question left for the policymaker was the terms under which such people labored. As James Gordon Bennett put it in an editorial in his New York *Herald* that supported passage of the Kansas-Nebraska Act, slavery was an "evil" only because "labor itself is an evil, inflicted as a curse upon mankind with the expulsion from 'Paradise Lost.'" He chided Northerners for refusing to recognize that "our hireling system of free labor" was "in truth . . . the white slavery system of the North." Evidence for these assertions was taken from the social statistics of the 1850 census: he compared the number of paupers and the deaf, dumb, blind, and idiotic in New England and six southern states. New England "boast[ed] the highest elements of Northern perfection, in free schools, free labor, free speech, and free men" yet it had an "average of more than three to one" of paupers compared with the southern states. While the black slaves and the poor whites "have generally enough to eat and air enough for health and wholesome ventilation," northern laborers were "crowded into close and unwholesome factories"; they lived in "unwholesome garrets and cellars" and were periodically threatened with "destitution" "for lack of employment."[35]

Both Helper's condemnation of the southern economy and proslavery attacks on the evils of northern wage labor generated strong rebuttals.

34. Hinton Rowan Helper, *The Impending Crisis of the South* (New York: Burdick Brothers, 1857), quotations on p. 25.

35. *New York Herald*, Feb. 9, 1854. See also James M. McPherson, *Ordeal by Fire: The Civil War and Reconstruction* (New York: Knopf, 1982), pp. 110–13.

Defenders of the social system in each section employed a variety of arguments, but most relevant for our purposes are the critiques of their opponents' statistical arguments. Initially Helper's book greatly infuriated the South, where it was banned as insurrectionary and attacked in newspaper reviews. Not until 1859, though, two years after publication, did the book generate a full critique. In that year a group of prominent antislavery men raised sixteen thousand dollars to reprint the book as a presidential campaign document. At that point, it became more than an antislavery text to be dismissed as propaganda. In the winter of 1859–60, John Sherman lost the Speakership of the House because he had been one of sixty-eight House members to endorse the work. In 1860 two full-scale critiques were published that found the errors in Helper's statistics and called in question his entire analysis.[36]

Most important, the critics noted that Helper had not corrected his data for differences in the northern and southern populations. If one used per capita measures of wealth, agricultural productivity, and the like, the South surpassed the North. Further, by the late 1850s, the 1850 census was out of date. Southerners proudly pointed to the fact that the South was unaffected by the Panic of 1857, that the price of cotton was rising, and that southern wealth was increasing. In short, *The Impending Crisis* was not, as its defenders claimed, a "thorough, reliable, demonstrating, overwhelming" document made up of "facts which cannot be denied or gainsaid." Rather, it was a compilation of statistical data by an amateur who was ignorant of the "rule of simple proportion," which "any schoolboy can calculate." Samuel Wolfe, who wrote the longest critique, considered it "too contemptible to notice" but for the fact that "the work has been brought to the attention of the public by Members of Congress."[37]

Defenders of the social system of the North were also quick to find fallacies in the proslavery uses of census data. After Edward Jarvis read Bennett's editorial in the *Herald,* he wrote to James DeBow, then working on the census *Compendium,* to urge that the mistaken impression of higher rates of pauperism in New England be corrected in the *Compendium* statistics. Jarvis pointed out that the paupers listed in the census were only those "whom the law compels the public to support." In other words, the data reflected state government policy, not the absolute number of paupers. He suggested that the *Compendium* statistics be accompanied by an explanation or "disclaimer of any inference to be drawn as to the amount of privation without first examining the laws respecting pauperism and the custom of relieving it from the public treasury."[38]

36. Potter, *Impending Crisis,* pp. 386*ff.*

37. Samuel M. Wolfe, *Helper's Impending Crisis Dissected* (Philadelphia: J. T. Lloyd, 1860), pp. 1–2, 38–56. See also Hugh Talmage Lefler, "Hinton Rowan Helper: Advocate of a 'White America,'" *Southern Sketches* 1 (Charlottesville, Va., 1935), esp. p. 20.

38. Quoted in Grob, *Edward Jarvis,* p. 146.

In short, though each side in the sectional debate used census data, neither side convinced the other of the virtue of its position. Nor did the arguments and their rebuttals generate more refined and precise social analysis of the labor systems of North and South. In the late 1850s, passions ran too high and events were moving too fast for the kind of dispassionate thinking that might have explored the relative efficiency of southern agriculture or the degraded conditions of wage laborers in northern cities. More common responses were grandiose rhetorical forms of praise or blame for the author. Helper was a "new Moses" or a "vile wretch," depending on one's point of view. These are not the evaluations usually reserved for statisticians.[39]

For the sake of argument, though, it might be useful to ponder why the census statistics shed so little light on the debates of slavery, on what kinds of information or forms of inquiry might have advanced the debate, and what difference it made to later generations of Americans that the analysis did not go forward.

First, it should be noted that most of the questions about the economic efficiency of southern agriculture and the well-being of slaves and wage laborers were empirical questions capable of empirical answers. As we know from the efforts of Robert Fogel, Stanley Engerman, and their critics, it is possible, even one hundred years later, to find data bearing on the profitability of southern farms and to evaluate the comparative productivity of different agricultural economies. Designed as they were simply to provide aggregate figures on crops produced, the published census statistics that Helper and his critics had were much too crude to be used to infer anything about the relative efficiency of individual farms or labor systems. Yet it is not inconceivable to imagine an amended 1860 census schedule that would have provided conclusive data on differential labor inputs on American farms and that might thus have provided an empirical resolution to Helper's charges. Congress was in session when the debates surrounding *The Impending Crisis* were at their peak; it would have been a relatively simple task to add several questions on the forms of labor used on American farms to the 1860 agricultural schedule. Such a census schedule would of course have been politically explosive—just as the 1850 census schedule was. Yet, that no one ever proposed such a solution to the great debates about slavery of the late 1850s indicates that the country was already past the point of compromise, debate, or rational investigation of the question of the "peculiar institution" and its future. Crucial elements of southern opinion were already bent on secession. It is instructive to watch James DeBow retreat from his nationalist tendencies of the early 1850s and embrace such inflammatory positions as a call for reopening the slave trade. And the Northern Republicans felt little need

39. Wolfe, *Helper's Impending Crisis*, p. 1; Lefler, "Helper," p. 19.

to conduct careful empirical investigations of the slave economy because they already sensed that history and demography were on their side. As Horace Bushnell had put it some years before, "the laws of population are themselves abolitionists." The Republicans knew they had a good chance of winning the presidency in 1860; soon the power to legislate an end to the hated system would be theirs.[40]

The tragedy is that the Civil War and the abrupt emancipation of the slaves in 1862 took place in the context of abysmal ignorance and misinformation on the part of northern policymakers with respect to black Americans. For years Southerners had defended their system by pointing out that abolition was impossible until some decision about what to do with the freed slaves had been made. Moderate northern opinion always stumbled on this question, since most Northerners had no desire to provide equal civil and political rights to blacks. Colonization did not seem a feasible solution, given the dismal record of the American Colonization Society. And as the antislavery movement broadened, the racial prejudice in its rhetoric became more common. The Republican party had a strong antiNegro wing; much of the popularity of Helper's *Impending Crisis* derived from its vitriolic racism and its condemnation of blacks for causing the degradation of southern whites.[41]

When Abraham Lincoln moved into the presidency in 1861, the next census had already been taken and most of the South had already seceded. When he got the census statistics on slaves, he confronted the awesome dimensions of the problem of abolition. There were almost 4 million slaves, according to the 1860 census. At current prices, they were worth well over $1.2 billion. The federal budget was about $65 million. Over the next four years, Lincoln requested information from the Census Office on how the nation might grapple with the problem of abolition. The data and analyses he got were not terribly illuminating. We know of course that abolition proceeded in any case, but the prejudices and fallacies born in the statistical debates of the 1850s haunted sociological and political analyses of black American life well into the twentieth century.

40. Robert Fogel and Stanley Engerman include a discussion of the legacy of Helper's and other scholars' analyses of the slave system in *Time on the Cross*, 2 vols. (Boston: Little, Brown, 1974), 1:158–90. On DeBow's later career, see Skipper, *J. D. B. DeBow*; Potter, *Impending Crisis*, pp. 395*ff.* For the Bushnell quotation, see Robert Wiebe, *The Opening of American Society* (New York: Vintage, 1985), p. 361.

41. See, e.g., Eric Foner, *Free Soil, Free Labor, Free Men: The Ideology of the Republican Party before the Civil War* (New York: Oxford University Press, 1970).

THREE

Counting Slaves and Freed Blacks:
War and Reconstruction by the Numbers

*It is a subject of congratulation that the unhappy state of affairs
which has interposed to impede the ordinary course of events
has not interfered with the rendition of complete returns from
all sections of our country, and that we are enabled to represent
the condition of all the great elements of a nation's prosperity as
they existed in the year 1860—a circumstance, probably, of no
trifling significance in facilitating the early and happy settlement of our domestic troubles.*
—*Joseph C. G. Kennedy*, Preliminary Report
of the Eighth Census, *1862*

Probably the one person who could have convinced Congress to use the census to address the great debates about
slavery in 1860 was Joseph C. G. Kennedy. But Kennedy
had good reasons for refraining from doing so. Though
officially fired as census superintendent in March 1853,
he remained in Washington after his dismissal and made
concerted efforts throughout the 1850s to clear his name
and get his old job back. He watched the Whig party
collapse, the Democrats take control of Congress and the
presidency, and the new Republican party grow. Unlike
many of his contemporaries, he never wholeheartedly
endorsed the emerging political rhetoric of either the
Republicans or the Democrats. He remained an "old fashioned free soil Whig" who maintained his political connections through the force of his personal and business
connections. He was one of the few reasonably high-level
federal officials who could claim by the late 1860s to have
worked equally well in Whig, Democratic, or Republican

THE GREAT TRIBULATION.

CENSUS MARSHAL.—"I jist want to know how many of yez is deaf, dumb, blind, insane and idiotic—likewise how many convicts there is in the family—what all your ages are, especially the old woman and the young ladies—and how many dollars the old gentleman is worth!"

[Tremendous sensation all round the table.]

5. The Great Tribulation, *Saturday Evening Post*, 1860. The census was always good raw material for cartoonists and humorists. This 1860 cartoon mocks the intrusiveness of the questions. The marshal is depicted as a boorish official meddling in the affairs of a respectable family.

administrations. In order to guarantee his own political future, therefore, Kennedy instinctively avoided involving his beloved census in the sectional controversies of the time.[1]

Kennedy achieved his goal of returning to run the 1860 census in 1858. That June Congress appropriated $3,500 to compile and publish the results of the 1850 manufacturing census. Pennsylvania Democrat

1. Joseph C. G. Kennedy to William Tecumseh Sherman, July 30, 1865, Sherman Papers, LC.

SCHEDULE 1.—Free Inhabitants in _____

State of _____ enumerated by me, on the _____

Post Office _____

Dwelling Houses— numbered in the order of visitation.	Families numbered in the order of visitation.	The name of every person whose usual place of abode on the first day of June, 1860, was in this family.	Age.	Sex.	Color.—{White, Black, or Mulatto.}	Profession, Occupation, or Trade of each person, male and female, over 15 years of age.
					DESCRIPTION.	
1	2	3	4	5	6	7
1						
39						
40						

No. white males, _____ No. colored males, _____ No. foreign born, _____ No. blind, _____

No. white females, _____ No. colored females, _____ No. deaf and dumb, _____ No. insane, _____

6—40

6. Schedule 1, Free Inhabitants, 1860. The 1860 schedule for free inhabitants demonstrated the expansion of census inquiries.

James Buchanan appointed Kennedy, a Pennsylvania Whig, to conduct the work. Kennedy was positioned to take over the superintendency of the imminent 1860 census.

In January 1859 Kennedy completed work on the manufacturing census and stayed on to begin the preparations for the 1860 census. Buchanan appointed him superintendent in May 1860. The preparations for the census were routine. Congress did not pass any new legislation. Kennedy modified the schedules and instructions to the enumerators to remedy the misunderstandings in 1850. From his experience in 1850 Kennedy knew how much work the tallying process would generate. He planned to increase the Washington clerical staff in the fall of 1860 as soon as he received the schedules.[2]

Kennedy had also grown into something of a national statistical spokesman by the late 1850s. He attended the International Statistical Congress meetings in Europe and corresponded with such prominent European statisticians as Adolphe Quetelet and Charles Babbage. He also promoted the development of statistics in the United States. In December 1859, for

2. *DAB*, 5:335–36; Carroll Wright and William C. Hunt, *History and Growth of the United States Census* (Washington, D.C.: GPO, 1900), pp. 50–52; Census Office, Eighth Census of the United States, *Instructions to Enumerators* (Washington, D.C.: Geo. W. Bowman, 1860).

	Page No.
――――――――――― in the County of ―――――――――――	
day of ―――――――, 1860.	
――――――――――――――――― , Ass't Marshal.	

VALUE OF ESTATE OWNED.		Place of Birth, Naming the State, Territory, or Country.	Married within the year.	Attended School within the year.	Persons over 20 years of age who can not read and write	Whether deaf and dumb, blind, insane, idiotic, pauper, or convict.	
Value of Real Estate.	Value of Personal Estate.						
8	9	10	11	12	13	14	
							1
							39
							40
		No. idiotic, ―――――				No. convicts, ―――――	
		No. paupers, ―――――					

example, he spoke to the American Geographical and Statistical Society (now the American Geographical Society) on "The Origin and Progress of Statistics." The address was infused with an optimistic nineteenth-century faith in the possibility of "improving the general condition of society" and ameliorating "the misfortunes of those who are morally or physically unable to assist themselves." The "mission of statistics," Kennedy asserted, was to carry out "the example of our Saviour while on earth, and by means of those agencies within man's control," to "confer" "the greatest boons upon suffering humanity, which He wrought by miracle." He pointed to the recent breakthroughs in the epidemiology of disease made by statisticians studying the differential geographical distribution of mortality data. And he discussed the improvements in the census during his tenure as superintendent. Kennedy thanked the society for its support and encouragement of federal statistics and hoped the society would continue its efforts. Looking to the year to come, 1860, he saw the eighth census as the opportunity to improve the system he had built in 1850. He even suggested that the United States might establish a permanent federal statistical bureau like those in European nations.[3]

In the next few years, the census and the science of statistics were

3. Joseph C. G. Kennedy, "The Origin and Process of Statistics," *Journal of the American Geographical and Statistical Society* 2 (1860–70): 92–120, quotations on p. 99.

harnessed for major new functions. But they were not the kind that Kennedy had described. The administration and processing of the 1860 census closely followed the pattern set in 1850. What did change were the uses and interpretations of census as the nation went to war and confronted the end of slavery.

For as it turned out, 1860 was not only an election year and a census year. It was also the year that "the cords which bind these states together in one common Union" broke apart. The immediate cause of the break was the collapse of the national party system and the election of a sectionally supported president. Abraham Lincoln was not even on the ballot in the South. Among the deeper processes that made Lincoln's victory possible—and made it seem so dangerous—was the growing demographic imbalance between the North and the South.

For the previous seventy years, Americans had extolled their rapid population growth and had worked out a variety of mechanisms to control the process in the political arena. Americans had become accustomed to thinking demographically, to celebrating the astounding 30 to 35 percent a decade growth rates evidenced in the census, and to coping with the decennial problems of redistributing political power according to the previous decade's growth and change. The constitutional requirements of apportionment thrust change into the public eye. In 1800 each of the 142 congressmen represented 33,000 people, in 1850 each of the 233 represented 93,432. The eastern states saw political representation shift to the west. Even Kentucky and Tennessee reached their peak congressional representation (13 members) in 1830. This demographic dynamism meant that the American political system was inherently unstable. Each decade the size and character of Congress and the electoral college changed; each decade politicians had to reassess their political strength.[4]

For the South, this change was becoming increasingly worrisome. After the 1850 census, the slaveholding South controlled only 35 percent of the seats in the House, and the 1860 apportionments would result in a further decline. As Roy Nichols commented some forty years ago, "The census seemed to be the South's worst enemy."[5]

It was in an atmosphere of crisis in the fall and winter of 1860 that Kennedy and his staff began the most critical phase of census tallying. By December the office staff was up to 130, and the majority of returns were in. Congress reassembled for its lame duck session and tried to cope with the secession movement and to fashion yet another compromise. From

4. Patricia Cline Cohen, *A Calculating People: The Spread of Numeracy in Early America* (Chicago: University of Chicago Press, 1982); Michel L. Balinski and H. Peyton Young, *Fair Representation: Meeting the Ideal of One Man, One Vote* (New Haven and London: Yale University Press, 1982).

5. Roy Nichols, *The Disruption of American Democracy* (New York: Macmillan, 1948), pp. 460–61.

Illinois Lincoln embarked on the delicate process of forming a cabinet. He refused to give assurances to the South that he would not move to restrict slavery. Kennedy, in alliance with a number of unionist congressmen, including Andrew Johnson, made one of the many efforts to avert the crisis. Kennedy used his clerical staff to work overtime mailing pro-Union speeches to voters in key southern districts.[6]

But compromise was no longer possible, and Congress adjourned. By the time Lincoln took office in March 1861, seven states had seceded. At the same time the normal processes of government continued. Kennedy was kept on by the Lincoln administration, and by early April he finished tallying the census for apportionment. Because new states had been admitted since the 1850 apportionment, the House would have to shrink by 5 seats back to Vinton's 233. The slave states would lose 6 seats; the free states would gain 1. Then events overtook the routine processes of political apportionment. On April 12 Confederate forces fired on Fort Sumter, South Carolina. On April 15 Lincoln declared a state of "insurrection" and called for 75,000 volunteers.[7]

For the next four years the nation was at war. And for the next four years the census office compiled and published the results of the 1860 census and aided in the war effort. The census was used to assess the military strength of the North and the South and to assess direct taxes to finance the war. It was mined to plan policy for the freed slaves. And it was used to reconstitute the national state and to reapportion political power after the end of the three-fifths compromise. The story of these uses provides evidence of the importance of the numbers in American political life and illustrates the strengths and weaknesses of the mid-nineteenth-century federal statistical system.

The initial and most obvious use of the census during the war was as an instrument to measure the relative military strength of the Union and the Confederacy. On the heels of Fort Sumter, Kennedy sent a report to Lincoln listing the number of white men from age eighteen to age forty-five in the free states, the "border slave" states (those that had not seceded), the seceded states, and the territories. Of the 5.5 million men of military age, 69 percent were in the free states. The seceded states could muster 9 percent. If all the remaining slave states joined the Confederacy, it could draw on another 1.1 million men. The prospects for the Union looked quite good. Similarly, over the next few months, Kennedy responded to Lincoln's requests for information about the capabilities of

6. Ibid., p. 404; Joseph C. G. Kennedy to Andrew Johnson, June 13, 1864, Johnson Papers, LC.

7. David Potter, *The Impending Crisis of the South* (New York: Harper & Row, 1976); James M. McPherson, *Ordeal by Fire: The Civil War and Reconstruction* (New York: Knopf, 1982). For a contemporary report of the 1860 apportionment, see *Harper's* 22 (May 1861): 836–37.

the Confederacy to manufacture saltpeter or sulfur for explosives. In January 1862 Congress passed a joint resolution on "war statistics" authorizing Kennedy to report data directly to the War Department. For the remainder of the war, the Census Office loaned clerks to the War Department for statistical work and performed such work in the Census Office itself. As Kennedy recalled after the war, his staff had tallied and published the basic tables in the eighth census reports (five volumes) at the same time that they prepared "[m]aps of each state by counties and congressional districts . . . for the Provost Marshal General" and "table after table of military apportionment demanded by differences of opinion between state and city authorities and the War Department." They also prepared "statistical maps for Generals in the field and military governors." These maps were perhaps the most important statistical innovation of the office. Kennedy's staff used postal route maps for counties in the South and annotated them with the results of the 1860 census. On the face of the map, data was written in for each county. Thus, for example, northern commanders had data on the number of whites, free blacks, and slaves for each county. They also knew the amount of improved land, the number of horses and mules, and the amount of wheat, corn, oats, and other crops produced in the county.[8]

General William Tecumseh Sherman made the most notable use of such statistical information in his march through Georgia to the sea. Sherman acknowledged the debt he had to the Census Office for the information both at the time of the march in 1864 and after the war. "No military expedition was ever based on sounder or surer data," he wrote to his daughter Ellen. The data made it possible for northern commanders to operate with short or no supply lines, to live off the land, and thus to move faster than traditional armies.[9]

In the summer of 1861 Congress and the Treasury Department also faced the problem of financing the war. Secretary of the Treasury Salmon P. Chase recommended a variety of taxes, including modest increases in tariffs, excise duties, and a direct tax apportioned among the states. Congress and the administration were relatively inexperienced in questions of taxation because the tariff had conveniently supplied all the

8. Joseph C. G. Kennedy to Abraham Lincoln, Apr. 27, Sept. 6, 1861, Lincoln Papers, LC; *Congressional Globe*, 37th Cong., 2d sess., 1862, p. 489; Joseph C. G. Kennedy to James Harlan, June 3, 1865, 1860 Census File, Office of the Secretary of the Interior, RG 48, NA. The maps are available in the Cartographic Archives Division, NA. For a description of the collection, see William J. Heynen, comp., *Agricultural Maps in the National Archives of the United States, ca. 1860–1930* (Washington, D.C.: National Archives and Records Service, 1976), pp. 3–4.

9. See Joseph C. G. Kennedy file, Walter Willcox Papers, box 36, LC; Lloyd Lewis, *Sherman: Fighting Prophet* (New York: Harcourt, Brace, 1932), p. 432.

federal revenue for the previous twenty years. Only as the war progressed did the difficulties of taxation and finance emerge as the massive problems they would later become.

For precedents for the direct tax, Congress literally returned to the statutory language used during the War of 1812 and apportioned twenty million dollars among the states—including the seceded states. The tax was apportioned on the basis of the representative population—that is, all free persons and three-fifths of the slave population—and was assessed on landed property. As it debated the bill, Congress began to recognize the difficulties with the proposed tax. How would the tax be collected in the insurrectionary states? What about the radically different values of assessed property between the older and richer states in the East and the developing West? Western states would pay a much higher relative levy than would eastern states. These difficulties prompted Congress to try to modify the tax. Congress provided for the sale of rebel property to pay the tax. Congress also levied the first federal income tax to balance the burden of the direct tax in the West. Lawmakers agreed that the income tax would fall most heavily on the citizens in the East, where incomes were higher. The income tax—not apportioned among the states on the basis of the census—was initially a tax of 3 percent on incomes above eight hundred dollars a year. Between 1862 and 1865, the tax was expanded to a 5 percent levy of incomes between six hundred and five thousand dollars; incomes above five thousand dollars were taxed at 10 percent. The tax was reduced after the war and was abolished in 1872.[10]

As it turned out, these modifications of the direct tax proposal had the most impact on the nation and on future national tax policy. The Civil War income tax generated $347 million over its existence, the direct tax only $15 million before it was repealed. The income tax showed itself to be a powerful revenue generator, the direct tax a feeble one. The income tax had a distinctly sectional impact. Seventy percent of the income tax was collected from residents in California, Connecticut, Massachusetts, New York, New Jersey, Maryland, Pennsylvania, and Rhode Island. (By way of comparison, these states accounted for about 30 percent of the population.) The direct tax was collected only in the loyal states, and the states themselves generally paid the tax, as they had during the War of 1812. Further, as noted above, because the states were also charged with raising and provisioning troops for the Union Army, state officials quickly discovered that they could offset some of their quotas for services and

10. Davis R. Dewey, *Financial History of the United States* (New York: Longmans, Green, 1924), pp. 272–306; E. R. A. Seligman, *The Income Tax* (1914; reprint, New York: August M. Kelley, 1970), pp. 430*ff.*; Joseph A. Hill, "The Civil War Income Tax," *Quarterly Journal of Economics* 8 (1894): 416–52, 491–98; Charles F. Dunbar, "The Direct Tax of 1861," *Quarterly Journal of Economics* 3 (1889): 436–61.

equipments against the state's direct tax bill. Thus the direct tax added no new revenue to the federal Treasury.

Collecting the tax in the insurrectionary states was another matter. It was feasible to collect the tax only in areas where the Union Army had established federal control. In most parts of the South, the tax went unpaid. But in several celebrated experiments—notably in the Sea Islands of South Carolina—federal officials seized plantation lands for unpaid taxes and used them to undertake dramatic experiments in reconstructing the southern social and economic system—including distributing valuable land to former slaves. These experiments, as we shall see, created further problems after the war as former landowners returned to claim their lands.[11]

Overall, then, Congress and federal officials concluded that the census apportionment of direct taxes was not a satisfactory constitutional mechanism. In a series of rulings after the Civil War, the Supreme Court declared that the Civil War income tax was not a direct tax and thus did not need to be apportioned on the basis of population. Congress never again attempted to levy a direct tax, and not surprisingly it did not occur to anyone to try to use the census to measure the tax capacity of the nation. Congress recognized that a land or capitation tax no longer effectively reflected the tax capacity of the citizenry. By the 1870s, federal revenue needs again were met by the tariff, and the debate about federal tax policy ended. When it reemerged in the 1890s, as we shall see, it was a debate about the income tax and the proper basis for determining the tax obligations of those who benefited from the wealth created in an industrial society.

Policymakers did call on the Census Office and on census data to address the most fundamental question raised by the war: What was to become of slavery and the slaves? It is generally recognized that the Lincoln administration only reluctantly took up the call for emancipation. Lincoln spent the first two years of the war trying to find a way to end the rebellion without freeing the slaves or to free the slaves and somehow to make it possible for the freed slaves to leave the United States. The first of these schemes foundered when the North discovered it could not win the war without the support of the black population—particularly black troops—and without appealing to the more militant wings of the antislavery movement. The second foundered when diplomatic efforts to secure "homelands" for the freed slaves did not materialize and when Northerners finally faced the numerical strength of the black population. There

11. Dunbar, "Direct Tax of 1861"; Willie Lee Rose, *Rehearsal for Reconstruction: The Port Royal Experiment* (New York: Bobbs-Merrill, 1964).

were almost 4 million slaves in the United States, according to the eighth census.[12]

Northerners had of course been reminded by Southerners of the dimensions of the problems of emancipation in terms of the capital investment in the slave population. As noted above, it was generally conceded that the American slave population was "worth" $1.2 billion or more, while the federal budget was about $65 million. These stark figures tended to discourage concrete plans for paid emancipation. But the cost of the war itself overrode those considerations. Early in the war, Lincoln wrote Kennedy asking for detailed data on the slave population in Delaware. He wanted to show that paid emancipation would ultimately be cheaper than civil war. Kennedy supplied the numbers, but the movement for paid emancipation did not take off. Lincoln ultimately agreed to immediate uncompensated emancipation not because he was committed to citizenship rights and equality for black Americans but because the war had made slavery untenable.[13]

That still left the extremely difficult question of the role of the freed slave after emancipation. It was here that the sheer quantitative dimension of the problem almost overwhelmed the best efforts of most of the political leaders involved. Further, rhetoric tended to emphasize abstract rights and high principles of political theory. As such there was little discussion on concrete questions of how many exslaves there would be, how they would earn a living, where would they live, and so forth. But the Census Office was in the business of understanding the quantitative dimensions of American social and economic life. It is extremely revealing to see how the office handled the issues relating to slavery and emancipation—particularly what George Fredrickson has called the "prognostications" of the future for black Americans.[14]

During the war, the Census Office published a series of reports and documents that contained implicit and explicit interpretations of the status and probable future tendencies of the American black population. The first was a population density map of the slave population in the American South as of 1860. Published in September 1861 and "Sold for

---

12. For an example of the conceptualization of the slavery issue in terms of the aggregate price of the slave population, see *Congressional Globe*, 39th Cong., 1st sess., 1866, pp. 1631–32, quoted in Joseph B. James, *The Framing of the Fourteenth Amendment* (Urbana, Ill.: University of Illinois Press, 1956), p. 94. For discussions of northern policy debates about emancipation, see George Fredrickson, *The Black Image in the White Mind* (New York: Harper & Row, 1971); James M. McPherson, *The Struggle for Equality* (Princeton, N.J.: Princeton University Press, 1964); and Mary Frances Berry, *Military Necessity and Civil Rights Policy* (Port Washington, N.Y.: Kennikat Press, 1977).

13. Joseph C. G. Kennedy to Abraham Lincoln, Nov. 26, 1861, Lincoln Papers, LC.

14. Fredrickson, *Black Image*, pp. xii–xiii.

the benefit of the Sick and Wounded Soldiers of the U.S. Army," this map could almost be considered a piece of art with its elaborate lettering and engraving. Statisticians developed this form of graphic presentation of data in the 1850s and publicized the innovation at meetings of the International Statistical Congress. The slavery map illustrated the relative strength and dispersion of the black population. It also revealed the overlap between the relative strength of Confederate sentiment and the density of the slave population. Its analytical power provided the Census Office with the motivation to explore further analyses of the character of the black population (fig. 7).[15]

Kennedy did so in the first major publication of the eighth census, the *Preliminary Report,* published in the spring of 1862. It is a remarkable document when one realizes that it extolled growth and expansion throughout the country even though the nation was in the midst of civil war. Kennedy hoped to reassure Northerners that the war was a "transitory" "evil" that the nation was strong enough to endure without impoverishment. He pointed out that the country had not experienced food shortages or even severe labor shortages since the war began. The census figures provided powerful evidence of the wealth of the nation: the population had increased 35 percent from 1850 to 1860, the "products of manufacture" 86 percent, banking capital almost 100 percent. The population could thus absorb "the national debt which has been incurred" in the war. From his perspective, "the truth as presented by the census, will teach us the importance of union and harmony, and stimulate a proper pride in the country and people as one and indivisible."[16]

Kennedy also sought to reassure Northerners that the problem of the fate of the slaves was not unsolvable. He endorsed the somewhat fashionable notion that blacks were demographically inferior to whites and thus, if emancipated, that they would not survive as a major element of the population. Kennedy managed to paper over the truly important demographic description of the black population revealed in his 1861 map: the black population had grown from 700,000 to 4 million since the first census. (This ninefold increase was a function of fertility, since there had been little or no immigration after the close of the slave trade.) Kennedy ignored this fact in his discussion of the "probable future population of the United States" and focused instead on the relative decennial growth rates of the white, free black, and slave populations. He noted that while the growth rate for whites was 38 percent between 1850 and 1860, that for slaves was 22 percent and that for free blacks was 12 percent. He

15. Heynen, *Agricultural Maps*; map also available in Cartographic Archives Division, RG 29, NA.

16. Census Office, *Preliminary Report on the Eighth Census* (Washington, D.C.: GPO, 1862), pp. 118–19.

projected that the emancipated slave population would grow at the rate of the free black population and thus the total black population in 1900 would be about 9 million. Their share of the total population would drop from 13 percent in 1870 to 9 percent in 1900. Emancipation would therefore lead to racial extinction.[17]

By 1864, when Kennedy published the final official report on the population of the United States in 1860, emancipation was a fait accompli and the Thirteenth Amendment to the Constitution was under consideration in Congress. Kennedy returned to his theme of the "competition" between the races and argued quite baldly that the census indicated "with unerring certainty," the "gradual extinction" of "the colored race." "[T]he mingling of the races is more unfavorable to vitality, than a condition of slavery," Kennedy wrote, so that insofar as a "mixed race" of mulattoes existed in the United States, they would lose out in competition with whites. And the "diffusion" of the "colored race," "will lead to a more rapid admixture, the tendency of which . . . will be to impair it physically without improving it morally." Black Americans would thus suffer the same fate as the Indians; since they "must in number and condition be greatly subordinate to the white race," they were "doomed to comparatively rapid absorption or extinction."[18]

It is tragic that the Census Office certified such notions of racial extinction during the Civil War era. We know now that such theories not only reflected the ingrained racism of nineteenth-century white society. They also were bad statistics. The numbers indicated that the black population was growing rapidly, just as the white population was. And focusing on differential growth rates for the various elements in society drew attention away from the real demographic issues confronting northern policymakers. What kind of political, social, and economic role would the four million freed slaves play in American life?[19]

The inadequacy of Kennedy's "prognostications" on the future of black Americans also undermined his continuing efforts to establish the Census Office as a permanent government bureau. Since Kennedy had little concrete information about the immediate role of the freed slave

17. Ibid., pp. 6–8.

18. Census Office, *Population of the United States in 1860* (Washington, D.C.: GPO, 1864), pp. xi–xii; John S. Haller, Jr., *Outcasts from Evolution: Scientific Attitudes of Racial Inferiority, 1859–1900* (Urbana, Ill.: University of Illinois Press, 1971), pp. 40*ff.*

19. For a statistical analysis of black population growth that drew quite different conclusions, see Robert Dale Owen, *The Wrong of Slavery: The Right of Emancipation and the Future of the African Race in the United States* (Philadelphia: J. B. Lippincott, 1864), pp. 84–101. Owen compared the number of slaves imported and the actual populations in the West Indies and the United States to show that the American black population was thriving and would thus tend to continue to do so after emancipation. For the context of Owen's work, see McPherson, *Struggle for Equality,* pp. 182–86.

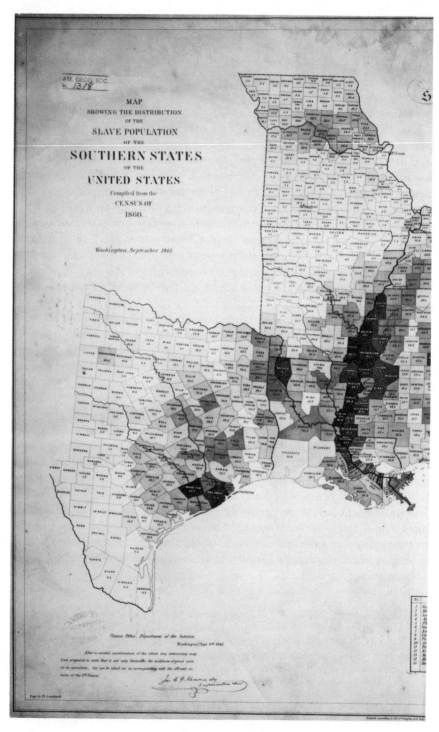

7. Map Showing the Distribution of the Slave Population of the Southern States of the United States . . . 1860. This 1861 map was one of the earliest census efforts to illustrate

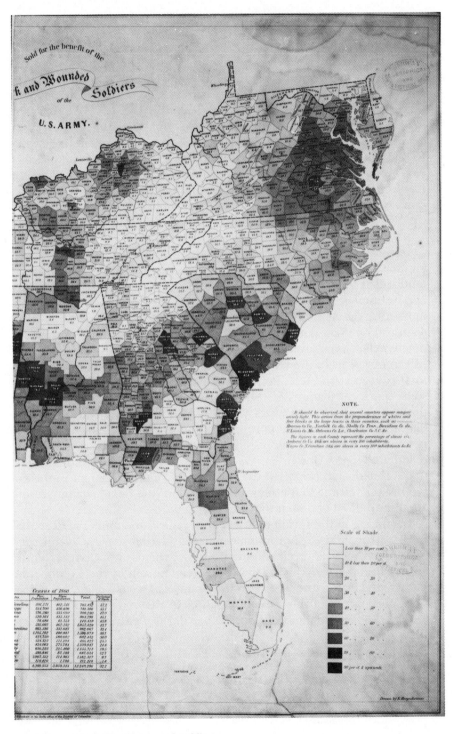

population patterns for the general public.

during Reconstruction, and since most Congressmen believed that sufficient data had already been published from the 1860 census, the office came under the critical scrutiny of the new Interior secretary, James Harlan, in the spring of 1865. Harlan could see no reason for keeping the office open since the war was over and the bulk of the census reports were in print. He was unimpressed with Kennedy's pleas for the need for more detailed agricultural statistics; nor did he, as a radical Republican, like Kennedy's old line Whig political leanings. Harlan closed the office in June 1865, fired Kennedy, and transferred the remaining work to the Land Office. Kennedy protested mightily but ineffectively. He did not claim that his statistics served the current policy debates about Reconstruction. As in the 1850s, he simply wanted his position back.[20]

Ironically, another demographic fact of life resurrected the demographic debates about Reconstruction just as the Census Office was being mothballed for the decade. That fact was, of course, the change in the apportionment formula for Congress and the electoral college set in motion by the Thirteenth Amendment and the end of the three-fifths compromise. Now not only was the South to receive political representation based on its exslave population; it was also to receive a bonus of about fifteen new seats in the House of Representatives and hence in the electoral college at the next apportionment. As northern Republicans did some quick calculations of the effect of this change on the balance of power between the two parties, they discovered that the Democratic party had a more than even chance of regaining control of the House and potentially of retaking the presidency once the Confederate states were readmitted to the Union. For the practical politician, it was little comfort that Kennedy had predicted the "extinction" of the black race in the not too distant future. These men thought about the next election season, and they did not like what they saw.[21]

Beginning in the spring of 1865, both radical and moderate Republicans confronted the apportionment issue as they debated the Reconstruction of the Union. Several solutions presented themselves. Congress could enfranchise the freed slaves, postpone readmission of the Confederate states to the Union until northern hegemony was secure, change the basis of apportionment from total population to the voting population, or reduce the representation of states that did not enfranchise the freed

20. Joseph C. G. Kennedy to William Seward, June 12, 1865, Office of the Secretary of the Interior, 1860 Census File, RG 48, NA; Kennedy to Thomas Ewing, June 13, 1865, Ewing Papers, University of Notre Dame Collection, microfilm, LC.

21. For the context of these debates, see McPherson, *The Struggle for Equality*; Joseph B. James, *The Framing of the Fourteenth Amendment* (Urbana, Ill.: University of Illinois Press, 1956); William Gillette, *The Right to Vote* (Baltimore: Johns Hopkins University Press, 1965); W. R. Brock, *An American Crisis* (New York: Harper & Row, 1963).

slaves. In the tumultuous debates of the Reconstruction era, all of these measures were seriously debated; all but the third—changing the basis of apportionment—were eventually tried. Each involved redefining the national polity and the relationship between the federal and the state governments. All parties agreed that the census would be needed to implement whatever constitutional changes were made.[22]

It is thus in the tangled history of the wartime amendments and the Reconstruction acts that one finds the germ of the next generation of debates about the role of the census and the federal statistical system. Kennedy's pseudo-Darwinian notions of racial extinction led policymakers up a blind alley. The reality of the need to reconstitute the state and redefine national citizenship after the Civil War revived political and intellectual interest in the census. While no official census machinery existed between mid-1865 and early 1870, a new generation of statisticians and statistically minded politicians who sought to fashion a census that would serve the needs of Reconstruction came of age. Among the most prominent of this new generation were James A. Garfield and Francis Amasa Walker.[23]

Abundant evidence indicates that, were it not for the bonus of representation that the South would receive as a result of abolishing slavery, Northern Republicans would not have spent much time championing the freed blacks' right to suffrage. By and large, northern states did not let free blacks vote, and several northern Republican states rejected black suffrage in 1865 and 1866. All bills proposing methods of reconstructing loyal governments in the South during the war assumed a white male electorate. But just as the North discovered it could not win the war without freeing and arming the slaves, Northerners also discovered that they could not reconstruct the Union without the political help of freed blacks. We know that Northern Republicans did so reluctantly, but they did ultimately lay the basis for black political participation in American life. The logic of representation and apportionment could not be resisted.[24]

Congress searched for methods to redefine the apportionment base as soon as the finality of formal emancipation was assured. One week after the House of Representatives passed the Thirteenth Amendment abolishing slavery, and hence the three-fifths compromise, Sen. Charles

22. William W. Van Alstyne, "The Fourteenth Amendment, the Right to Vote, and the Understanding of the Thirty-ninth Congress," *Supreme Court Review* (1965): 33–86.

23. Burke A. Hinsdale, ed., *The Works of James Abram Garfield*, vol. 1 (1882; reprint, Freeport, N.Y.: Books For Libraries Press, 1970); James Phinney Munroe, *A Life of Francis Amasa Walker* (New York: Henry Holt, 1923).

24. James, *Fourteenth Amendment*; Gillette, *Right to Vote*; McPherson, *Ordeal by Fire*; Brock, *American Crisis*. For early versions of reconstruction bills, see S. 538, 37th Cong., 3d sess., Feb. 17, 1863, and S. 365, 37th Cong., 2d sess., June 23, 1862.

Sumner proposed another constitutional amendment in the Senate to change the apportionment base from the total population to the voting population of a state. The bill died with the expiration of the Thirty-eighth Congress in March. That summer, northern Republican congressmen began to propagandize their districts about the need to develop methods to secure Republican hegemony in the South. For example, Rep. James Garfield spoke to a Fourth of July audience at Ravenna, Ohio, and called for black suffrage on the grounds of both political right and expediency. The "negro" stood by the Union "in the hour of our sorest need, and by his aid, under God, the Republic was saved." Freed slaves thus deserved the vote. But Garfield urged his audience to ponder "another consideration," the consequence of the change in representation. "If the negro be denied the franchise, and the size of the House of Representatives remain as now," Garfield warned,

> we shall have fifteen additional members of Congress from the States lately in rebellion without the addition of a single citizen to their population, and we shall have fifteen less in the loyal States. This will not only give six members of Congress to South Carolina, four sevenths of whose people are negroes, but it will place the power of the State, as well as the destiny of 412,000 black men, in the hands of the 20,000 white men (less than the number of voters in our own Congressional district) who, under the restricted suffrage of that undemocratic State, exercise the franchise.[25]

By the fall, prominent Republican newspapers reported the effect of various proposals for changes in representation. The *Chicago Tribune* published a state-by-state report of the changes in representation that would result from the end of the three-fifths compromise and an allocation of representation on the basis of the voting population within each state. The former slave states would gain sixteen seats in Congress from abolition; if the apportionment was changed to the voting population, these same states would instead lose eighteen seats. The need for action on the apportionment formula was obvious.[26]

What to do was less obvious. The regulation of suffrage had always been a state matter, and the different states had a bewildering variety of rules. Many congressmen balked at the notion of federalizing control over the franchise. Congress could stop short of regulating the franchise by simply changing the apportionment base to the voting population, but that might encourage a mad rush among the states to increase the electorate by enfranchising foreigners and women as well as blacks. Some states already allowed aliens to vote, and the infant women's suffrage movement was pressing for the enfranchisement of women along with the freed blacks. Further, New Englanders discovered by January 1866 that

25. Hinsdale, ed., *Words of Garfield*, pp. 90–91.
26. James, *Fourteenth Amendment*, p. 23.

an apportionment based on voters would severely reduce their representation. New England had more women than men, a large number of unnaturalized immigrants, and relatively restrictive franchise rules. So New England congressmen quickly moved to oppose an apportionment rule based on voters. The nub of the problem was that northern states did not allow blacks to vote, and it was not clear how to write a national apportionment rule that would enfranchise southern blacks without also enfranchising Northern blacks.[27]

These issues were debated at length during the first session of the Thirty-ninth Congress. The Committee on Reconstruction finally wrote a politically acceptable solution in what became Section 2 of the Fourteenth Amendment:[28]

> Representatives shall be apportioned among the several States according to their respective numbers, counting the whole number of persons in each State, excluding Indians not taxed. But when the right to vote at any election for the choice of Electors for President and Vice-President of the United States, Representatives in Congress, the executive and judicial officers of a State, or the members of the Legislature thereof, is denied to any of the male inhabitants of such State, being twenty-one years of age and citizens of the United States, or in any way abridged, except for participation in rebellion, or other crime, the basis of representation therein shall be reduced in the proportion which the number of such male citizens shall bear to the whole number of male citizens twenty-one years of age in such State.

If the South would not enfranchise the freed slaves, their congressional representation would be reduced proportionately. Northern states that did not allow blacks to vote would be similarly punished, but, since the number of such voters was inconsequential, there was little likelihood that disenfranchisement would cost them a congressional seat or electoral vote. And the amendment avoided the question of women's suffrage by penalizing a state only for denying men the right to vote.

Section 2 passed with the rest of the amendment in June 1866. Prominent northern Radicals, who supported universal suffrage, were not completely happy with the provision. They were willing to accept it in order to assure the Republican ascendancy in Congress and the electoral college, but they continued to agitate for congressionally mandated universal suffrage. In July 1868 the amendment was ratified, and Republicans began to think about implementation.[29]

Implementation of Section 2 never came. The clause became a dead

27. Ibid., pp. 55ff.
28. George David Zuckerman, "A Consideration of the History and Present Status of Section 2 of the Fourteenth Amendment," *Fordham Law Review* 30 (1961): 93–136; George Smith, "Republicans, Reconstruction and Section 2 of the Fourteenth Amendment," *Western Political Quarterly* 23 (1976): 829–53.
29. Van Alstyne, "Fourteenth Amendment."

letter, or, as the Congressional Research Service put it in their official annotation of the Constitution, "little more than an historical curiosity." Why Congress never implemented Section 2 has a number of explanations, and they do have some merit. The most obvious is that by the time the 1870 census was taken, the Fifteenth Amendment to the Constitution had been ratified and blacks had the constitutional right to vote in both the South and the North. There was thus no need to penalize states for refusing the franchise to particular classes of voters. Later in the century, when blacks were systematically denied the franchise in the South, in this view, Congress had lost its will to enforce Section 2.[30]

Nevertheless, there is more to the story of the effort to implement Section 2. It is tied to moves to reform and harness the census for political reconstruction. This effort failed, but it left a legacy of ideas and experience about the possibilities and limitations of congressional power and statistical apportionment. And it prompted Congress to question the nature and goals of the census more generally and then to refocus federal statistical efforts on the impact of the burgeoning urban industrial sector of the economy.

In December 1868 the Fortieth Congress convened its third session. On the agenda were the proposals for what became the Fifteenth Amendment as well as calls for implementation of Section 2 of the Fourteenth Amendment in time for the upcoming 1870 census. In the Senate, James Harlan proposed a resolution "directing the Senate Judiciary Committee to prepare a bill for the apportionment of Representatives in compliance with section 2 of the fourteenth amendment." The resolution passed the Senate but died in the House. The House did, however, move to deal with census legislation and appointed a select committee headed by James A. Garfield of Ohio. This committee reported a bill in March 1869 that passed the House but died in the Senate. Garfield's committee then met during the summer months when Congress was out of session and prepared an elaborate report on the ninth census in preparation for reintroducing the census bill in December 1869.[31]

Garfield's bill and the committee's report provide some of the best evidence of Congress's intention to use the census to administer the political penalties in Section 2 of the Fourteenth Amendment and thus to promote black suffrage in the South. Garfield proposed that the census collect two types of information. First, the census would question adult men to determine if they were "citizens of the United States being twenty-one years of age, whose right to vote is denied or abridged on other grounds than rebellion or crime." Second, the committee compiled infor-

30. Congressional Research Service, *The Constitution of the United States: Analysis and Interpretation* (Washington, D.C.: GPO, 1972), pp. 1528–29; Gillette, *Right to Vote.*
31. Zuckerman, "Consideration of Section 2," pp. 107*ff.*

mation from state laws on the particular suffrage restrictions operative in various states to estimate the potential electorate. With this information Congress could calculate an apportionment that would recognize and penalize suffrage restriction.[32]

But Garfield and his committee went much further. When they put out a public call to experts to come and testify about improving the census, they discovered, as had Joseph C. G. Kennedy twenty years earlier, that many statisticians and public officials had ideas about how to improve the census. Garfield, eclectic and something of an intellectual himself, became fascinated with the new field of statistics and welcomed the new ideas and suggestions. His census report thus contained many more proposals to improve the census. His model bill radically revamped the existing 1850 legislation.[33]

Garfield proposed to remove the responsibility for the field enumeration from the U.S. marshals and instead appoint field supervisors for each congressional district. He proposed a wide variety of new inquiries on all the schedules. He proposed that the system of compensation for the enumerators be changed. He also proposed that the time allowed for the enumeration be shortened from months to days.

Unfortunately, all the proposals to improve the basic census machinery served to arouse suspicion about Garfield's ultimate intentions and thus led the Senate to sabotage the bill. In December 1869 Garfield reintroduced his bill in the House. In the course of the debate it became obvious that the timing of the ratification of the Fifteenth Amendment could affect the apportionment penalty as written in Garfield's bill. The census was to be taken within six months, and Garfield's legislation required an automatic reduction in representation to those states that refused blacks the right to vote. What would happen, several congressmen asked, if immediately on the conclusion of the census, the Fifteenth Amendment should be ratified and all state laws restricting black suffrage nullified? Should a state suffer a decade of reduced representation? Garfield agreed that this might present difficulties and thus recommended that the apportionment section be deleted and reintroduced in a separate bill.[34]

What then occurred was both comic and tragic. The House passed the amended bill; the Senate tabled it because it no longer addressed the great questions raised by the Fourteenth Amendment and black suffrage. Garfield's bill merely reformed the census machinery—legislation that few senators thought necessary and some thought downright insidious. What

32. "Ninth Census," H.R. Rept. 3, 41st Cong., 2d sess., 1870 (Serial 1436), quotation on p. 53. The report detailed the various restrictions on suffrage that would be pertinent to enforcing Section 2 of the Fourteenth Amendment (pp. 71–99).

33. Wright and Hunt, *History and Growth*, pp. 52–54; Hinsdale, ed., *Works of Garfield*, pp. 443–76.

34. Zuckerman, "Consideration of Section 2," pp. 109–10.

offended the Senate most, according to the *Nation*'s postmortem of the legislative debate, was the change in the field administration of the census. Federal marshals were appointed on the recommendation of senators, and hence the census was a form of senatorial patronage. Garfield proposed to shift the field administration to congressional districts—and hence to a form of House patronage.[35]

The census of 1870 was thus taken under the plan of the 1850 legislation. Garfield, though, was not completely unsuccessful in his attempts to modernize and streamline the census bureaucracy. He had drawn together a wide variety of experts during that 1869 summer of effort in the basement of the Capitol, and he had identified one young man who would continue to make a career of the census for the next twenty-five years: Francis Amasa Walker. Walker had come to work in the Treasury Department under David Wells in January 1869, and he prepared schedules and reports for Garfield's committee. In January 1870, as the Senate was killing Garfield's census bill, President Grant nominated the twenty-nine-year-old Walker as census superintendent. From his position as census superintendent Walker became a nationally respected expert on statistics, economics, and public policy.[36]

At the time of his appointment, Walker merely faced a difficult administrative task. He had no new legislation to streamline the census bureaucracy, but he was under considerable pressure to take an accurate, efficient census. Commentators of all stripes were tremendously interested in the changes in the American population after a decade of civil war and social upheaval. The South especially was politically unstable; white elites were resistant to federal authority, recalcitrant about Reconstruction, and generally unwilling to yield to postwar realities. The West was wild, unsettled, and difficult to enumerate. Eastern cities were exploding with migrants, both native- and foreign-born. Walker thus had to superintend the count and determine the numbers that would be used to address the potentially charged question of apportionment penalties.[37]

Walker achieved mixed results in the 1870 census; in the successes and failures one can glimpse the end of one era of federal statistical effort and the beginning of another. Commentators have generally praised Walker for his innovations in industrial statistics, for his improvements in the Washington statistical bureaucracy, for his cartography. On the other hand, the 1870 census suffered from extremely poor field procedures and some badly worded questions. It was plagued with undercounts, local demands for recounts, and inadequate responses to questions. These

35. H. Adams, "Imbroglio about the Census," *Nation* 10 (1870): 116.

36. Munroe, *Life of Walker*, pp. 101–26.

37. Walker gives a vivid description of these problems in his own introduction to vol. 1 of the 1870 population report. See Census Office, *Ninth Census: The Statistics of the Population of the United States*, vol. 1 (Washington, D.C.: GPO, 1872), pp. ix–xliv.

COUNTING SLAVES AND FREED BLACKS   79

weaknesses directly affected the 1872 congressional apportionment, and thus contemporary criticisms of the census overshadowed praise. Since neither the infant statistical community nor the key players in Congress knew how to remedy these technical problems with the census, they concluded either that Section 2 of the Fourteenth Amendment could not be implemented or that its undesirable side effects made it an unworkable mechanism for Reconstruction. The ironies ran deep.[38]

In December 1871 Francis Walker reported the results of the 1870 census to Congress for apportionment. One of the first questions that Congress had to address was the size of the House after the next apportionment. Walker reported that U.S. population had grown to 38.1 million. The decennial growth rate had slowed to 22 percent. Given continued westward expansion, there was a great deal of sentiment to increase the number of representatives to minimize the loss of congressional seats in the older eastern states and to make sure that congressional districts did not get too large. Walker therefore reported apportionments for a House of Representatives with anywhere from 241 to 300 members. Differential population growth made it necessary, Walker indicated, to increase the size of the House by at least 40 members to minimize the loss of seats in the East, particularly in New England.[39]

Congress also wanted to know what effect the end of the three-fifths compromise was going to have on the relative distribution of seats in Congress. Clearly, the South should gain as a result of the full counting of the freed slaves. Walker therefore produced data indicating the increases in the representative population for the southern states. He reported that the end of the three-fifths compromise had increased the representative population of the southern states by almost 14 percent. In Alabama, Florida, Georgia, Louisiana, Mississippi, and South Carolina the change had increased the representative population between 20 and 30 percent.[40]

Congress also wanted to know how many male citizens were disfranchised according to the language of Section 2 of the Fourteenth Amend-

38. Munroe, *Life of Walker*; Margo Anderson Conk, "The Census, Political Power and Social Change," *Social Science History* 8 (Winter 1984): 81–106; Robert Barrows, "The Ninth Federal Census of Indianapolis: A Case Study in Civic Chauvinism," *Indiana Magazine of History* 73 (1977): 1–16.

39. *Ninth Census*, vol. 1:xiii–xv. Walker had the unpleasant task of telling Congress that the growth rate of the population had declined radically over the decade. See chap. 4, below. He reported three calculations for the population to soften the impact: the population for apportionment was 38.1 million; that for the states and territories was 38.6 million; that for what he called the "true population"—including "Indians not taxed" and whites in Indian country and Alaska—was 38.9 million. The figure generally in use today, which corrects for the 1870 undercounts, is 39.8 million. See Bureau of the Census, *Historical Statistics of the United States: Colonial Times to 1970,* pt. 1 (Washington, D.C.: GPO, 1975), pp. 1, 8.

40. *Ninth Census*, 1:xiii–xv.

ment and therefore how the representative population of the various states was to be calculated. Walker reported to the House that only forty thousand men were disfranchised according to the language of Section 2—out of a total potential electorate of over eight million. He also reported through the secretary of the Interior that he was "disposed to give but little credit to the returns made by assistant marshals in regard to the denial or abridgement of suffrage." The numbers were bad; he did not specify why the desired information had not been correctly collected.[41]

The numbers were not so trivial that they could be ignored with impunity. James Garfield noted that if the House recalculated the representative population on the basis of the forty thousand disfranchised men, both Rhode Island and Arkansas could lose a representative. He used the opportunity of the census report to castigate his colleagues for not passing the census reform legislation in the winter of 1869–70. Better census machinery, he pointed out, might have avoided this constitutional dilemma.[42]

Garfield's message was lost in the complexities of the debate. In the next months Congress reapportioned the House without applying the strictures of Section 2. In some ways Congress also violated the original constitutional requirements for apportionment according to population. In February 1872 the size of the House was set at 283 members. Only New Hampshire and Vermont, according to this apportionment, lost representation compared to the 1860 apportionment. Nevertheless, Congress was unsatisfied. In May, Congress added 9 representatives, bringing the size of the House to 292. Vermont and New Hampshire each regained their 1860 allotment of 3 representatives each. Pennsylvania, Indiana, Tennessee, Louisiana, and Alabama also gained one seat each. But then the shenanigans began. Florida gained a seat, though it did not deserve one; New York gained one seat, though it deserved two. Illinois deserved an additional seat under an apportionment of 292 but did not get one.[43]

Finally, and perhaps most ironically, after all the controversy about the end of the three-fifths compromise, the former slave states did not increase their share of representation in Congress at the 1870 census. The bonus of full counting of the freed blacks merely allowed the South to maintain the status quo. This happened for several reasons. First, population growth had taken place primarily in the West during the decade. All of the eastern states suffered relative population loss. California, Iowa, Michigan, Minnesota, Missouri, and Oregon, for example, had decennial growth rates of over 50 percent. Second, the war itself had taken an enormous toll on the southern population and had impeded population

41. Zuckerman, "Consideration of Section 2," pp. 110*ff.*
42. Ibid., pp. 112*ff.*; Hinsdale, ed., *Works of Garfield*, pp. 761–65.
43. Balinski and Young, *Fair Representation*, pp. 37*ff.*; *Ninth Census*, 1:xv.

growth. Finally, though this was not obvious until 1880, the census had probably undercounted the southern population by 1.26 million.[44]

Congress and Francis Walker concluded from the 1870 experience that it was necessary to reform the census before statistics could be used to regulate the franchise. They eliminated the questions about suffrage restriction in the 1880 census schedule. They were never reintroduced. Walker continually pointed to the weaknesses of using the federal marshals as field administrators. As census director, he had no control over either these supervisory agents or the assistant marshals who actually did the house-to-house census.[45]

With the advantage of hindsight, we might note further flaws in the 1870 census effort. First, neither the Garfield committee nor Walker were willing to initiate a long-term effort to study the statistical issues involved in measuring voter participation and voting restrictions. They did not try to estimate the number of male citizens who did not vote because of apathy or subtler obstacles to participation. They expected the assistant marshals to report if the individual was denied the vote whether or not the individual knew if he could vote. Questions were weakly framed, and several additional questions could profitably have been added to clarify ambiguities inherent in the inquiry. Finally, Walker could have used the opportunity presented by the passage of the Fifteenth Amendment to lessen the pressure from Congress for high-quality data. He could have experimented in future censuses with new questions. He could have used his authority to appoint a special agent to investigate the problems of collecting electoral statistics.[46]

Because Walker and later census officials did none of these things, Congress was ill-prepared to deal with the problem of suffrage restriction at the turn of the century, when the southern states systematically restricted black suffrage. In the first decade of the twentieth century, Congress again debated using the census to measure suffrage restriction and thus to reduce southern representation in the House. During the consideration of the 1900 apportionment legislation in 1901, Republicans introduced a motion to ask the census director to report the "total number of male citizens . . . over 21 years of age in each of the several States of the

44. Francis A. Walker, "The Colored Race in the United States," in *Discussions in Economics and Statistics*, ed. Davis R. Dewey, vol. 2 (1899; reprint, New York: Burt Franklin, 1970), pp. 129*ff.* See also Chap. 4, below.

45. *Ninth Census*; Francis A. Walker, "Report of the Superintendent of the Census," 45th Cong., 3d sess., 1878, H.R. Ex. Doc. 1 (Serial 1850), pp. 839*ff.*; "Interview with Prof. Francis A. Walker, Superintendent of the Census," 45th Cong., 3d sess., 1878, S. Misc. Doc. 26 (Serial 1833).

46. Walker was well aware of the possibility of using special agents to collect certain types of statistics, such as assessed valuation or social statistics, which had been gathered through the analysis of local government records since 1850. See Walker, "Report of the Superintendent," p. 845.

Union," and the "total number of male citizens of the United States over 21 years of age who, by reason of State constitutional limitations or State legislation, are denied the right of suffrage." On the key vote of this effort to enforce Section 2, the measure failed, 94 to 136. The lost opportunity of 1870 meant that no tradition of collecting data on suffrage or suffrage restriction in the census was established. Section 2 became a dead letter; the decennial reapportionment proceeded, but the discrepancy between the size of an area's population and its actual electorate grew enormously. Voter turnout in the South was half that of the North in the twentieth century. Not until the passage of the Voting Rights Act and the civil rights movement of the 1960s were the patterns reversed.[47]

The census, of course, formed only a fraction of the effort to change the political structure of the South during Reconstruction. Its failure to collect systematic information on suffrage and suffrage restriction as mandated by Section 2 of the Fourteenth Amendment was clearly only part of a more general "retreat from Reconstruction," as William Gillette has put it. Yet the failure should still be noted, precisely because the census is such an unobtrusive recorder of our national life. Walker's impatience with his field staff and his increasing inattention to southern questions in favor of those regarding urbanization and industrialization had a cost. The men who wrote the wartime amendments understood all too well the transitory nature of politics; they wanted Reconstruction mechanisms that would remind Americans of their duties to equal suffrage and civil rights long after the passions of the war years had waned. In that duty the 1870 census failed. It did not maintain the statistics on suffrage restriction and civil rights, and later generations of Americans suffered the consequences of that failure.

47. William Gillette, *Retreat from Reconstruction, 1869–1879* (Baton Rouge, La.: Louisiana State University Press, 1979); J. Morgan Kousser, *The Shaping of Southern Politics: Suffrage Restriction and the Establishment of the One-Party South, 1880–1910* (New Haven and London: Yale University Press, 1974); Ben Margolis, "Judicial Enforcement of Section 2 of the Fourteenth Amendment," *Law in Transition* 23 (1963): 128–63; Zuckerman, "Consideration of Section 2," pp. 116*ff.*

FOUR || The Census and Industrial America
in the Gilded Age

A new work, and in many respects, a different mode of life, now offered themselves to the people of the United States. . . . [About 1840] manufactures, on the large scale, were to be established. . . . [T]hat career was to be undertaken which . . . was, in half a century, to lead the United States to the proud position of the first industrial nation of the world.
—*Francis Amasa Walker, 1889*

During the late nineteenth century, American census takers, like the broader community of policymakers, slowly turned their attention away from the problems of the South and of American race relations. Instead they took up the emerging social issues presented by urbanization, industrialization, and the end of the western frontier. As they did so, they refashioned the machinery of the census.

Between the 1870s and the turn of the century, several innovations in census taking emerged. They included two major pieces of census legislation. In 1879 Congress gave the Census Office control over the field administration of the census. The superintendent of the census received the authority to appoint the supervisors and to approve the appointment of enumerators. Legislation in 1902 made the Bureau of the Census a permanent federal agency. Further, census officials introduced machine tabulation of the data at the 1890 census, and they made major breakthroughs in cartography and the presentation and organization of data.

These innovations meant that the U.S. Census Office in 1900 bore only slight resemblance to the organizations that

Kennedy and Walker had run during the Civil War and Reconstruction eras. By and large, these were years in which census controversies, like other federal issues, were not life and death struggles. Party battles abounded, shaping the growth and character of the census. However, they did not ultimately paralyze legislation or prevent statistical innovations from being tried.

By a wide variety of indicators, the census became a much more elaborate enterprise in the late nineteenth century than it had been before the Civil War. The number of published volumes of data increased from five in 1860 and 1870 to twenty-three in 1880 and thirty-two in 1890. Francis Walker tripled the size of the Washington office staff between 1860 and 1870 and then tripled it again in 1880 (to 1,495). By 1900 over 3,500 people worked in the Washington Census Office. The field enumeration staff grew similarly. In 1870, 62 marshals and 6,530 assistant marshals took the census. By 1900, 300 supervisors and almost 53,000 enumerators took the census. In turn, the per capita cost of the census grew. In 1860 the count cost 6.3¢ a person; by 1900 it cost 15.5¢ a person.[1]

The growth of the census was a function of the changes in the nature of American society. By the late nineteenth century, Americans had managed to people most of the continental United States; as the census takers documented in 1890, there was no longer a frontier line. In 1893 Frederick Jackson Turner pointed out that the closing of the frontier would necessarily force major changes in the society. The Founding Fathers had looked West and had seen limitless acres of open land that guaranteed opportunity for centuries. The Americans of the late nineteenth century saw a continent filled with people; westward migration was still the norm, but it would necessarily be a slowly dying phenomenon.[2]

Further, the overwhelming majority of Americans of the early Republic had worked in agriculture. By 1880, the census documented that half the American labor force worked in manufacturing, mining, trade, transportation, or services. The census devised new and more elaborate statistics on the nonagricultural labor force to describe these changes and thus to document the increasing diversification of the economy. In addi-

1. On the growth of the Census Office, see Carroll Wright and William C. Hunt, *History and Growth of the United States Census* (Washington, D.C.: GPO, 1900), pp. 52–84, and A. Ross Eckler, *The Bureau of the Census* (New York: Praeger, 1972), pp. 3–11, 24. On "statebuilding" generally in the period, see Morton Keller, *Affairs of State* (Cambridge, Mass.: Harvard University Press, 1977); Stephen Skowronek, *Building a New American State* (Cambridge, Mass.: Harvard University Press, 1982); and Leonard White, *The Republican Era, 1869–1901: A Study in Administrative History* (New York: Macmillan, 1958).

2. Gerald Nash, "The Census of 1890 and the Closing of the Frontier," *Pacific Northwest Quarterly* 71 (July 1980): 98–100; Frederick Jackson Turner, "The Significance of the Frontier in American History," *Annual Report of the American Historical Association* (1893): 199–227.

tion, the census began its statistics on the urban population to document the remarkable growth of cities; between one-fifth and one-fourth of the population lived in "urban" areas in 1870, and the trajectory of growth was upward. These population changes prompted new and more detailed cross-tabulations of the answers on the census, which in turn prompted new interpretations of the meaning of the changes. The new efforts were primarily exploratory and descriptive and were thus divorced from the traditional role of the census as an apportionment mechanism. By the early twentieth century, though, as we shall see, the methods, classifications, and descriptions of the Gilded Age census takers began to work their way into policy debates and ultimately into new population apportionment mechanisms.[3]

In these years, the economic censuses, and what came to be called "social statistics," also came into their own. As the American economy diversified, Congress called on the decennial census to document, for example, the growth of transportation, manufacturing, mining, agriculture, electrical utilities, and insurance industries. The office also worked on improving vital statistics and the statistics on the "defective, dependent, and delinquent classes." These new efforts led to a differentiation in the structure of the Census Office and the expertise of the statisticians. The statisticians discovered they had created new constituencies for the data. In the early nineteenth century, as we have seen, congressmen, local politicians, and almanac publishers were among the most interested users of census data. By the late nineteenth century, business associations, reformers, and the new university men also lobbied for data that would fit their needs. As interest in the new initiatives grew, the traditional role of the census as a mechanism to apportion political representation faded in importance. The statisticians began to think of apportionment as merely a necessary but relatively routine and unimportant footnote in the whole census effort.

In short, during these years, the purpose of the census changed. Though still a political apportionment mechanism, the census also became a full-fledged instrument to monitor the overall state of American society. Self-defined professional statisticians began to take control of the census. They saw themselves as creating new and more sophisticated interpretations of the numbers. We have seen that important statements about social policy were always embedded in the census data. Nevertheless, major innovations in the "science of statistics" in the late nineteenth century did invest the numbers with greater interpretive power. And

3. Margo Anderson Conk, *The United States Census and Labor Force Change: A History of Occupation Statistics* (Ann Arbor, Mich.: UMI Research Press, 1980). For a description of the urban/rural classifications used in the census, see Bureau of the Census, *Historical Statistics of the United States: Colonial Times to 1970,* pt. 1 (Washington, D.C.: GPO, 1975), pp. 2–3.

perhaps more importantly, universities and, somewhat later, private research organizations grew and began to codify the science of statistics.
Universities began to teach statistics as part of their curricula. These new
courses defined an authoritative methodological and interpretive tradition. In turn, these newly trained statisticians went to work for statistical
agencies or popularized statistics to the general public.[4]

As a result, the men who administered and interpreted the census in
the late nineteenth century played a crucial role in explaining to the
society at large just what was happening as America entered its urban
industrial phase. They saw the population spread across the country and
drew maps that made Americans aware of the "closing of the frontier."
They documented the arrival of the "new immigrants" and their pen-
chant for settling in cities. They pointed out that many of the older rural
counties of the country populated by native white Americans were losing
population. And they documented the social class structure of the urban
industrial regions that seemed to be the most dynamic growth areas of the
country.

By the turn of the century, the census takers and many in Congress
were calling for the creation of a permanent federal agency to take the
census. They made two arguments for the proposal. First, they pointed
out that Congress and the public were demanding so much data that the
Census Office de facto existed for seven to eight years of the decade. It
would be more efficient to create a permanent agency and schedule the
work throughout the decade. Second, they used demographic changes in
the population as evidence of the continuous need to monitor and interpret the statistical health and well-being of American society. At the turn
of the century the statisticians achieved their goal. The 1902 legislation
completed the fundamental shift in the role of the census. Congress
recognized that legislative apportionment was only one of many uses of
census data and, hence, that census taking had to be placed on a new
footing to meet the new demands.

Francis Walker (fig. 8) probably did not realize how much his accep-
tance of President Grant's appointment as census superintendent would
affect both his personal career and the character of the census. Like
Kennedy twenty years earlier, Walker was a relative newcomer to Washington political life and the world of federal statistics. One year earlier,

4. On the development of higher education in the late 19th c., see Alexandra Oleson
and John Voss, *The Organization of Knowledge in Modern America, 1860–1920* (Baltimore:
Johns Hopkins University Press, 1979). The first major text was Richmond Mayo-Smith, *The
Science of Statistics,* pt. 1: *Statistics and Sociology,* and pt. 2: *Statistics and Economics* (New York:
Macmillan, 1895, 1899). See also Helen Walker, *Studies in the History of the Statistical Method*
(Baltimore: Williams & Wilkins, 1929), pp. 148–56, and A. Hunter Dupree, *Science in the
Federal Government* (Cambridge, Mass.: Harvard University Press, 1957).

8. Francis Amasa Walker, Superintendent of the Census Office, 1870 and 1880.

Walker had taken a position as chief of the Bureau of Statistics and assistant to David Wells in the Treasury Department. That year he became acquainted with the statistical workings of the federal government and made a name for himself by reorganizing the bureau and publishing several well-received reports.

Walker was also the son of Amasa Walker, a major antebellum political economist. He grew up in an atmosphere where economics and political questions were discussed and subjected to rudimentary quantitative analysis. He had also distinguished himself during the Civil War. He rose to the rank of adjutant general in the Army of the Potomac and fought in some of the most brutal combat of the war.[5]

Still, at twenty-nine, Walker had little experience running a large administrative undertaking like the census and minimal formal training in statistics. He had gained most of his knowledge of the census during the months that he had worked on Garfield's staff to write a new census bill. He knew, he felt, what he wanted to avoid: the type of operation that Kennedy had run in 1860. Walker felt that Kennedy's office was too slow in processing the data. He believed that Kennedy had prolonged the

5. James Phinney Munroe, *A Life of Francis Amasa Walker* (New York: Henry Holt, 1923).

tabulation process to perpetuate his own position. Walker vowed to publish the census volumes as quickly as possible and to disband the office.

Walker also wanted to expand the detail in the reports and change tabulation methods. He published a biting, but by and large accurate, attack on the occupation statistics in 1860 and called for detailed data on the employed population in cities. He wanted to dispense with the third copy of the schedules then deposited with the local county clerks around the country. The existence of these schedules, he felt, was an invasion of privacy and an unneeded clerical expense. And of course he wanted to take the field administration of the census away from the control of the U.S. marshals and to appoint a field staff responsible to the Census Office and the Interior Department.[6]

Although most of his proposals eventually proved sound, Walker incurred some political wounds during his tenure that hampered his ability to implement his ideas. In particular, Walker underestimated the political liabilities of attacking Kennedy too heavily. Kennedy was still in Washington and lobbying among his political friends for reappointment to the census post. In the summer of 1869, Kennedy testified against Garfield's bill. By 1870, when Walker was appointed, Kennedy began sniping at the young superintendent in the press and in letters to Congress. Kennedy continued to hope for his own restoration to the census post, as had occurred in 1860.[7]

Walker thus started his career in the Census Office with a vocal critic close at hand and without the reform legislation that he had wanted. He administered the 1870 census under the 1850 legislation and concentrated his administrative and statistical efforts on those aspects of the census process that he could control directly. The field administration of the census was not one. It derived from the U.S. marshal system. Some of the sixty-two marshals worked in urban regions with millions of people, others in sparsely settled frontier regions. The marshals appointed their assistants themselves, so Walker had control neither over the quality nor, in precise ways, over the number of assistants who were appointed.

Walker could control the processing of the census in Washington, so he took steps to make up for some of the inefficiencies inherent in the field administration system by improving the central office procedures. Walker was committed to shortening the period between the taking of the census and its publication. He tripled the size of the Washington office. By December 1870, four hundred clerks worked to tabulate the census.

6. Francis Amasa Walker, "American Industry in the Census," *Atlantic Monthly* 24 (December 1869): 689–701; Walker, "Report of the Superintendent of Census to the Secretary of the Interior," in *Ninth Census of the United States: The Statistics of Population*, vol. 1 (Washington, D.C.: GPO, 1872), pp. xxi–xlviii.

7. *Congressional Globe*, 41st Cong., 2d sess., 1870, pp. 1147*ff.*

He created a clearly defined divisional structure in the office and administered qualifying examinations to applicants for the clerical positions.

These efforts yielded results. By December 1871, Walker could report that the population census was substantially completed. He published the main volume of the population report in 1872, one to two years earlier than had Kennedy or DeBow. Three more volumes of the census appeared in 1873; a statistical atlas appeared in 1874. In accordance with his previous commitment to run an efficient operation, Walker disbanded the census office in July 1873.

Nevertheless, Walker still faced serious problems in taking the census that he felt he had only partially solved. The problems derived from the field administration system, the unsettled conditions in the South, and from demographic changes in the population itself. Walker was the first census superintendent who had to contend with demands for recounts from irate city boosters unhappy with the bureau's figures. The bureau ordered a recount of several places—including the cities of Indianapolis, Philadelphia, and New York. In both New York and Philadelphia, the popular notion of the population was considerably above what the bureau counted. New Yorkers believed that they had passed the 1 million mark, but the bureau initially counted only 923,944. Philadelphia's first count was 657,277, while the local boosters had predicted 800,000. In Philadelphia and New York, the second count was 2 to 2.5 percent above the first, far below the claims of 10 to 20 percent undercounts. In Indianapolis, the new numbers were significantly higher. The city, a Republican stronghold, had hoped to reach a population of 50,000 at the ninth census and was thus devastated to learn that the initial count was under 41,000. It was also the home of the powerful Republican senator Oliver Morton. After a complicated series of appeals and discussions, Walker authorized a recount that resulted in a 19 percent increase in the Indianapolis population. The city managed to "grow" by annexing land in the fall of 1870 and using the redrawn boundaries for the recount.[8]

More apt criticism could be made of the 1870 census for undercounting the Southern population—particularly its black population. Interpolation back from the 1880 figures indicate a potential total undercount of 1.2 million in the South and a black undercount of over .5 million—over 10 percent of the black population. In the 1870s, though, little was made of this undercount, both because the southern states were already reaping a bonus in congressional seats and electoral votes from the aboli-

8. *Ninth Census,* 1:xx–xxi; Robert G. Barrows, "The Ninth Federal Census of Indianapolis: A Case Study in Civic Chauvinism," *Indiana Magazine of History* 73, no. 1 (1977): 1–16; John B. Sharpless and Ray M. Shortridge, "Biased Underenumeration in Census Manuscripts: Methodological Implications," *Journal of Urban History* 1 (1975): 409–39.

tion of slavery and because few whites were seriously looking for robust growth in the black population.[9]

Finally, Walker faced difficulties counting the sparsely settled frontier regions of the West. Transportation and communication between Washington and the Far West had improved considerably since Kennedy had coped with the destruction of the 1850 returns from California, but Walker still had to arrange for the safety of the assistant marshals in parts of the territories "menaced by Indian attack, or frequented by lawless bands of Whites." Even the geography of some areas was open to dispute. Walker tried to provide additional compensation for the marshals in such regions, because, as he told Congress, "the enumeration of many Subdivisions in these Territories involves the organization and equipment of a small expedition," including "guides[,] interpreters, and even [army] escorts, being often necessary for the performance of the duty."[10]

In short, the United States of 1870 was demographically diverse and, if anything, becoming more so. In Walter Nugent's language, the "frontier-rural" style of life had been dominant in America since the early eighteenth century. While it was still dominant in many parts of the West, it was changing rapidly in parts of the East. The changes had several facets. In the northeastern states, large cities such as New York, Philadelphia, Baltimore, and Boston were becoming major commercial and industrial centers. Smaller market towns were growing into cities in their own right, as were the manufacturing villages scattered through the region.[11]

Further, the population growth rates in the older rural areas of the country were declining noticeably. By the 1860s, statisticians in Massachusetts, for example, had begun to document the decline in the birth rates of the populations in these areas. High fertility characterized frontier regions but not the older settled farm areas of the East.[12]

Third, in the 1840s, 1850s, and 1860s, 6.6 million European immigrants had arrived in the United States. By and large, they did not "melt" into the English-speaking white Protestant majority of the society. They

9. *Eleventh Census of the Population: 1890*, vol. 1 (Washington, D.C.: GPO, 1895), pp. xi–xii.

10. Francis Amasa Walker to Jacob B. Cox, May 10, 16, 1870, Walker to Columbus Delano, Dec. 6, 1871, Records of the Secretary of the Interior relating to the Ninth Census, RG 48, box 3, NA.

11. Walter Nugent, *Structures of American Social History* (Bloomington, Ind.: Indiana University Press, 1981). For example, the cities of New York, Philadelphia, Boston, and Baltimore contained about 2 million people; the western states of California, Minnesota, Kansas, Nebraska, Oregon, and Nevada contained about 1.6 million.

12. Nathan Allen, "The Foreign Element in Massachusetts, 1866," in *Historical Aspects of the Immigration Problem*, ed. Edith Abbott (Chicago: University of Chicago Press, 1926); Maris Vinovskis, *Fertility in Massachusetts from the Revolution to the Civil War* (New York: Academic Press, 1981).

THE CENSUS.

CENSUS-TAKER. "Good-morning, madam; I'm taking the census."
OLD LADY. "The what?"
C.-T. "The c-e-n-s-u-s!"
O. L. "For lan's sake! what with tramps takin' everythin' they kin lay their han's on, young folks takin' fotygrafs of ye without so much as askin', an' impudent fellows comin' roun' as wants ter take yer senses, pretty soon there won't be nothin' left ter take, I'm thinking."

9. The Census, *Harper's Weekly,* 1890. This cartoon humorously treats the problem of whether the "respondent" understands the functions of or questions on the census.

formed identifiable ethnic communities and elaborated local cultures that set them apart from the native white Protestant population. The Irish and many Germans were Roman Catholics. The Germans maintained their language. And, though many immigrants migrated west to settle new farms like other Americans, most immigrants tended to settle in cities. Immigrants also seemed fond of alcoholic beverages at a time when the temperance movement was gaining strength in the native population. They thus added cultural strains to the dominant society.

In other words, in 1870, 28 percent of the population was black or immigrant while 26 percent lived in urban places. More important for demographic trends, the dynamic areas of the population were no longer only the rural frontier areas. Rapid growth characterized cities and manufacturing towns, as well as immigrant neighborhoods and regions.

These trends prompted Francis Walker and his staff to find ways to illustrate the demographic changes in the population for the general public in several ways. First, Walker fostered the development of new classification systems, increased the amount of detail in the published data, and codified rules for data analysis. Second, he wrote numerous articles interpreting the results of the census for popular and scholarly journals. A lively essayist, Walker published pieces on general demographic trends—"The First Century of the Republic: Growth and Distribution of Population"—as well as on what the census had to say about particular aspects of American life—"Our Domestic Service," for example, or "Our Foreign Population."[13]

Walker also instituted the publication of the census *Statistical Atlas* with its multicolored maps and charts of the most important trends in the population. The atlas allowed the general public to see at a glance demographic characteristics that only the statistically trained could easily glean from the dry compilations of numbers in the tables themselves. In particular, Walker and his staff devised some of the best known visual indicators of American population change, including population density maps and the concept of the center of population (fig. 10).

Walker included a number of these maps in the census volumes themselves; he drew population density maps for particular subgroups of the population—blacks and whites, native-born and foreign-born. He calculated the "center of population" for every census between 1790 and 1870 and placed the series of stars representing the theoretical point of balance of the "weight" of the population on a map to illustrate the consistent westward thrust of the population (fig. 11). These innovations earned

13. See the bibliography of Walker's writings in Munroe, *Life of Walker*, pp. 420–39; Francis Amasa Walker, *Discussions in Economics and Statistics*, ed. Davis R. Dewey, 2 vols. (New York: Henry Holt, 1899).

DENSITY OF POPULATION, 1790

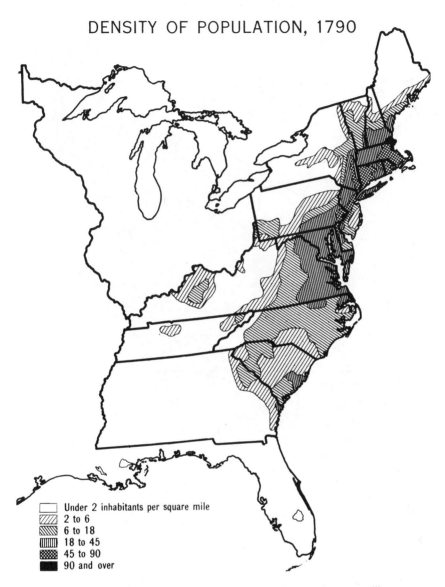

Under 2 inhabitants per square mile
2 to 6
6 to 18
18 to 45
45 to 90
90 and over

10a–e. Density of Population, 1790, 1830, 1860, 1890, and 1930. These maps illustrate population growth over time and should be viewed in sequence. Note that the 1860 map depicted only the eastern half of the country, although U.S. land stretched to California by 1850.

him the reputation of a great statistician. The 1874 *Statistical Atlas* won critical praise and awards from the international statistical community.[14]

14. H. G. Funkhouser, "Historical Development of the Graphical Representation of

CENTER OF POPULATION: 1790 TO 1980

["Center of population" is that point at which an imaginary flat, weightless, and rigid map of the United States would balance if weights of identical value were placed on it so that each weight represented the location of one person on the date of the census]

YEAR [1]	North latitude			West longitude			Approximate location
	°	'	"	°	'	"	
1790 (Aug. 2)	39	16	30	76	11	12	23 miles east of Baltimore, Md.
1850 (June 1)	38	59	0	81	19	0	23 miles southeast of Parkersburg, W. Va.
1900 (June 1)	39	9	36	85	48	54	6 miles southeast of Columbus, Ind.
1950 (Apr. 1)	38	50	21	88	9	33	8 miles north-northwest of Olney, Richland County, Ill.
1960 (Apr. 1)	38	35	58	89	12	35	In Clinton Co. about 6½ miles northwest of Centralia, Ill.
1970 (Apr. 1)	38	27	47	89	42	22	5.3 miles east-southeast of the Mascoutah City Hall in St. Clair County, Ill.
1980 (Apr. 1)	38	8	13	90	34	26	¼ mile west of De Soto in Jefferson County, Mo.

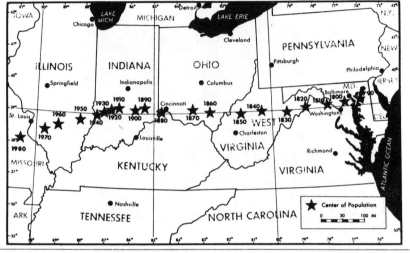

[1] For dates of admissions of the States and changes in areal definition, see "State Origins and Boundaries," *United States Summary, U.S. Census of Population: 1960*, vol. I. For year of admission to statehood, see table 326.

Source: U.S. Bureau of the Census, *1980 Census of Population, Vol. 1*.

---

11. Center of Population, 1790–1980. This map also illustrates the westward thrust of the population over time.

such legislation, and Walker and James A. Garfield, still one of the main legislators interested in statistical matters, were more adept at writing a bill that would pass. The Reconstruction debates that had prompted the earlier effort at census reform were no longer on the legislative agenda. Improving the census could be considered as a matter in its own right. It made good administrative sense to give the Census Office control over its own field administration. It also seemed both possible and reasonable to expand and improve the amount of data collected and published. A nation that would top fifty million people in 1880 could well afford a census that would adequately detail the character of its population, economy, and social life.

Accordingly, in 1878 Walker and a small group of interested legislators drew up a bill to revise the census machinery. In January, Walker submit-

DENSITY OF POPULATION, 1790

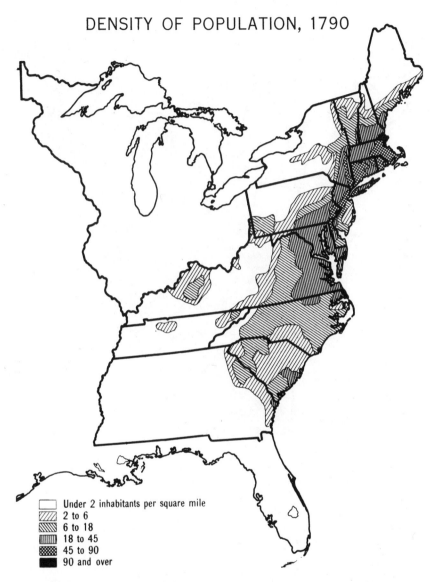

Under 2 inhabitants per square mile
2 to 6
6 to 18
18 to 45
45 to 90
90 and over

10a–e. Density of Population, 1790, 1830, 1860, 1890, and 1930. These maps illustrate population growth over time and should be viewed in sequence. Note that the 1860 map depicted only the eastern half of the country, although U.S. land stretched to California by 1850.

him the reputation of a great statistician. The 1874 *Statistical Atlas* won critical praise and awards from the international statistical community.[14]

14. H. G. Funkhouser, "Historical Development of the Graphical Representation of

DENSITY OF POPULATION, 1830

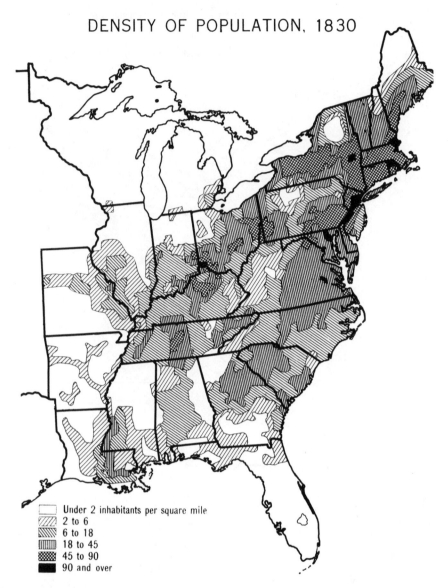

Under 2 inhabitants per square mile
2 to 6
6 to 18
18 to 45
45 to 90
90 and over

10b. Density of Population, 1830.

After a stint in 1872 as commissioner of Indian Affairs, Francis Walker left government service to become a professor of political economy at the Sheffield Scientific School of Yale University. Except for a brief period in

Statistical Data," *Osiris* 3 (1937): 269–404; Paul J. Fitzpatrick, "Leading American Statisticians in the Nineteenth Century," *JASA* 52 (September 1957): 301–21.

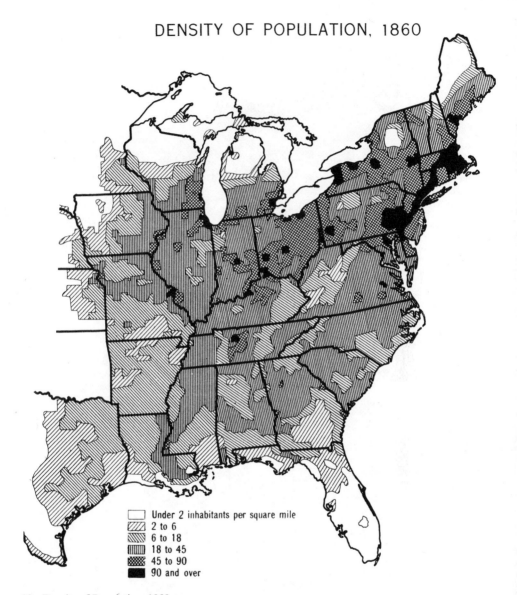

Under 2 inhabitants per square mile
2 to 6
6 to 18
18 to 45
45 to 90
90 and over

10c. Density of Population, 1860.

the summer of 1876 when he served as an official at the Philadelphia
Centennial Exhibition, he remained at the university until 1879, when he
returned to Washington to superintend the 1880 census. During the
1870s, though, Walker maintained an unofficial position as superintendent of the census. He lobbied for a quinquennial census in 1875 and
testified in detail in 1878 about the need to revise the 1850 census law.

By the late 1870s Congress was more disposed to look favorably on

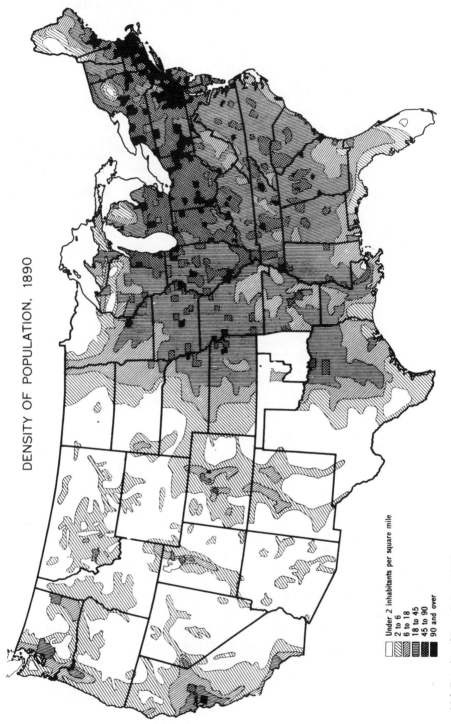

DENSITY OF POPULATION, 1890

Under 2 inhabitants per square mile
2 to 6
6 to 18
18 to 45
45 to 90
90 and over

10d. Density of Population, 1890.

DENSITY OF POPULATION, 1930

Under 2 inhabitants per square mile
2 to 6
6 to 18
18 to 45
45 to 90
90 and over

10e. Density of Population, 1930.

CENTER OF POPULATION: 1790 TO 1980

["Center of population" is that point at which an imaginary flat, weightless, and rigid map of the United States would balance if weights of identical value were placed on it so that each weight represented the location of one person on the date of the census]

YEAR [1]	North latitude			West longitude			Approximate location
	°	′	″	°	′	″	
1790 (Aug. 2)	39	16	30	76	11	12	23 miles east of Baltimore, Md.
1850 (June 1)	38	59	0	81	19	0	23 miles southeast of Parkersburg, W. Va.
1900 (June 1)	39	9	36	85	48	54	6 miles southeast of Columbus, Ind.
1950 (Apr. 1)	38	50	21	88	9	33	8 miles north-northwest of Olney, Richland County, Ill.
1960 (Apr. 1)	38	35	58	89	12	35	In Clinton Co. about 6½ miles northwest of Centralia, Ill.
1970 (Apr. 1)	38	27	47	89	42	22	5.3 miles east-southeast of the Mascoutah City Hall in St. Clair County, Ill.
1980 (Apr. 1)	38	8	13	90	34	26	¼ mile west of De Soto in Jefferson County, Mo.

[1] For dates of admissions of the States and changes in areal definition, see "State Origins and Boundaries," *United States Summary, U.S. Census of Population: 1960*, vol. I. For year of admission to statehood, see table 326.

Source: U.S. Bureau of the Census, *1980 Census of Population, Vol. 1.*

11. Center of Population, 1790–1980. This map also illustrates the westward thrust of the population over time.

such legislation, and Walker and James A. Garfield, still one of the main legislators interested in statistical matters, were more adept at writing a bill that would pass. The Reconstruction debates that had prompted the earlier effort at census reform were no longer on the legislative agenda. Improving the census could be considered as a matter in its own right. It made good administrative sense to give the Census Office control over its own field administration. It also seemed both possible and reasonable to expand and improve the amount of data collected and published. A nation that would top fifty million people in 1880 could well afford a census that would adequately detail the character of its population, economy, and social life.

Accordingly, in 1878 Walker and a small group of interested legislators drew up a bill to revise the census machinery. In January, Walker submitted a report to Carl Schurz, secretary of the Interior, detailing his recommendations for a new "census scheme." In May, Garfield introduced a bill based on these recommendations, but it was not acted upon. At the third session of the Forty-fifth Congress, in January 1879, another bill was introduced, was modified in committee, and passed on the last day of the session. Walker and Garfield had finally achieved their goal of revising the 1850 law. Walker was appointed superintendent for the 1880 census on April 1, 1879.[15]

The 1880 law empowered Walker to control the field administration of the census, to expand the scope of the reported statistics, and to appoint special agents to collect statistics on particular industries, social problems, or related phenomena. He also had the authority to expand the size of his Washington clerical staff. He immediately began preparations for the tenth census—for what was truly to be the "jumbo of censuses."

Walker began by creating what eventually became the geography, or field, division of the Census Office. He hired Henry Gannett from the U.S. Geological Survey and systematically mapped the country into supervisory districts. These 150 field officials replaced the federal marshals. For the first time, the Census Office determined before the census was taken the size of the field staff units. Such planning led to more serious geographical analysis of the population as a whole. One had to know, for example, just where the population was concentrated, where enumerators would experience difficulty in counting an area, where particularly rapid growth had taken place in the last decade that would affect the size of enumeration districts.

Walker also had the authority to expand radically the enumeration and clerical staff. There had been about 6,500 enumerators in 1870; there were to be over 31,000 in 1880. Further, he planned to triple the size of the Washington clerical staff to process the data more quickly. This expansion enabled the 1880 census to shorten the period of enumeration to two weeks in cities and a month in other areas.

Walker pursued these changes in the name of efficiency and statistical quality. More and better data were to be collected and published by a larger and better qualified and trained staff. Walker turned to the new universities to recruit his special agents and higher-grade staff. The list of men who worked on the 1880 census reads like a log of the late nineteenth-century academic elite. Congress, however, saw the new census legislation differently. They saw increased political patronage in the new armies of clerks and enumerators. They also expected, somewhat contra-

15. Wright and Hunt, *History and Growth*, pp. 58–69; Annual Report of the Superintendent of the Census, 1878, 45th Cong., 3d sess., 1878, H.R. Ex. Doc. 1 (Serial 1850), pp. 839–57; Interview . . . with Francis Amasa Walker, December 1878, 45th Cong., 3d sess., 1878, S. Misc. Doc. 26 (Serial 1833).

dictorily, that Walker would make good on his claim that he could save one-third of the cost of taking the census with better legislation.

Walker was thus besieged with pressure for clerical and enumerator jobs, both from applicants and from congressmen eager to fortify party machines. Walker insisted, as in 1870, on testing his clerks for their statistical aptitude. In the absence of civil service testing machinery elsewhere in the government, Walker also had to take on the task of a huge personnel agency. When Walker continued to insist on competency as the test for appointment, he began to lose his support in Congress. In this, the most patronage-ridden era of machine politics and unstable party majorities on the federal level, Walker's actions appeared high-handed and politically suicidal to Republican loyalists. Walker, the good-government Mugwump who disparaged the logrolling politics of the day, refused to appoint the candidates of the bosses.[16]

In mid-1881, his policies came back to haunt him. Walker abruptly ran out of money in early 1881 and submitted a request for an additional appropriation above the $3 million that had been included in the 1879 law. Congress did not act on the request, and Walker was forced to lay off half his clerical staff—some seven hundred people. The remaining seven hundred worked without pay until Congress came back into session and voted a deficiency appropriation the following year. Walker was treated badly in the press. Joseph C. G. Kennedy, still feuding with Walker, published two scathing satirical attacks on Walker's administration. In November 1881, Walker resigned to become president of the Massachusetts Institute of Technology. Charles W. Seaton, Walker's chief clerk, took over the position of superintendent.[17]

Thus, two years after Francis Walker and James Garfield celebrated the passage of their census reform bill, the Census Office was again in crisis. This time it was caught between the patronage demands of the party politicians and the pressures for scientific quality coming from the new academic world. Both groups had been interested in expanding the scope of the census, but now they battled for control of the new office. Political leaders could justify the increased expense of Walker's elaborate census if the work provided jobs to party regulars. If the jobs were to go to the politically uncommitted or to the opposition, the money was wasted. Since Walker and his supporters refused to bow to the pressures of the party leaders, they had to find a way to maintain the volume of data collected on a lower budget.

16. Munroe, *Life of Walker*, pp. 197, 204.

17. Report of the Superintendent of the Census, Nov. 1, 1881, 47th Cong., 1st sess., H.R. Ex. Doc. 1, vol. 10, pt. 5:665–727; Joseph C. G. Kennedy to the U.S. Congress on the Tenth Census, Feb. 22, 1881, Files of the Secretary of the Interior relating to the 1870 Census, RG 48, NA; see also Communication from Joseph C. G. Kennedy, May 31, 1879, 46th Cong., 1st sess., S. Misc. Doc. 45.

The demographic results of the census were also somewhat problematic. The population did top fifty million, and the decennial growth rate rose again to 30 percent. But the results also raised questions about the accuracy of the 1870 population count. In particular, according to the census of 1880 the southern population—particularly in South Carolina—had grown so dramatically during the 1870s that Walker was charged with "census fraud" in the form of overcounting. Walker dispatched Henry Gannett, census geographer, to investigate. Gannett concluded that the 1880 count was correct and that the 1870 count was probably low. Congress concluded that the turmoil of the Reconstruction era was the cause. But, since Reconstruction had ended, nothing needed to be done. Further, Walker reported a disturbing characteristic of Vinton's apportionment method as he calculated apportionments for various House sizes. Calling the problem "the Alabama paradox," Walker noted that in a House of 299 members, Alabama received 8 members. In a House of 300 members, Alabama's portion dropped to 7. Balinski and Young have explained that Vinton's method is prone to such paradoxes because of the way it treats remainders. As usual, Congress was unimpressed with the niceties of the mathematics and uninterested in solving the paradox. As they would for the next thirty years, they simply found another House size that avoided the paradox and prevented any state from losing seats. They finally settled on a House of 325 members—effectively using Webster's apportionment method. The census was again proving to be a somewhat troublesome and unpredictable instrument to measure and apportion representation, but there was no political reason to do anything about it.[18]

In the short term, Walker or his successors could do little to remedy the problems with the census or improve their relations with Congress. The Census Office continued to process the data slowly and to request supplemental appropriations from Congress. It was an uneasy relationship. Congress passed appropriations in 1882 and 1884 that called for "the completion of the work . . . and closing the bureau." Each time, the closing order was repealed and the work continued. In 1885 the formal office was abolished; it reopened the next day as a charge of Carroll Wright's new Bureau of Labor. In 1888 the final volumes of the 1880 census were published.[19]

Despite these problems, the 1880 census was a truly remarkable effort, encompassing twenty-two volumes plus a compendium. Walker pub-

18. Census Office, *Compendium of the Tenth Census*, pt. 1 (Washington, D.C.: GPO, 1885); Henry Gannett, "The Alleged Census Frauds in the South," *International Review* 10 (1881): 459–66; Michel L. Balinski and H. Peyton Young, *Fair Representation: Meeting the Ideal of One Man, One Vote* (New Haven and London: Yale University Press, 1982), pp. 38–45.

19. Wright and Hunt, *History and Growth*, p. 922.

lished one major volume each for the population, manufactures, agriculture, and vital statistics of the nation. In addition, in keeping with his goal of making the census a memorial to the nation's centennial, he added new volumes dealing with the industrial and economic growth of the nation. These latter studies were compiled and written by "special agents"—men with particular expertise in a branch of industry or trade. These volumes combined statistical presentations with interpretive text to explain the data. Walker was criticized for the appointment of these several dozen special agents. The appointments seemed to be costly and extraneous academic patronage. Those familiar with the internal workings of the Census Office, though, knew that the real crisis facing the Census Office was tallying or cross-tabulating the population data.

In 1880 the office was still tallying the population census as it had in 1850, by marking a condensing sheet for each particular cross-tabulation desired. But with double the population and with much more interest in detailed breakdowns of the data, the process had become unwieldy. Walker had begun to encourage development of mechanisms to facilitate tabulation in 1870. The "Seaton device," invented by the chief clerk, placed the condensing sheet on rollers and allowed the clerk to roll the paper back as it was filled. The tallying was still done by hand, though, and required the labor of hundreds of clerks. If a means could be found to mechanize this tallying, this labor could be saved and the cost of taking the census could be reduced considerably.[20]

Walker and his staff thus began systematic efforts to develop a method of mechanical tabulation of the data. In the summer of 1881, amid the turmoil engendered by the fiscal crisis, Herman Hollerith, a young Columbia graduate who had worked on the mining census, went to work in the bureau's Population Division with the sole purpose of devising a mechanical method of tabulating population returns. He had been encouraged to tackle the question of mechanical tabulation by John Shaw Billings, the census official in charge of vital statistics and a family friend. Over the next few years, Walker and his friends nurtured Hollerith's efforts both scientifically and politically. Walker hired Hollerith at MIT as an instructor in mechanical engineering for the 1882–83 academic year; Hollerith found a position in the Patent Office in 1883–84. By 1884 he was ready to build a working model of his electrical tabulating machine. By 1887 he had secured the necessary patents and, with the help of Billings, had begun to test the system in tabulating the vital statistics of Baltimore. By 1889 Hollerith and the major statisticians in the Census Bureau felt the system was sufficiently perfected to use in the 1890 census (see figs. 12, 13, and 14).[21]

20. Leon Truesdell, *The Development of Punch Card Tabulation in the Bureau of the Census, 1890–1940* (Washington, D.C.: GPO, 1965).

21. Geoffrey Austrian, *Herman Hollerith: Forgotten Giant of Information Processing* (New York: Columbia University Press, 1982).

A WEEKLY JOURNAL OF PRACTICAL INFORMATION, ART, SCIENCE, MECHANICS, CHEMISTRY, AND MANUFACTURES.

Vol. LXIII.—No. 9.
Established 1845.

NEW YORK, AUGUST 30, 1890.

[$3.00 A YEAR.
Weekly.]

THE NEW CENSUS OF THE UNITED STATES—THE ELECTRICAL ENUMERATING MECHANISM.—[See page 132.]

12. The New Census . . . Electrical Enumerating Mechanism, *Scientific American*, 1890. The electrical tabulating system, introduced in 1890, captured the public imagination. This magazine cover illustrated the various stages of the new process—from receiving the schedules to punching the cards to tabulating the results.

13. 1890-model tabulating machine with sorting attachment. The operator placed each card, representing the information on one individual, in the tabulator. The clock dials advanced for the appropriate categories, and the card was removed and placed in the sorting box, right, for the next tabulation.

In the late 1880s, Walker also searched for an administrative solution to the problems of patronage and political pressures on the Census Office. In the wake of James A. Garfield's assassination by a disappointed office seeker in 1881 and the political fallout during the 1882 congressional elections, leaders of both political parties were willing to consider passage of a civil service law. The Pendleton Act, passed in January 1883, created the possibility of developing a professional civil service for such specialized and technical positions as statisticians. Walker proposed in January 1888 that the census be located administratively in the Bureau of Labor under Carroll Wright's watchful eye. In effect Walker was proposing the creation of a permanent census office in a relatively politically neutral office. With this proposal he was also ruling himself out as superintendent in 1890.[22]

22. Francis Amasa Walker, "The Eleventh Census of the United States," *Quarterly Journal of Economics* 2 (January 1888): 135–61; James Leiby, *Carroll Wright and Labor Reform: The Origin of Labor Statistics* (Cambridge, Mass.: Harvard University Press, 1960).

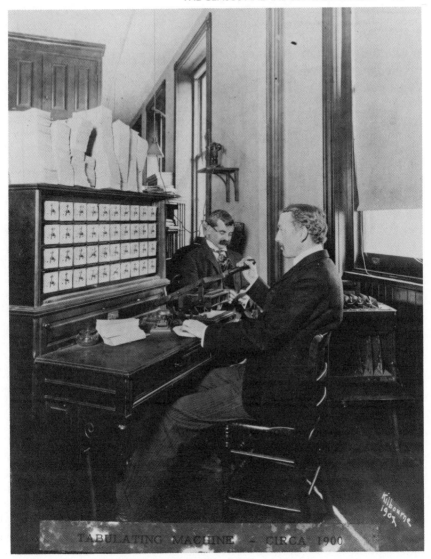

14. Tabulating machine, circa 1900. This man operated the tabulator. The sorting box is at right.

The proposal had considerable administrative merit and was modeled after the Massachusetts system, where the Bureau of Labor took the state census. It also seemed politically savvy since Carroll Wright had been appointed as commissioner of Labor by Republican Chester Arthur and had maintained the position during Democrat Grover Cleveland's administration. Whoever won the 1888 presidential election, Walker hoped, would be satisfied with Wright's political credentials.

But Walker again misjudged the political situation. Grover Cleveland did not win reelection, and Benjamin Harrison wanted the patronage from the census jobs for the Republican party. In 1889, Harrison appointed Robert Porter as superintendent. Porter, a British-born newspaper editor, had served as a special agent at the 1880 census and had written the report on valuation, taxation, and public indebtedness. The law governing the 1890 census did not require appointees take civil service examinations. Patronage remained the chosen method for appointing the almost 47,000 enumerators and more than 3,000 clerical workers. The office was again a temporary agency within the Department of Interior. And, though some of the more esoteric subjects investigated in 1880 were not redone in 1890, the 1890 census devoted entire volumes to special study of such areas as mineral industries, churches, mortgage indebtedness, transportation industries, and insurance, in addition to the standard volumes on population, agriculture, manufactures, and national vital statistics.[23]

Not surprisingly, therefore, the 1890 census suffered from as many administrative difficulties as had the 1880 census. Again the office was besieged by office seekers. Again the office had to train thousands of new clerks in the difficult duties of statistical tabulation. Again the publication of the census results was delayed by the sheer difficulty of processing the data and the need for additional appropriations.

But two new issues complicated matters further. First, the installation of Hollerith's electrical tabulation system brought a whole new set of concerns about how to make the system function efficiently and how to ensure that the new machine tabulators did not make mistakes or vitiate the accuracy of the census. Second, the results of the 1890 census showed the rate of population growth to be slowing considerably for the nation as a whole, and the public quickly blamed the Census Office for undercounting the population. These issues made the taking of the 1890 census both controversial and turbulent.

The field administration of the count went smoothly. Every return was in by early November 1890; the official hand count of the population for apportionment was reported by the end of November. The schedules were then sent to punching clerks, primarily women, who entered the data on the schedules on punch cards, one to a person. When cards for a particular geographic area, for example, an enumeration district, were punched, they were tabulated by placing them, one by one, in Hollerith's tabulating machine. The machine, a wonder of efficiency for its day, was in fact an extremely primitive counter. The operator placed the punched card on the press and lowered the upper portion of the press onto the card. The upper press contained metal pins that passed through the

23. Wright and Hunt, *History and Growth*, pp. 69–76.

punch holes on the card and closed an electrical circuit. The circuit activated a clock-dial counter that advanced one space. The circuits could be connected by relays to make simple counts for one variable, such as the number of males and females, and cross-tabulations of the data, for example, the number of white males, white females, and nonwhite males and females. Once a batch of cards was run through the machines, the counters were read and recorded for further totaling, and the clock dials were set to zero in preparation for a new set of cards.

Hollerith also installed a set of electrically activated sorting boxes to further subdivide the already counted cards. Since the statisticians intended to read the cards several times for various tabulations, the sorting boxes allowed the clerks to set up the cards in the proper order to facilitate the next tabulation. For example, for the occupation count, it was unnecessary to run all 62 million cards through the tabulating machines. One only had to use the cards for the employed population. These could be physically separated out while tabulating the previous data and reserved for the occupation count.

The new machinery greatly facilitated the tabulation of the population data and prompted statisticians to attempt much more complex cross-tabulations. The results of the 1890 census are much more detailed than those of previous censuses, and no American population census was ever again hand tabulated. Porter, Hollerith, and those close to the work of the new electrical system were extraordinarily pleased with its performance, though of course the system had "bugs." For example, for each tabulation the relays had to be soldered by hand, a specialized and cumbersome process. Since the census office was leasing the machines from Hollerith, Porter wanted to use the tabulators as efficiently as possible. From late 1890 to the spring of 1891 two shifts of clerks ran the tabulators—women during the day and men in the evening. This procedure was stopped because statisticians found it difficult to coordinate the workload of the two shifts. They finally determined to contract with Hollerith for more machines.[24]

Initial press reaction to the census was favorable. Reporters were fascinated with the new machinery; the work of tabulation and reporting in bulletin form seemed to be proceeding apace. When, in late 1890, the actual population count was reported, however, objections began to be heard. The growth rate for the decade had dropped, according to the reported figures, to about 25 percent—some 5 percent below the rate of 1870 to 1880 and almost 10 percent below the rates that had prevailed from 1790 to 1860. Only the Civil War decade had shown a slower rate of growth. Census statisticians responded that their data were correct, that the 1870 census had been in error—to the tune of a 1.26 million person

24. Austrian, *Hollerith*, pp. 58–73; Truesdell, *Punch Card Tabulation*, pp. 26–83.

undercount (about 3 percent). If the 1870 census were corrected for such an undercount, then the growth rate from 1860 would indicate that the population had in fact been growing at the rate of about 25 percent a decade since 1860.

In the spring of 1891, Francis Walker entered the fray and published two articles casting doubt on the accuracy of the 1890 data. The absolute growth the population between 1880 and 1890 was 12.5 million people. He pointed out that over 5 million immigrants had come to the United States in the 1880s, "twice as much [sic] as during the immediately preceding or any preceding decade." If the 1890 population data were to be believed, Walker argued, a sharp decline in the American birth rate during the 1880s would have to have occurred. Walker was then beginning to promote a virulent racist immigration restriction movement in the name of preserving American society from the "degradation" of Europe. He knew that the later tabulations of the census data would detail the composition of the growth of the population. If the census were correct, the data would show a decline in the age cohort under ten years old. But he found the conclusion that immigrants contributed almost half the decennial population growth extremely unpalatable and was thus willing to cast doubt on the census. As a respected statistician, his public criticism of the census was sufficient evidence to undermine seriously Porter's office.[25]

As the complex work of tabulation and reporting of the data wore on, therefore, the Census Office came under increasing critical scrutiny. Porter had hoped to establish a permanent census office during his tenure and had begun to recommend legislation as early as his first annual report in 1889. In 1890 the National Board of Trade joined in the lobbying effort. In February 1891 the senate requested the secretary of the Interior to draft a bill for a permanent office for the first session of the upcoming Congress. By the time that the bill was introduced in December 1891, however, the reputations of Porter and the Census Office had been tarnished, and the bill died in committee. In 1892 the House also held hearings and reported on the need for a permanent bureau, but the Democratically controlled House also investigated the office for patronage abuse, corruption, waste, and malfeasance. The Democrats swept the presidency and both houses of Congress in 1892, and the chances for permanent Census Office legislation died.[26]

25. Walter Willcox, "The Development of the American Census since 1890," *Political Science Quarterly* 29 (1914): 438–59; Francis Amasa Walker, "The United States Census," and Walker, "The Great Count of 1890," both in *Discussions*, vol. 2, quotation on p. 124. See also Census Office, *Compendium of the Eleventh Census: 1890*, pt. 1: *Population* (Washington, D.C.: GPO, 1892), pp. xxxv–xliv.

26. Willcox, "American Census since 1890"; Permanent Census Bureau, H.R. Rept. 2393, pts. 1, 2, 52d Cong., 2d sess., 1893 (Serial 5141), pt. 1:1–109, pt. 2:1–3; Investigation

Robert Porter resigned in July 1893 with the change in administration, and the work of finishing the census was again turned over to Carroll Wright in the Department of Labor. Much of the census material had been issued in bulletin form before formal publication, but the final volumes were not published until 1897. Even the second volume of the population report—until that time, one of the earliest published volumes—was dated 1897.

The 1890 census cost eighteen cents per capita. In the long run, it was, as Francis Walker called its predecessor, a "marvel of cheapness." It was also a technical wonder and an administrative disaster. It is even reasonable to suggest that the major achievement of the 1890 census—the successful introduction of a system of machine tabulation—resulted from the peculiar disabilities American census takers faced. The constraints of a political system dominated by partisan patronage in conjunction with the need to record and report the data quickly for constitutional purposes had prompted significant technological innovations in data processing. In the politically turbulent 1880s and 1890s, Congress and major sectors of public opinion had demanded more and better census data. But the nation did not create a central statistical office to collect and publish information about the economy and society in its own right. And so the census faced broad demands but inadequate funding and administrative support. Within ten years, though, Congress would change its position, and the Census Office would become a permanent part of the federal government.

Changes in the broader American political and social arena prepared the way for the creation of the permanent Census Office. First and foremost, the destabilizing factor of turbulent national party politics ended. After 1896, the Republican party gained secure electoral control over Congress and the presidency. Census reform would therefore ultimately have to appeal mainly to Republican interests. Second, advocates of a permanent bureau—particularly Carroll Wright of the Department of Labor—moved to coordinate a systematic lobbying effort of groups interested in a permanent office. By the mid-1890s, these included such business organizations as the National Board of Trade, the professional organizations of university-based scholars (particularly the American Economic Association and the American Statistical Association), and some Republican political leaders. Third, the natural opposition to creating more federal agencies began to evaporate at the turn of the century as Congress considered a wide variety of new initiatives. Opponents to a

of the Census Bureau, July 16, 1892, H.R. Rept. 1933, 52d Cong., 1st sess. (Serial 3048), pp. 1–180; Anne S. Lee, "The Census under Fire: The Press and the 1890 Census" (paper presented at the Annual Meeting of the Population Association of America, Minneapolis, Minn., May 1984).

permanent office had always asked what a permanent census office would do during the middle years of a decade. This question seemed less damaging if Congress were willing to consider adding other functions to the Census Office.[27]

Ironically, but perhaps predictably, the successful campaign for a permanent census office got going in earnest at a point when the constitutional purposes of the census seemed so innocuous and routine that the statisticians could be called on to do new and different things. Reconstruction was over, and the census would not be needed to address questions on the rights of the black population. The reapportionment process was fairly routine, since Congress enlarged the size of the House each decade. States might lose relative but not absolute numbers of House seats. And, in the 1890s, a series of laws and court decisions effectively rendered the census apportionment of direct taxes a dead letter and finally decoupled the census and the tax system.

We have seen that the census apportionment of direct taxes was used only in wartime and that even then it was not a successful way to raise revenue. By the Civil War, congressmen from western agricultural states objected that such direct taxes on land discriminated against their section. Since property values were so much higher in the East, direct taxes fell more heavily on the West. Westerners proposed that income taxes were more effective revenue generators. There was some question about whether income taxes were direct or indirect taxes. The Supreme Court determined the Civil War income tax to have been an indirect tax that did not have to be apportioned among the states.

In the 1880s and early 1890s, the question of the proper level and basis for federal taxation again arose in Congress. Southern and western farmers faced agricultural distress and falling prices. The industrial economy suffered from periodic cycles of boom and bust that severely hurt workers' incomes. The federal Treasury again showed an embarrassing surplus, and Congress debated a wide variety of measures to spend the surplus to help the dispossessed or to reduce taxes. The Populists—primarily from the West and South—demanded currency expansion and lower tariffs. In this environment, congressmen, especially from the southern states, demanded that Congress remit or return the taxes from the direct tax of 1861. In 1891, Congress returned the taxes to the states that had paid them and remitted the unpaid sums. The landowners in the Sea Islands of South Carolina who had lost their lands for nonpayment of taxes received compensation for their losses. As Charles Dunbar remarked in his analysis of the experience with the tax, this repayment "close[d] a

27. Willcox, "American Census since 1890"; Keller, *Affairs of State*; Skowronek, *New American State*.

singular chapter in the history of taxation,—a chapter the repetition of which, we may be sure, our people will not be tempted to risk hereafter."

On the heels of the Panic of 1893 and amid increasing sectional strife, Congress passed another income tax in an effort to lower the federal government's dependence on the tariff. Positions on the bill reflected sectional interests. Southerners and Westerners supported the tax; northeastern congressmen generally opposed it. Opponents of the bill considered it "rank class legislation" derived from theories of "anarchism and communism." In 1895 the Supreme Court declared the income tax unconstitutional, ruling that it was a direct tax that had to be apportioned among the states. This ruling, although made by a split court, effectively killed the possibility of a federal income tax until the Constitution was amended and effectively ended the relationship between the census and federal taxation. Attempts to pass an amendment began in 1895. In 1909 Congress passed the Sixteenth Amendment to the Constitution; it was ratified in 1913.

The amendment, the first since Reconstruction, permitted Congress "to lay and collect taxes on incomes, from whatever source derived without apportionment among the several States and without regard to any census or enumeration." Congress acknowledged that income and wealth in an industrializing society were so unequally distributed that a per capita distribution of tax burdens would be politically intolerable. A population census was no longer an effective measure of the distribution of wealth. Accordingly, until 1940, when a question on individual income was added to the schedule, the population census did not treat questions of income and wealth.[28]

The campaign to revive the issue of a permanent census office began in 1896. Carroll Wright prepared a bill for the Fifty-fourth Congress, but it died with the adjournment of Congress in the spring of 1897. Learning from these experiences, census advocates narrowed their goals and reintroduced bills in the Fifty-fifth Congress to take the 1900 census. Such a bill became law in March 1899.

Supporters of a permanent office did not have sufficient strength during the Fifty-fifth Congress to legislate permanent status for the 1900 census office. Both the House and the Senate versions of the bill contained the phrase that "nothing herein contained shall be construed to establish a census bureau permanent beyond the twelfth census." Despite

28. Charles Franklin Dunbar, "The Direct Tax of 1861," *Quarterly Journal of Economics* 3 (1889): 436–61, quotation on p. 461; Sidney Ratner, *Taxation and Democracy in America* (New York: John Wiley & Sons, 1967), pp. 145–215, 298–320; E. R. A. Seligman, *The Income Tax* (1914; reprint, New York: Augustus M. Kelley, 1970).

this subterfuge, the tenor of the debates on the bill indicate that the issue of the permanency of the office was foremost in the legislators' minds. They continually returned to the issue and discussed whether the office should be an independent agency or housed within a cabinet department, whether the staff should be covered by civil service rules, and whether the office could complete the work during the census period. These questions had been discussed during previous census debates; only the prospect of a permanent office prompted Congress to discuss them again.[29]

Further, though the proposed legislation superficially resembled the 1890 census law, small but significant differences in language again presaged permanent status. The areas of investigation and field procedures remained the same. So did procedures for hiring the Washington staff. However, for the first time Congress set priorities specifying which data were to be collected and published first. In particular, they specified that only the statistics of population, mortality and vital statistics, agriculture, and manufactures were to be published as official census reports. These were to be issued by July 1902. The director was charged not to begin collection of other data—mining, social statistics of cities, and so on—until after the statistics of agriculture and manufacture were completed. The director had considerable administrative independence in the Department of Interior to hire and staff his agency. And the 1899 law created a position for an assistant director, as well as for five chief statisticians, all of whom were to be "persons of known and tried experience in statistical work." These officials were to oversee the technical aspects of the census. Congress thus recognized the expertise of the new university men who contributed to the development of census methods and were one of the major groups to use census data. In addition, Congress freed the census director from the technical questions of census taking and recognized that he should concern himself with the overall administration and political conduct of the office.

William McKinley appointed William Merriam, a prominent Republican organizer and former governor of Minnesota, as census director in March 1899. Merriam had no previous statistical experience, but he quickly became known as an able administrator and political representative of the census. The 1900 census ran smoothly even though it was taken during an election year and positions were still allocated by patronage rules. The reporting of the population for apportionment went smoothly. In December 1901, President Theodore Roosevelt recommended that the office be made permanent.[30]

It is clear from the actions of the high-level officials of the Census

29. Wright and Hunt, *History and Growth*, pp. 79–84, 950.

30. Eckler, *Bureau of the Census*; W. Stull Holt, *The Bureau of the Census: Its History, Activities and Organization* (Washington, D.C.: Brookings Institution, 1929), pp. 31–37.

Office that they directed much of their work toward the goal of convincing Congress to make the office permanent. From his position as chief statistician in the newly created Division of Research and Results, for example, Walter Willcox sponsored special population studies to address pressing public policy issues. Willcox hired several men who were to become prominent statisticians and policymakers in later years, including Wesley Mitchell, W. E. B. Dubois, Allyn Young, and Thomas Sewall Adams. Their work, Willcox felt, would testify to the possibilities for analysis within the permanent office.

William Merriam spent much of his time and energy working with Congress and soothing concerns about creating an unnecessary government agency. He was willing to run the 1900 census under the old patronage system to generate political capital, at the same time that he proved that it would not necessarily impede efficiency. And he even used his employees' lack of civil service protections as a weapon to insure continuation of the office. Walter Willcox recalled, for example, that Merriam allowed his clerks—particularly his female clerks—to pressure their local congressmen to make the office permanent and thus guarantee their jobs after 1902.[31]

Finally, statisticians who had had connections with previous censuses demonstrated how a permanent census office could conduct ongoing surveys between census years. Their opportunity arose from a most unlikely source, given the dominant Republican political complexion of the staff, but it proved to Congress and other opponents just how a permanent census office might branch into new areas and obviate the need to create another statistical office elsewhere in the federal bureaucracy.

The opportunity came as the office collected statistics of cotton production for the 1900 census. At the turn of the century, cotton was, as it had been for most of the century, America's premier export item. The 1899 crop was about 9 million bales; three-fourths was exported. For the previous twenty years cotton acreage and production had been increasing dramatically while the price had been declining. Many cotton-growing areas of the South were severely distressed—particularly by a rise in tenancy and debt. Good production statistics were necessary to guarantee a decent price to the farmer, yet the trajectory of prices pointed down. Hence, foreign buyers, primarily English cotton mill representatives, followed a practice of overestimating the size of the crop to force the price down.

The Department of Agriculture had a crop estimation service that

31. David Michael Grossman, "Professors and Public Service, 1885–1925: A Chapter in the Professionalization of the Social Sciences" (Ph.D. diss., Washington University, 1973), pp. 23–72; Eckler, *Bureau of the Census*, pp. 9–10; William R. Merriam, "Need of a Permanent Census Office," *North American Review* 174 (January 1902): 105–12.

reported the size of the crop. It was both unreliable and not designed to provide timely information of the current market conditions facing the farmer. The Census Office saw an opportunity and a need to step in and provide better service.

The avenue it took was both ingenious and illustrative of the role that a permanent statistical office could play. The innovations were made in the Division of Manufactures, headed by Chief Statistician Simon Newton Dexter North. North had been involved with the census since 1880, was a former lobbyist for the wool manufacturing industry, and became census director in 1903. In 1900 he authorized the collection and publication of cotton production statistics through the census of manufactures—namely, through the records of the production of cotton gins. The 1900 census thus reported the data for 1899. As a by-product of this data, the office acquired a list of gins that could be and was resurveyed the following year. To oversee the work, North hired Daniel Roper, a South Carolina Democrat with good connections to southern congressmen. By 1902 Roper had built such a successful record of crop statistics that the annual collection of cotton statistics was proposed in the 1902 law that made the office permanent. For the first time, the Census Office hired a permanent, if only part-time, staff of field agents to survey the ginners each fall and winter. The data also guaranteed a new constituency of southern farmers and merchants to support the office's continuation and prosperity.[32]

Merriam and his staff's efforts bore fruit. In March 1902 Congress made the Census Office permanent, mandating the continuation of the office's major initiatives. Cotton statistics were to be collected annually. The director was charged with completing the other inquiries postponed until after the main population data were reported. The census of manufactures was made quinquennial. The office staff came under civil service.

The lobbying efforts of the previous fifteen years were finally successful. The office retained its premier role of administering the decennial census of population for apportionment while it also conducted general statistical work for the federal government between the counts. It maintained its role as the major statistical agency of the federal government at the same time that it spread its workload to better accomplish the task. The officials finally had the luxury of planning for the future and of maintaining staff continuity.

Within a year, however, the situation would change again. As the permanent census law was being debated, Congress conducted a parallel

32. Holt, *Bureau of the Census*, pp. 40*ff.*; Annual Reports of the Bureau of the Census for the years, 1899, 1900, 1901, and 1902 (Washington, D.C.: GPO, 1899–1902); Julius H. Parmelee, "Statistical Work of the Federal Government," *Yale Review* 19 (November 1910/ February 1911), pp. 376*ff.*; Daniel C. Roper, *Fifty Years of Public Life* (Durham, N.C.: Duke University Press, 1941), pp. 107–22.

debate to create a new cabinet-level Department of Commerce. The Census Office was slated to be moved from Interior to Commerce if that bill passed. Eleven months later it did, and the Census Office, along with several other statistical bureaus, moved to the new department. With this move, a new era of census politics and problems began; within a decade, the Census Office was again fighting for its life.

|| Building the Federal Statistical System
in the Early Twentieth Century

*The present Bureau of the Census has been called frequently a
statistical laboratory. Except during a few brief intervals, this name
has not been justified. A laboratory is a place for analysis and
original research, where great discoveries in the scientific world are
worked out. The Bureau of the Census may be more correctly called
a figure factory. It has tabulated an infinite variety of statistical
facts, but it seldom offers anything but raw material.*
—*William Rossiter, 1914*

The establishment of the permanent census office marked a
major transition in the history of statistics in the United
States. Congress finally acknowledged the need for a general
federal agency to gather statistics on a wide variety of topics
irrespective of the requirements of the decennial census. No
longer would statistical data collection be commonly rele-
gated to the decennial census, to special investigating commissions, or to special projects of other government offices.
Congress further recognized that the collection and analysis
of statistics required several skilled statisticians, hundreds of
clerks, tabulating machinery, and a permanent organizational structure. Because Congress assumed that the absolute size
of the office would fluctuate with the requirements of its
workload, the size of the future permanent census office was
not fully defined in the 1902 legislation. Nevertheless, it was
clear from the outset that the office would be large by contemporary federal standards. In 1903, the office employed
about a dozen high-level staff members and over 700 clerks.
By 1906–7, during the lull between the decennial census
booms, the office still employed 650 people. By comparison,

the Department of Labor of 1902 (containing the Bureau of Labor Statistics) employed 80 people. The Bureau of Statistics of the Treasury Department contained 48.[1]

In short, the 1902 legislation created a new, large, and potentially powerful federal agency with few administrative functions beyond its traditional one to provide data for apportionment. The political controversies that surrounded the census in the first quarter of the twentieth century derived from this basic situation. Congress, the statisticians, and the incumbents in the executive branch debated the appropriate administrative location and role of the Census Office. Should the office become the central statistical bureau for the entire government? Should the office concentrate on population and social statistics or on economic and business statistics? How should the office manage the radical surges in workload resulting from the periodic censuses and coordinate them with the increasing number of annual or even more frequent surveys?

These same statisticians and policymakers also debated what might best be called population policy. As we have seen in the earlier debates about the abolition of slavery and Reconstruction, the peculiar character of the American state and polity turned issues of population growth and dispersion into profoundly political questions. The original apportionment rules in the Constitution created a mechanism for redistributing political power to regions with growing populations—primarily the West. The three-fifths compromise required Americans to count slave and free separately; later they also counted blacks and whites and natives and foreigners separately. In the late nineteenth and early twentieth century new population issues were added to these earlier concerns as Americans confronted rising immigration, radical urban growth, the end of the frontier, a declining native white birthrate, and, in some areas of the country, rural depopulation. Such new demographic trends automatically set in motion the apportionment mechanisms that were designed to redistribute political power to the growing areas. As had occurred in the 1850s when the South faced decreasing power on the national scene, those identifying with old stock Americans worried over the increasing power of cities and immigrants.[2]

Again the census was embroiled in the debates as Congress debated immigration restriction and refused to reapportion itself after the 1920 census. And again the Census Office tailored much of its data collection

1. W. Stull Holt, *The Bureau of the Census: Its History, Activities and Organization* (Washington, D.C.: Brookings Institution, 1929); Department of Commerce and Labor, *Organization and Law of the Department of Commerce and Labor* (Washington, D.C.: GPO, 1904), pp. 78–96, 599. This last source reprints the Senate report (no. 569), the text of the law with amendments, and the full congressional debate.

2. Walter Nugent, *Structures of American Social History* (Bloomington, Ind.: Indiana University Press, 1981).

and analysis to the questions of apportionment and the nature of population growth and change in the period.

The stories of these two debates—the administrative structure of the permanent census office, and the population policies needed for an urban industrial society—are intertwined. Nevertheless, it is useful for the sake of clarity to tell them separately. In this chapter I treat the administrative history of the census from the creation of the permanent bureau through the mid-1920s. In the following chapter, I examine the contemporary population debates and their impact on the form and content of the census and the American state.

The March 1902 census law was simple in form. "The Census Office temporarily established in the Department of the Interior," the legislation stated, ". . . is hereby made a permanent office." The work of completing the tabulation and publication of the twelfth census was to continue. The inquiries that had been postponed during the decennial period were taken up. Not much changed in the office.

Around the same time, though, the Senate passed a bill to create a new cabinet department, Commerce and Labor, which would include the Census Office. That bill passed the Senate on January 28, 1902, and was sent to the House for its consideration. As the Census Office conducted its first year of permanent existence, the Commerce and Labor bill remained dormant. One year later, in January 1903, it emerged from committee with amendments supported by President Roosevelt; it was debated in the full House. The fate of the bill was uncertain, since conservative Republicans were distinctly unhappy with the potential investigatory powers of the proposed Bureau of Corporations. To prod the House to act, Roosevelt called in the Washington press, threatened to call a special session of Congress if the bill did not pass, and told members of the House that opposition to the bill was coming from John D. Rockefeller and other large industrialists. The public outcry that resulted from this not entirely accurate assessment prompted Congress to pass the bill. By mid-February 1903, Roosevelt appointed George Cortelyou, his private secretary, as secretary of Commerce and Labor. The business of organizing the new department began.[3]

Establishing the new department was no easy task. It involved transferring many government offices from other departments as well as establishing the two new bureaus: Corporations and Manufactures. In addition to the transfer of the Census Office, the Organic Act mandated the transfer of the Coast and Geodetic Survey, the Light-House Board, the Treasury's Bureau of Statistics, the State Department's Bureau of Foreign

3. Henry F. Pringle, *Theodore Roosevelt* (New York: Harcourt, Brace & World, 1956), pp. 239–41; Department of Commerce and Labor, *Organization and Law*, pp. 22–34.

Commerce, the Bureau of Standards, the Steamboat Inspection Service, the Bureau of Fisheries, the regulation of seal and salmon fisheries, the Bureau of Labor, the Bureau of Navigation, and the Department of Labor. In the official language, the purpose of the new department was "to foster, promote, and develop the foreign and domestic commerce, the mining, manufacturing, shipping, and fishing industries, and labor interests, and the transportation facilities of the United States."[4]

By the summer of 1904, the secretary boasted that the new Department of Commerce and Labor had a staff of ten thousand and a budget of about two million dollars. But it was not yet an integrated whole or even a coherent functioning unit. Overall, the functions of the new department tended toward fact-finding and data-gathering, but it also encompassed regulatory functions. The Bureau of Corporations had the authority to recommend to Congress more new forms of business regulation on the order of the Interstate Commerce Commission.

Further, the statistical bureaus that made up the new Department were of radically different sizes. They brought with them varied traditions. They had served different constituencies; they had exercised different levels of autonomy. The Census Office, the largest of the new bureaus, had more than seven hundred employees, a tradition of independence developed in its years as a temporary agency in the Interior Department, and was headed by a number of high-paid officials. The Bureau of Labor, the next largest office, on the other hand, served the labor movement, had been headed by Carroll Wright since its inception, and had eighty employees. The American Federation of Labor had objected to its inclusion in the new department. The Bureau of Foreign Commerce in the State Department had six employees and was headed by a clerk who made $2,100 a year.[5]

It was Cortelyou's task to get the new behemoth moving in a unified fashion. One of the major subtasks in the process was to consolidate the duplications in the statistics gathered by the several bureaus. In the course of its debates, Congress repeatedly stated that the new department would allow the secretary to centralize the statistical system. Section 4 of the act authorized the secretary to consolidate bureaus; Section 12 allowed the president to move statistical offices from elsewhere in the government to Commerce and Labor. The details were left undetermined.

Theodore Roosevelt appointed a Committee on the Scientific Work in Government to consider consolidation. The committee included such noted statisticians as Walter Willcox, as well as such powerful Roosevelt officials as Gifford Pinchot and James Garfield, son of the late president.

4. Department of Commerce and Labor, *Organization and Law*, p. 25.
5. Ibid., pp. 23, 446–49, 599.

Simon Newton Dexter North, the new census director, also clearly saw centralization as one of his major goals. But the efforts quickly ran into snags as other statistical offices objected to losing their independence, and the various technical and political difficulties of consolidation became apparent. Within a year, Cortelyou resigned to run Roosevelt's 1904 presidential campaign; the issue was dropped.[6]

The proponents of consolidation retreated and waited for another opportunity. In the Census Office North moved in new directions; he hoped to become the central statistical agency by virtue of collecting the most statistics on the widest variety of topics.

At the time, this appeared to be a viable strategy. In the early years of the century, the bureau expanded its statistical work in a variety of ways. It compiled the reports of the 1900 census. It began to compile immigration statistics, and it conducted a manufacturing census in 1905. Congress mandated the collection of new data on banking, railways, and power in 1906. The bureau conducted a Philippine census in 1903, a Cuban census in 1907–8, a census of Oklahoma in 1907. It completed the *Official Register of the United States* after 1906. It set up a machine shop and began to manufacture its own tabulating machinery between 1905 and 1907. It published special reports on marriage and divorce in the United States; it published the returns of the 1790 census and added several interpretive volumes on the history of population growth.[7]

In other words, the permanent bureau broke away from the tradition of collecting data only at the decennial census and moved toward frequent and timely surveys. In line with the overall thrust of federal policy during the Progressive Era, most initiatives were in the field of business and economic statistics. Between 1903 and 1933, the leadership of the bureau came from the Division of Manufactures in the bureau or from statisticians and politicians outside the bureau interested in business regulation. Business statistics were both the center of controversy and the locus of power in the period, and statisticians accordingly turned their resources toward producing them.

Nevertheless, the bureau was unsuccessful in achieving its somewhat imperial goal of becoming the central statistical bureau by default. Several factors worked against the effort. First, officials and statisticians in other bureaus within the government resisted being subsumed into the Census Bureau. By the turn of the century, many federal agencies routinely collected and published statistical data. Usually these data were a by-

---

6. David Michael Grossman, "Professors and Public Service, 1885–1925: A Chapter in the Professionalization of the Social Sciences" (Ph.D. diss., Washington University, 1973), pp. 51*ff.* See also the Annual Reports of the Bureau of the Census, 1903–1910, published with the Annual Reports of the Department of Commerce and Labor.

7. Holt, *Bureau of the Census*, pp. 37–52.

product of administrative processes—collecting taxes, recording the arrival of immigrants, fostering agricultural improvements through experiment stations. Officials in the agencies that generated this data saw little need to turn it over to a central statistical agency. They were uninterested in modifying administrative procedures to standardize reporting systems, classification schemes, or questionnaires. The professional statistician's interest in uniform and comparable series as an end in itself was generally not shared by other bureaucrats. And, as John Cummings put it in an article surveying the American statistical system, centralization could lead to new problems. A larger central statistical bureaucracy could result in "reducing those in charge of important statistical inquiries to the position of subordinates, subject to a control which, while it may not materially increase efficiency or effect any material economy, may, nevertheless, so distribute responsibility as to diminish personal interest and pride, and *esprit de corps*." In short, census officials would have to offer positive services to the constituencies served by other data collection efforts if they wished to centralize the statistical system. At the time, the officials in other agencies did not see the need to centralize.[8]

Another major impediment to centralization resulted from conflict over the division of authority between the Commerce Department and the Census Bureau. During the years that the Office had been a temporary agency, it had developed a tradition of operating relatively independently of departmental control. This resulted partly from the need to hire, operate, and then dismantle the Washington office and the field staff of thousands within one or two years, partly from the Interior Department's lack of interest in controlling the bureau. In fact, during the Gilded Age, the major pressure for particular appointments came from patronage demands, not from administrators in Washington who wished to create a clean, well-oiled bureaucracy.[9]

By the early years of the twentieth century, though, administrative reform was in the air, and the older informal hiring and disbursement patterns of the Census Bureau seemed dangerously anarchic. Thus Director North and the secretary of Commerce and Labor's office soon became locked in a series of conflicts over relative authority. Some issues, such as whether the seal of the office should be coordinated with that of

8. John Cummings, "Statistical Work of the Federal Government of the United States," in *The History of Statistics: Their Development and Progress in Many Countries*, ed. John Koren (New York: Macmillan, 1918), pp. 571–689, quotation on p. 686.

9. Holt, *Bureau of the Census*, pp. 37–38; Walter Willcox, "The Development of the American Census Office since 1890," *Political Science Quarterly* 29 (September 1914): 438–59. See also Stephen Skowronek, *Building a New American State: The Expansion of National Administrative Capacities, 1877–1920* (New York: Cambridge University Press, 1982), and Leonard White, *The Republican Era, 1869–1901: A Study in Administrative History* (New York: Macmillan, 1958).

the department, seemed petty and symbolic. Others were more substantive: would the census schedules be open to scrutiny to other department officials, for example, those in the Bureau of Corporations? The bureau, by this time, had developed a professional commitment to data confidentiality and thus successfully resisted releasing raw schedules. Could the director hire and fire without sanction of the Commerce and Labor secretary? Even the name of the Census Bureau became a matter of controversy. The Secretary wanted to use "Bureau" to standardize all the divisions within the department. The Census Office objected and insisted on remaining an "office." Both had been used in common parlance and in statutes, but "bureau" in the context of the administrative fight connoted lesser status. As Chief Clerk William Rossiter wrote at the time, it meant the subjugation of the "strong, lusty temporary office" to "the Department Bureau curse."[10]

The issue raged from 1903 on and was a matter of controversy during the hearings for the legislation for the 1910 census. Throughout, despite repeated decisions by the attorney general in favor of the Census Office's autonomy and new congressional language supporting the office, the Commerce and Labor Department slowly gained the upper hand in administrative matters. The cost of the battle was great for the Census Office. The secretary of Commerce and Labor and the president soured on the idea of making the Census Office the central statistical office.

Nevertheless, the obvious duplications of some statistical series forced the issue to the fore again. In 1907, Oscar Straus, the third secretary of Commerce and Labor in four years, appointed a second interdepartmental committee to determine if the statistical offices in the department should be consolidated—particularly if the Bureau of Statistics (formerly in the Treasury Department and charged with publishing the statistics of foreign and domestic commerce) should be consolidated with the Census Bureau. Again, the committee held lengthy hearings and recommended that the two not be merged—ostensibly because the consolidation would result in few savings. In fact, the staff of both bureaus opposed the merger. The committee did recommend the appointment of a committee to determine uniform methods, eliminate duplications, and keep the various statistical offices "abreast of the most modern methods." The Interdepartmental Statistical Committee was appointed but by 1911 had made no public recommendations.[11]

10. William S. Rossiter, "The Present Status of Statistical Work and How It Needs to be Developed in the Service of the Federal Government," *JASA*, n.s., 106 (June 1914): 85–96, quotations on pp. 91–94; Willcox, "Development of the American Census Office."

11. Committee on Statistical Reorganization, *Statistical Reorganization* (Washington, D.C.: GPO, 1908), quotation on p. 20. The committee members were Lawrence Murray, assistant secretary of Commerce and Labor, S. N. D. North, census director, Herbert Knox

In short, by 1910, Julius H. Parmelee, surveying the state of the "Statistical Work of the Federal Government" could report that "statistical concentration has probably gone far enough"; he predicted that "intelligent cooperation is unquestionably the watchword of the morrow." As the 1910 census approached, it appeared that the bureau was insufficiently powerful to absorb the other statistical offices, nor, as the largest statistical office in the government, would it let itself be subsumed into another bureau.[12]

The census of 1910 forced the bureau back to its central mission—taking the decennial census—and to determining what new initiatives it might want to make. The census would be the first under the permanent bureau and thus under more than the usual scrutiny as a test of the permanent agency. With the change of administration in 1908, Edward Dana Durand, former deputy commissioner of the Bureau of Corporations, became the new census director. Durand was the first professional academic statistician to head the bureau since Francis Walker in 1880. To bureau insiders he was also a "department" appointment, someone who would side with Commerce and Labor on issues of hiring, disbursements, and policy.[13]

As usual Congress battled over new census legislation. The question of patronage appointments for enumerator and clerical posts was again a sore point. Theodore Roosevelt vetoed one census bill in February 1909 because it failed to include the clerical staff in the civil service. In July 1909 Congress backed away from its position and passed a bill that included the office staff in the civil service. Preparations for the decennial census began immediately.[14]

The census of 1910 was ambitious but mired in difficulties. The permanent staff prepared for many new tabulations—for example, of labor force and industrial data—but officials soon found that a number of political and technical problems hampered their efforts. Congress moved the date of the enumeration back from June 1 to April 15 and thus shortened the planning period before the actual count. In March 1910, one month before the enumeration, Congress added a question on mother tongue to the population schedule, necessitating radical changes in

Smith, commissioner of Corporations, Charles P. Neill, commissioner of Labor, and O. P. Austin, chief of the Bureau of Statistics. E. R. A. Seligman of Columbia University, J. W. Jenks of Cornell University, and H. Parker Willis of Washington, D.C., acted as advisers to the committee.

12. Julius H. Parmelee, "The Statistical Work of the Federal Government," *Yale Review* 19 (November 1910/February 1911): 289–308, 374–91, quotation on p. 391.

13. Willcox, "Development of the American Census Office," p. 456. Edward Dana Durand, *Memoirs of E. Dana Durand* (typescript, 1954, at Census Bureau Library, Suitland, Md.).

14. Roosevelt's rationale for the veto is quoted in Holt, *Bureau of the Census*, p. 54.

coding and tabulating procedures. (The question was designed to determine the ethnic background of immigrants and their children who could not be identified by country of birth—for example, Jews or other ethnic minorities from central and eastern European empires. It was also used to determine the size of the non-English-speaking population.)[15]

The bureau also intended to use its own tabulating machinery in 1910 to save the expensive rental charges it had paid to Herman Hollerith's Tabulating Machine Company. Bureau mechanicians felt they could design a better tabulator and save money at the same time. Unfortunately, the new census procedures and machinery did not function at peak efficiency. Thirty-one cities were recounted or had their schedules examined for padding or undercounting. In the worst case, Tacoma, Washington, reported an initial population of over 116,000; the bureau finally credited the city with under 84,000. The automatic tabulating machinery did not live up to expectations. The bureau had to use older machines, which had to be hand fed. Though the data were reported in timely fashion in bulletin form, a change in the manner of presentation in the final reports delayed the publication of the last volumes. The data were printed by state in separate volumes. This format required that all the data for each state—including agriculture and manufacturing census results—be completed before the report could be printed.

In July 1912 the decennial census period ended, and the bureau was slated to lay off the temporary staff and return to its smaller permanent organization. The thirteenth census reports were far from ready for the printer. Congress passed a $500,000 deficiency appropriation. By the election of Woodrow Wilson to the presidency, it was clear that these funds were insufficient and that the bureau was in crisis.[16]

The Democrats came to town in 1913, and the bureau's fortunes turned from bad to worse. The census had been run by Republicans since the Civil War era. Its leadership had come, by and large, from East Coast elite universities or from reform Republican circles. The emerging leadership of the statistically minded academic community had come to think of the bureau as a training ground for aspiring graduate students. With its large staff and its fluctuating workload, the bureau was a good place to find a student a summer position, to search for a dissertation topic. The bureau also served the academic community by making special tabulations for faculty and by being receptive to calls for new types of data collection.[17]

15. Ibid., pp. 54–61.

16. Herman Hollerith was obviously unhappy with the bureau's decision to manufacture its own machines. His side of the controversy surrounding this decision is detailed in Geoffrey D. Austrian, *Herman Hollerith: Forgotten Giant of Information Processing* (New York: Columbia University Press, 1982), pp. 221–37, 267–305.

17. Grossman, "Professors and Public Service," pp. 23–72.

All this changed when the Democrats took over. Wilson was a minority party president with limited ability to enact his legislative agenda. He quickly acknowledged the power of the party leadership to deliver the goods in return for patronage appointments in federal agencies. The Census Bureau became one of those agencies. In the spring of 1913, Director Durand resigned under duress; William J. Harris, a prominent Georgia politician, replaced him in July. Harris appointed a committee to determine what should be done about the unfinished thirteenth census work. Former census directors William R. Merriam and S. N. D. North, Walter F. Willcox, former chief clerk William S. Rossiter, and Daniel C. Roper, who began the cotton statistics program and then served as the first assistant postmaster general, reported in September 1913. They recommended that major tabulations be canceled and that other work be abbreviated to finish the census and publish the data by 1914.[18]

The academic community and professional statisticians responded with alarm. A spate of articles appeared in late 1913 and 1914 assessing the history of the permanent bureau and evaluating its current problems. The *Journal of Political Economy* called the situation in the bureau "wretched." Authors debated the causes of the bureau's decline. Was it merely that the decennial census had gone badly? Was Durand a poor administrator? Had the change of administration hindered the work? Or were there deeper problems that required more radical solutions?[19]

The generation of statisticians who had lobbied for the permanent bureau needed answers. They had repeatedly argued that most of the problems of the decennial census up until 1900 resulted from the diffi- culties of recreating a census bureau every ten years. A permanent bu- reau, they had assured the public, would solve these problems. Now it seemed that the permanent bureau did not guarantee an efficient, accu- rate, and thorough enumeration. Did the intercensal work then justify the bureau's existence? As former census official John Cummings noted, the bureau spent $1.2 million to $1.4 million a year during the seven years between decennial censuses. Such funds were "sufficient to provide for all the running expenses of a city of 100,000 inhabitants, or one of our larger

18. Holt, *Bureau of the Census,* p. 61.
19. See, e.g., Willcox, "Development of the American Census Office"; Rossiter, "Present Status of Statistical Work"; John Cummings, "The Permanent Census Bureau: A Decade of Work," *Journal of the American Statistical Association* 13 (December 1913): 605–38; "The Recurring Census Problem," *Journal of Political Economy* 22 (July 1914): 691–93; "Re- organization of the Census," ibid. 21 (October 1913): 770–73; "Statistical Work of the United States Government," *American Economic Review* 5 (March 1915), suppl.: 162–208; and "Work of the Bureau of the Census," *Independent* 79 (July 20, 1914): 101. Koren's commemorative volume of essays, *The History of Statistics,* was also begun in late 1913. It was both a tribute to the seventy-fifth anniversary of the American Statistical Association and an effort to counter the problems in the bureau. See especially S. N. D. North's essay, "Seventy Five Years of Progress in Statistics: The Outlook for the Future," pp. 15–49.

universities." If, he continued, this work was "a sort of statistical fly-flapping without practical social value," then the statisticians should close up shop, return the census office to its status as a temporary agency, and retire their plans for a central statistical bureau. This was an ominous warning only ten years after the creation of the permanent bureau.[20]

The statisticians blamed their difficulties on party politics, bureaucratic infighting, and inadequate funds. But in many ways census officials had always faced these problems and there was no indication that they would go away in the future. In fact, the bureau failed in its more ambitious efforts during the 1910 census period because the statisticians tried several new initiatives without restructuring the agency to handle them.

During the second half of the nineteenth century, the Census Bureau had grown into a huge but undifferentiated bureaucracy. The director had the authority to hire legions of entry-level clerks and keypunch operators, but the size of the higher-level staff was severely limited. The 1902 legislation recognized only five positions for trained statisticians in the entire bureau. Only twenty permanent clerical positions were above entry level. The agency thus had no mid-level staff with any sophisticated statistical training. Nor was the bureau a good place to make a career because one had little possibility of advancement. When the bureau tried in 1910 to develop, for example, new occupation and industry statistics, the effort bogged down in the technical difficulties of devising a classification system. In short, the bureau's only strength at the turn of the century was in compiling and tabulating a great volume of data. It lacked the capacity to devise innovative solutions to the emerging technical questions it faced. Theoretically minded statisticians and research scholars were beginning to create new forms of statistical organizations to foster their endeavors. Many bureau statisticians went to work for such new organizations as the National Bureau for Economic Research, the Brookings Institution, and the Carnegie Endowment. The new private foundations, research bureaus, and academic institutes could focus on scientific questions and had the flexibility to work on problems of measurement, theory, or conceptualization. Statistical innovations in these arenas— particularly the development of probability methods and sampling— were not introduced into the bureau. This situation remained unchanged until the 1930s, when the bureau faced another administrative and technical crisis.[21]

Nevertheless, a radical move to dismantle the bureau did not emerge. Institutional inertia, the Democrats' needs for patronage places, and the academic community's obvious interest in maintaining the bureau all

20. Cummings, "Permanent Census Bureau," pp. 609–10.

21. Holt, *Bureau of the Census*, p. 172; Helen M. Walker, *Studies in the History of Statistical Method* (Baltimore: Williams & Wilkins, 1929).

prevented such an effort. But the malaise severely lowered the agency's morale, led to resignations of higher-level staff, and halted further talk of consolidating the federal statistical system. In July 1914, William Harris resigned to become the head of the newly created Federal Trade Commission. Almost a year went by until Samuel L. Rogers of North Carolina, another Democratic politician with no statistical training, became director. The bureau returned to its intercensal staff of six hundred to eight hundred employees and to the other censuses and surveys that would occupy its time until 1920. Again the workload was heavy: the census of manufactures in 1915, the special censuses of several rapidly growing cities—Tulsa, Oklahoma; El Paso, Texas; and Hamtramck and Highland Park, Michigan—and new statistical series on births and state finances.[22]

Working conditions in the bureau were not ideal. The *Annual Reports* of Director Rogers and other sources are sprinkled with complaints about the minor insults the statisticians endured. The bureau crowded its own staff as 40 employees from the new Federal Trade Commission moved into their office space. When the bureau returned to its intercensal staffing levels in the early 1910s, 185 employees were demoted and took pay cuts. Throughout the period the director did not have the power to reclassify and restructure clerical positions to fit the varying work load. Clerks soon learned that if they wanted to advance their careers, they had to leave the bureau.[23]

The complaints and pleas for remedial legislation fell on deaf ears in the mid-1910s, as administrative reform bogged down throughout the federal system. Statistical observers recognized that little would be done before the 1920 census. They also knew, though, that the next decennial census would again force the issue of the quality and competency of the Census Bureau. All sides retreated and waited.

The American entry into World War I in April 1917, however, forced the issue of the capacities of the national statistical system three years ahead of schedule. The story of the mobilization of the national bureaucracy for war and the creation of the emergency wartime agencies is relatively familiar, but the effect of these activities on the Census Bureau and its capacities is not. As during the Civil War, the bureau suddenly found itself in the limelight as other agencies and policymakers turned to them for data on everything from explosives and manpower sources to leather stocks. This time, however, a coterie of former census officials and statisticians were poised to take advantage of the situation and to use the emergency to justify expansion and reform of the federal statistical system.

The bureau initially became involved in war work in May 1917 when it

22. Holt, *Bureau of the Census*, pp. 61–69.
23. Cummings, "Permanent Census Bureau," p. 612.

prepared estimates and apportionments of draft-age men. The bureau classified registrants and draftees by occupation so that recruits could be channeled into the appropriate tasks. It also searched its population records for age data to prosecute draft dodgers. Further, the Census Bureau compiled industrial statistics to plan the war mobilization. These included statistics and capacity of such materials as iron and steel, wool, leather, kapok, nitrites, antimony, graphite, and coal. In 1917–18, the equivalent of 44 bureau employees worked on war statistics; by 1918–19, the number had risen to 143.[24]

The transition to war work was not smooth. Neither the bureau nor the other statistical agencies were geared toward rapid publication of estimates or current production levels of commodities. In the area of import and export and shipping statistics, the situation was most critical, since the entire American war effort hinged on the ability of the government to get men and materiel to Europe efficiently. When in late 1917 the Allies upgraded the American war contribution, the need for the statistics became critical.

In early 1918, therefore, the Wilson administration created a powerful statistical and planning effort under the coordination of Edwin Gay, dean of the Harvard Business School. To regulate imports Gay built the Division of Planning and Statistics in the U.S. Shipping Board and War Trade Board. In June 1918 Wilson created the Central Bureau of Planning and Statistics with Gay at its head to oversee the statistical war effort throughout the government. By the armistice Gay had one thousand people working directly or indirectly for him. His higher-level associates included many disaffected former census officials, such as Wesley Mitchell and William Rossiter, who saw in the Central Bureau a new possibility for the creation of a central statistical system.[25]

The war did not last long enough for the Central Bureau to prove its usefulness beyond solving the emergency tasks. Gay tried to turn the Central Bureau into a planning agency for reconversion, but, in the battles between president and Congress, the bureau's appropriations ended in June 1919.

Others made efforts to institutionalize the experience of the war effort. The most successful was the creation of the joint Census Advisory Committee of the American Statistical Association and the American Economic Association in November 1918. This committee, composed of men who had played a major role in census history and in the statistical war mobilization, began to meet in 1919 and has since continued to advise the

24. Annual Reports of the Bureau of the Census, 1917, 1918, and 1919 (Washington, D.C.: GPO, 1917–19); Holt, *Bureau of the Census*, pp. 70–71.

25. Herbert Heaton, *A Scholar in Action: Edwin F. Gay* (Cambridge, Mass.: Harvard University Press, 1952), pp. 97–138; Lucy Sprague Mitchell, *Two Lives: The Story of Wesley Clair Mitchell and Myself* (New York: Simon and Schuster, 1913), pp. 363ff.

bureau. The committee was chaired initially by former chief clerk William Rossiter, then of Rumford Press, and included Carroll Doten of MIT, Edwin Gay, Wesley Mitchell, E. R. A. Seligman of Columbia University, and Walter Willcox of Cornell University. The committee effectively served as a policymaker in the absence of strong bureau leadership. Over the years its members testified before Congress, wrote reports on sensitive issues, determined the form and content of census schedules and set priorities for special census studies. These men also became the institutional memory of many bureau traditions and forged a tangible link between the government and the academic community.[26]

They could not, however, achieve their own goals of institutional improvement in the Census Bureau. In the aftermath of the war experience, administrative reform again became a matter of debate in Washington as Progressives pointed out the limitations of the capacities of the American state. Reformers resubmitted Taft's proposal for a Bureau of the Budget and more efficient federal planning and auditing mechanisms in 1919. The Budget and Accounting Act of 1921 created a Bureau of the Budget in the Treasury Department and a General Accounting Office as an auditing arm of Congress. In 1919, Congress commissioned the Bureau of Efficiency to consider restructuring the federal statistical system. In 1922, this bureau recommended that the Bureau of the Census be restructured as the Bureau of Federal Statistics with control over all nonadministrative federal statistics.[27]

By the time the report was issued, "normalcy" had returned and progressive reform was in decline. Statistical reform was a lesser priority than budget reform, and the report took a back seat in the reconversion debates. Moreover, the 1920 census was, as we shall see, a controversial count that prompted a reapportionment crisis in Congress. Congress was in no mood to embark on administrative reorganization of the statistical system.

Ironically, in the early 1920s, statistical improvement became the watchword of the Commerce Department leadership, not the bureau leadership, as Herbert Hoover took over as secretary of Commerce. Hoover's interests lay in continuing some of the production statistics started during World War I. He fostered the creation of the monthly *Survey of Current Business* in 1921 and pressed for a census of distribution in 1926. Information gathering and statistics played a prominent role in Hoover's theories of the "associative state," as Ellis Hawley calls it. The

26. Holt, *Bureau of the Census*, p. 71. For the records of the committee, see esp. Records of the Census Advisory Committee, series 148, RG 29, Records of the Bureau of the Census, NA.

27. Skowronek, *Building a New American State*, pp. 200–211; *The Statistical Work of the Federal Government* (Washington, D.C.: GPO, 1922), also available as H.R. Doc. 394, 67th Cong., 2d sess., 1922.

bureau's energies in the 1920s were directed toward the improvement of business statistics, toward fostering cooperation between industry, government, and academic experts in the area of economic statistics, and toward the collection of data that might foster improvements in the national economy without the heavy hand of government "planning."[28]

Throughout the 1920s, though, the bureau's efforts in business statistics were shadowed by the problems created by the patterns of population growth and change. In the 1920s, immigration restriction and congressional and legislative apportionment became pressing issues on the national legislative agenda. On one level both were "caused" by the census numbers. Congress ended the traditional American policy of open immigration by apportioning quotas on the basis of the "national origins" of the population. At the same time, Congress froze the size of the House of Representatives and then stalemated over reapportioning itself because rural areas with declining populations would lose representatives. Both crises resulted from major structural changes in the American population. Urbanization and industrialization brought changes in class structure and ways of life. As the producer and interpreter of the data that defined these issues, the Census Bureau was drawn into the debates. The statisticians classified, calculated, and organized the census results for the policymakers' needs. The particular character of the data that the statisticians created in the 1920s has reverberated through American social policy, scholarly discourse, and politics ever since.

28. Holt, *Bureau of the Census*, pp. 77–86; Ellis Hawley, *The Great War and the Search for a Modern Order: A History of the American People and Their Institutions, 1917–1933* (New York: St. Martins, 1979); Hawley, "Herbert Hoover and Economic Stabilization, 1921–22," in *Herbert Hoover as Secretary of Commerce*, ed. Ellis Hawley (Iowa City, Iowa: University of Iowa Press, 1981); Carolyn Grin, "The Unemployment Conference of 1921," *Mid-America* 54, no. 2 (1973): 83–107; Peri Ethan Arnold, "Herbert Hoover and the Department of Commerce: A Study of Ideology and Policy," (Ph.D. diss., University of Chicago, 1972); Arnold, *Making the Managerial Presidency: Comprehensive Reorganization Planning, 1905–1980* (Princeton, N.J.: Princeton University Press, 1986); Barry Karl, "Presidential Planning and Social Science Research: Mr. Hoover's Experts," *Perspectives in American History* 3 (1969): 347–409; Guy Alchon, *The Invisible Hand of Planning: Capitalism, Social Science and the State in the 1920s* (Princeton, N.J.: Princeton University Press, 1985). This literature is also useful for the story of how former census officials continued much of their research and organizational efforts outside the government and created large-scale private research organizations (the National Bureau of Economic Research and the Brookings Institution, for example) and university-based institutes in the 1920s. See also chap. 7, below.

SIX | The Tribal Twenties Revisited:
National Origins, Malapportionment,
and Cheating by the Numbers

*Then came the foreigner, making his way into the little village,
bringing—small blame to him!—not only a vastly lower standard of
living, but too often an actual present incapacity even to understand
the refinements of life and thought in the community in which he
sought a home.*

—*Francis Walker, 1890*

*These people . . . are beaten men from beaten races; representing the
worst failures in the struggle for existence.*

—*Francis Walker, 1896*

The Census Bureau of 1920 had little advance warning of the
political crisis that would flow from the results of the fourteenth census. The preparation for the count was routine; the
chief statisticians planned the tabulating schedule; they developed procedures to deal with the irate city boosters who felt
that their cities had been undercounted. The statisticians modified the tabulation procedures to avoid the processing delays
of 1910. Some worried over the effect of demobilization on the
census effort—particularly in terms of paying the enumerators, given the wartime inflation. Overall, however, the statisticians expected that they would, as they had since 1880, count
the population, report the data for apportionment by the end
of the census year, and then cross-tabulate the detailed data on
the census form for social and economic analysis.[1]

1. W. Stull Holt, *The Bureau of the Census: Its History, Activities and Organization* (Washington, D.C.: Brookings Institution, 1929), pp. 71–80.

15. The Center of Population . . . 1920. The Census Bureau reported that 50 percent of the American population lived in urban areas in 1920. Yet this photo of the center of population for that year conveys a very different story. Rural Americans claimed cultural and moral, if not numerical, dominance (see also fig. 11).

The political situation in the nation as a whole, though, was hardly normal. The 1920 census was taken in January amid the turmoil of the reconversion from World War I. The war itself had ended in November 1918, yet its aftermath still shook the country in early 1920. Woodrow Wilson had lost his political mandate in the 1918 congressional elections, when both houses of Congress turned Republican. In December 1918 Wilson went to Versailles; he returned in the spring of 1919 but could not convince the Senate to support either the treaty or the League of Nations. In September he was incapacitated by a stroke. The nation lacked leadership at a crucial time.

On the domestic front, labor strife broke out as workers attempted to recover the real wages that they had lost to wartime inflation. During 1919, 22 percent of the work force went on strike at some time. In Seattle, a general strike swept the city; in Boston the police struck. In the steel industry, 360,000 workers, primarily immigrants from southern and eastern Europe, struck from September 1919 to January 1920 to end the twelve-hour day and gain union recognition. Most strikes carried overtones of revolutionary rhetoric as strike leaders compared the American situation with the Russian Revolution and other revolutionary upheavals then taking place in Europe.

The Justice Department responded to these developments by making mass arrests of radical political activists and union organizers in late 1919 and early 1920. On January 2, 1920, the same day the census was to be taken, agents rounded up 2,700 people in thirty-three cities. Attorney General A. Mitchell Palmer stretched his powers under the immigration laws and rode roughshod over the civil and political rights of thousands of Americans, holding them without bail or destroying their union offices on the pretense that the radicals were destabilizing American society.

A series of race riots and ethnic battles resulting from the rapid migrations of the war years also wracked the nation. These attacks were, by and large, of whites against blacks or natives against foreigners. In 1917, for example, forty-eight were killed in a race riot in East St. Louis. After months of tension between blacks and whites, a similar race riot erupted in Chicago in the summer of 1919. Thirty-eight were killed in several days of rioting. In August 1920, a mob in southern Illinois attacked Italian immigrants who worked in the local mining industry and who allegedly had robbed banks and kidnapped two boys. Hundreds fled the area as the mob dragged people from their homes, beat them, and burned their houses.[2]

Underlying the political turmoil were dramatic social and demographic changes in American society—many of which had been coming for decades—but which nevertheless were newly frightening in the context of the postwar crisis. Urban industrial society in particular seemed the locus of economic unrest, ethnic and racial conflict, and corrupt politics. Though cities had been growing rapidly since the mid-nineteenth century, in the context of the postwar crisis, they appeared as a monstrous perversion of American ideals and ways of life.

Census statisticians had, of course, been monitoring these changes for decades and had produced the detailed interpretations of the data that allowed the public to understand what was happening. Men such as Francis Amasa Walker, Richmond Mayo Smith, Walter Willcox, and Carroll Wright had produced the classifications to define the urban and rural population; they had calculated the differential growth rates of the various states, regions, social classes, and ethnic and racial groups of the nation. They had provided, if you will, the language to debate the sources of the social turmoil, and, not surprisingly, politicians and the general

2. Robert Murray, *Red Scare: A Study in National Hysteria, 1919–1920* (Minneapolis, Minn.: University of Minnesota Press, 1955); David Brody, *Labor in Crisis: The Steel Strike of 1919* (New York: Lippincott, 1965); William M. Tuttle, *Race Riot at East St. Louis, July 2, 1917* (Carbondale, Ill.: Southern Illinois University Press, 1964); August Meier and Elliott Rudwick, *From Plantation to Ghetto* (New York: Hill and Wang, 1970); Tuttle, *Race Riot: Chicago in the Red Summer of 1919* (New York: Atheneum, 1970); John Higham, *Strangers in the Land* (New York: Atheneum, 1974), esp. pp. 264–65; James Green, *The World of the Worker* (New York: Hill and Wang, 1980), pp. 93–99; P. K. Edwards, *Strikes in the United States, 1881–1974* (New York: St. Martin's Press, 1981).

public looked to the 1920 census results for explanations and clues to the changing nature of American society.

The census results seemed to confirm the pessimist's worst fears. The population had grown by about 14 million during the decade—or only about 15 percent. The Far West had continued to grow, but so had the densely settled cities of the Northeast and Midwest. The most dramatic calculations showed that the urban population had grown by 19 million, while the rural population had declined by 5 million. Relatedly, the figures showed that the urban areas formed the home of immigrants and their children. Seventy-two percent of the foreign stock population lived in urban areas; 41 percent of the natives born of native parents lived in urban areas. The initial congressional apportionment figures, published at the end of 1920, indicated that nineteen states would gain or lose congressional seats unless the size of the House of Representatives were increased. In New England, Maine, Vermont, and Rhode Island were slated to lose one seat each; Connecticut would gain one. In the South, Louisiana, Mississippi, and Kentucky would lose one seat each; North Carolina and Texas would each gain one. California was to gain three seats; Michigan and Ohio were each to gain two. Indiana, Iowa, Kansas, Nebraska, and Missouri would lose. States with rapidly growing urban areas benefited; those without them lost.

Reaction in the popular press to these developments captured the contemporary concern. They termed the trend "dangerous," "a condition dreaded by sociologists and patriots." "The United States is becoming overindustrialized," the *New York World* noted. For the first time in the history of the nation, the Census Bureau reported, a majority of Americans lived in "urban" places—modestly defined as those places with populations of 2,500 or more. Would there be a sufficiently large farm population to supply food to the nation, several papers wondered.[3]

The statistics were troublesome because, for the previous half-century, many commentators and social critics had worried what the changing population distribution meant and had used population patterns in political debates to support particular social policies. We have seen how the interpretations of the differential growth patterns of the northern and southern populations, or the slave and free populations, entered into the discussions of slavery extension or the apportionment of representation after the Civil War. In the same manner, during the Gilded Age and

3. Walter Nugent, *Structures of American Social History* (Bloomington, Ind.: Indiana University Press, 1981); Michel L. Balinski and H. Peyton Young, *Fair Representation: Meeting the Ideal of One Man, One Vote* (New Haven and London: Yale University Press, 1982). For contemporary reaction, see, e.g., "A Census 'Thunderclap,'" *Literary Digest* 67 (Oct. 23, 1920): 16–17; "Our Decreasing Increase," ibid. 66 (July 17, 1920): 17; "Doubtful Good of Our City Growth," ibid. 66 (Sept. 18, 1920): 17; "City Growth and Rural Loss," ibid. 65 (May 29, 1920): 22; and "The Triumph of Cain," *Independent* 105 (Apr. 2, 1921): 346.

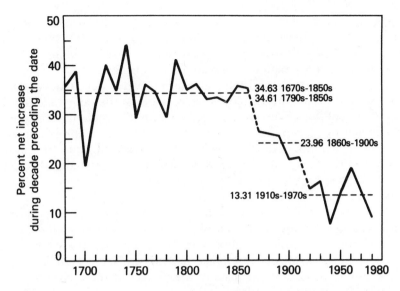

16. The Three Plateaus, Rates of Population Growth by Decade. Population growth rates have displayed remarkable continuity over time with sharp breaks in the late nineteenth and early twentieth centuries.

Progressive Era, the new generation of academic statisticians debated the differential growth rates evident in the native and foreign-born populations and in the rural and urban populations.

Central to these discussions were notions about the traditional "natural" patterns of population growth and change in the United States. These notions were themselves the result of a century or more of observation about the growth of the population. As Walter Nugent has shown in his *Structures of American Social History,* major continuities were evident in the growth and settlement patterns of the American population from the early eighteenth century through the Civil War decade. The population grew at a consistent rate of 33 to 36 percent a decade; it consistently moved west through the settlement of frontier-rural farms. Birth rates were highest on the frontier; they slowed considerably by the second or third generation. The Vermont and New Hampshire of the 1790s, the Illinois of the 1830s, and the Dakotas of the 1880s displayed similar demographic patterns (see fig. 16).

In the late nineteenth century, these patterns continued in the West but gave way to newer patterns of population change in the East and Midwest. Nugent has called this period "the great conjuncture." The populations of the settled rural areas of the nation stabilized or even declined. Relatedly, urban growth accelerated in these same regions as manufacturing and trade became more important forces in the national economy. This new industrial economy also spawned a "laboring," or "working," class of industrial wage earners, which grew to about 40 percent of the American labor force by 1910. By the 1920s, about three-fourths of these industrial wage earners were concentrated in 155 industrial counties of the nation (5 percent of all counties).

Further, as early as the 1860s, statisticians had noticed that rural birth rates were declining in the older eastern states at the same time that the population of the urban areas was growing rapidly—and that the growth was fueled by foreign immigration. Dr. Nathan Allen, for example, reported such findings to the Massachusetts Board of State Charities in 1867. He asked the board to consider whether these changes were the result of "our higher civilization" or an indication of "a more artificial mode of life and the unwholesome state of society."

Massachusetts was one of the first states in the nation to experience these changes because it had an old commercial economy and was the locus of the new textile and shoe manufacturing industries. A relatively small state in area, Massachusetts also had no rural hinterland, as did New York and Pennsylvania, to cushion the impact of these changes on its political life. Many of the nation's most influential institutions of higher education made their home in Massachusetts, and thus it contributed a large share of the old stock intellectual elite who analyzed the processes of change. These men disliked the shift in political influence to the cities. They were also heavily represented among the leading statisticians in the Census Bureau from Francis Walker's time through the 1920s.[4]

These self-defined representatives of the old stock Americans were troubled by the demographic shifts for several reasons. First, much republican political theory and Jeffersonian political theory in particular presupposed a independent yeomanry and artisanry to guarantee political liberty. In this view, the urban laboring classes could not be trusted to exercise independent political positions. They were too dependent on their employers or to the siren calls of demagogues to be trusted to maintain a republic. Well into the late nineteenth century, mainstream American political leaders, as well as those of the infant labor movement, considered a permanent wage-laboring class a perversion of American ideals.[5]

4. Nugent, *Structures*, pp. 54–86. Allen's statement is reprinted as "The Foreign Element in Massachusetts," in *Historical Aspects of the Immigration Problem: Select Documents*, ed. Edith Abbott (Chicago: University of Chicago Press, 1926), pp. 337–45. See also Hal S. Barron, *Those Who Stayed Behind: Rural Society in Nineteenth-Century New England* (New York: Cambridge University Press, 1984); Margo Anderson Conk, "The Census, Political Power and Social Change: The Significance of Population Growth in American History," *Social Science History* 8 (Winter 1984): 81–106; and Conk, *The United States Census and Labor Force Change* (Ann Arbor, Mich.: UMI Research Press, 1980), pp. 71–82.

5. For discussions of the ideological positions of the new academics, see the essays by John Higham, Edward Shils, and Lawrence Veysey in *The Organization of Knowledge in Modern America, 1860–1920*, ed. Alexandra Oleson and John Voss (Baltimore: Johns Hop-

Second, the reapportionment mechanisms of the census automatically and relentlessly shifted political power to the areas with growing populations. During the first seventy years of the Republic, political representation shifted westward. As we have seen, Virginia, Massachusetts, Connecticut, Vermont, New Hampshire, and Maryland saw their congressional delegations peak by 1820. Ohio's House delegation grew from 6 to 21 from 1810 to 1880, Indiana's from 1 to 13. Between 1850 and 1910, the Iowa delegation grew from 2 to 11, the Illinois from 9 to 27. After the late nineteenth century reapportionment increasingly transferred political power to states with large urban populations. New York, for example, had 40 congressmen in 1830 in the period before rapid urbanization. New York's congressional delegation declined to 31 in 1860 as population grew rapidly in the West. By 1910, though, its delegation had again risen—to 43 members—as urban growth fueled the power of the Empire State.

Third, the shift in political power was troublesome because much urban growth was obviously a function of European immigration. Until the mid-nineteenth century, high birth rates fueled population growth and westward expansion. After midcentury, immigration played an increasingly important role in population growth. Nativists at midcentury questioned whether the Irish and Germans would subvert American political traditions. By the 1880s, as John Higham documented, such fears reemerged when a strike wave swept the country. Urban political machines also seemed especially offensive to republican ideals. When these commentators noticed that the sources of immigration were shifting in the late 1880s and 1890s, a full-blown immigration restriction movement emerged that based its objections to open immigration squarely on the supposed "racial" differences between the older northern and western European stock population and the newer immigrants from southern and eastern Europe. Francis Walker was a leading theorist of this movement. After his death in 1897, other major census statisticians, such as Assistant Director Joseph Hill, Director S. N. D. North, and Chief Clerk William Rossiter, promulgated his ideas. The federal Immigration Commission, founded in 1907, incorporated these ideas in its official reports and warned the country about the problems the thirteen million immigrants presented to the nation.[6]

kins University Press), and John Higham, with Leonard Krieger and Felix Gilbert, *History* (Englewood Cliffs, N.J.: Prentice Hall, 1965). For labor attitudes toward the development of American capitalism, see, e.g., Eric Foner, *Free Soil, Free Labor, Free Men: The Ideology of the Republican Party before the Civil War* (New York: Oxford University Press, 1970); Sean Wilenz, *Chants Democratic: New York City and the Rise of the American Working Class* (New York: Oxford University Press, 1984); Leon Fink, *Workingmen's Democracy: The Knights of Labor and American Politics* (Urbana, Ill.: University of Illinois Press, 1983); and David Montgomery, *Beyond Equality: Labor and the Radical Republicans, 1862–1872* (New York: Knopf, 1967).

6. Higham, *Strangers in the Land*; Barbara Miller Solomon, *Ancestors and Immigrants* (Cambridge, Mass.: Harvard University Press, 1956). Hill was a statistician for the Immigra-

These interpretive threads resonated through the census figures in the fall of 1920. Similar concerns had, of course, arisen from the data for previous censuses. But this time they played a greater role in the public debate because the traditional countervailing mechanisms that Congress had used to soften or delay the impact of the demographic changes no longer existed. There seemed no way to avoid the transfer of power to the cities and hence to immigrants and a growing urban working class.

Congress did not face this reality after previous censuses because it could still look west. Reapportionment is always a destabilizing and traumatic political event. In a society as demographically volatile as the United States, it is not surprising that politicians devised mechanisms to control the political shifts that resulted from reapportionment. For the previous century, western settlement and the admission of new states had forced eastern states to relinquish some of their relative power in congressional seats and the electoral college. Congress thus had developed mechanisms to deal with this shifting balance of power.

One involved mitigating the effects of reapportionment by regulating the pace of admission of new states. Population growth increased a state's power in the House, where population and representation had a direct relationship. But the creation of new states added two new members to the Senate regardless of population. Thus a sparsely populated state in the West could be admitted to be the political ally of the party or faction of an older eastern state that was facing a relative population decline. In the first half of the nineteenth century, of course, it was precisely the unraveling of this dynamic that provided one cause of the sectional crisis between the slave and the free states. By midcentury, the South had lost its ability to muster a majority in the House; it thus had to rely on its control of the Senate to guarantee the continuation of the slave system.

After the Civil War rapid population growth continued and new states were admitted to the Union, but the rules changed. In the era of unstable party majorities, Congress admitted new states in response to particular hopes for political advantage. Democrats had hoped that Colorado, admitted in 1876, would aid their presidential efforts. When Colorado's three electoral votes went to Hayes, the Democrats cooled on the idea of admitting more states. In 1889–90, for only the second time since the war, the Republican party took control of both houses of Congress and the presidency. Six sparsely populated western states (North and South Dakota, Idaho, Washington, Montana, and Wyoming) were abruptly admitted to the Union. The new states sent twelve senators and seven

tion Commission. Rossiter wrote for the popular press and wrote the census monograph *A Century of Population Growth.* For the position of S. N. D. North, see his discussion of "race admixture" in his essay "Seventy Five Years of Progress in Statistics: The Outlook for the Future," in *The History of Statistics: Their Development and Progress in Many Countries,* ed. John Koren (New York: Macmillan, 1918), pp. 41–43.

representatives—all Republicans—to Congress. By way of comparison, Arizona and New Mexico, which had Democratic tendencies, had to wait for admission until 1912, when splits within the Republican party required it to make other legislative compromises to pass its tariff measures.[7]

After 1912, of course, no more territories could be admitted, so political majorities could not be strengthened by the creation of new states. Further, the more recently admitted western states were not growing rapidly enough to balance the growing strength of the urban areas. Of the eleven states admitted after 1870, only one, Oklahoma, had as many as eight representatives in 1910. The eleven combined had only thirty-one representatives. The representatives from these states thus composed 7 percent of the House but 23 percent of the Senate. To put the matter slightly differently, the city of Chicago had roughly the same population in 1890 as did the six states admitted in 1889–90.

Congress had also mitigated the declining power of the older rural areas of the nation by increasing the size of the House after each census to guarantee that states would not lose House seats. From 1870 to 1910 the size of the House increased from 292 to 435 members; no state lost a seat. By 1910, however, the House chamber was becoming crowded, the cost of running the Congress was growing, and conducting business was becoming unwieldy. Congress resolved after the 1910 census to maintain the House at 435 members. Reapportionment after the 1920 census would be a zero-sum game.[8]

Finally, from 1896 to 1910, the Republicans had secured control of the national government. Woodrow Wilson's presidency broke this hegemony only because of a Republican party split. In the years after 1896, the growing strength of the cities did not seem to threaten Republican ascendancy; the immigrants voted Republican in sufficient strength to prevent the immigration restriction movement from making headway in Congress. By 1920, though, the rising power of the urban areas began to threaten this Republican ascendancy. It was clear from Wilson's presidency that urban areas were beginning to vote more decisively Democratic. The small but growing Socialist movement also had strong appeal in cities.[9]

7. Frederic L. Paxson, "The Admission of the 'Omnibus' States, 1889–90," *Proceedings of the State Historical Society of Wisconsin* (Madison, Wis.: State Historical Society, 1912): 77–96; Roy Nichols, *The Disruption of American Democracy* (New York: Macmillan, 1948), pp. 460–61. Utah, admitted in 1896, also faced problems in achieving statehood because its Mormon population was considered "deviant."

8. Congressional Quarterly, *Guide to U.S. Elections* (Washington, D.C.: Congressional Quarterly, 1975), pp. 519–41.

9. I rely here on the insights from the new political history, particularly from the discussions of critical elections. Walter Dean Burnham in particular discusses the procedural

In short, when the Republican-controlled Sixty-sixth Congress received the apportionment figures from the Census Bureau in the fall of 1920, they did not like what they saw. The numbers indicated that they were to take away 11 House seats from ten rural states and give them to 8 urbanizing states. At the same time, foreign immigration resumed in full force as shipping schedules returned to their prewar patterns. By late 1920, 52,000 immigrants were arriving in the United States each month. The demographic patterns that presented the 1920 apportionment dilemma showed every indication of continuing.

For the next ten years the Republican-controlled Congress wrestled with the political implications of the 1920 census results and struggled to devise new mechanisms to minimize the impact of reapportionment. They radically restricted immigration and refused—for the only time in the nation's history—to reapportion the House of Representatives. These actions became the new core mechanisms for controlling population change and hence the shifts in political power in later decades. And, as in the previous debates about population change, the language and legislation of the 1920s are rich with ideological assumptions about the true nature and goals of American society.

Both immigration restriction and reapportionment were on the legislative agenda as Congress reassembled for the short lame-duck session of the 66th Congress in December 1920. Republican Isaac Siegel of New York, member of the House Census Committee, prepared a reapportionment bill to increase the size of the House to 483 so that no state would lose a seat. Republican Albert Johnson of Washington introduced an "emergency" bill to suspend immigration for two years. The reapportionment bill was amended to keep the size of the House at 435; eleven states would lose House seats. Both bills passed the House in early 1921 and moved to the Senate. At this point their fate diverged. The senators from the eleven states that would have lost representatives blocked action on the bill. Action on reapportionment bill would have to await the Sixty-seventh Congress.[10]

The immigration bill faced a more positive response from the Senate Committee on Immigration. Leaders of the committee sympathized with

barriers to democratic participation passed in the early 20th c., especially voter registration, at-large elections, and primaries. The changes in reapportionment methods described below were another technique to limit participation. See, e.g., Paul Kleppner, *Who Voted? The Dynamics of Electoral Turnout, 1870–1980* (New York: Praeger, 1982), and Kleppner, "Critical Realignments and Electoral Systems," and William Dean Burnham, "The System of 1896: An Analysis," both in *The Evolution of American Electoral Systems,* Paul Kleppner et al. (Westport, Conn.: Greenwood Press, 1981), pp. 3–32, 146–202.

10. The legislative history of the immigration bill is described in Higham, *Strangers in the Land,* pp. 300–324; for the reapportionment bill, see *Congressional Digest* 8, no. 2 (1929): 46.

the goals of Johnson's bill but thought it too severe a measure. These eastern Republicans wanted to cut down on the number of immigrants from southern and eastern Europe, but they also recognized the needs of the employers of immigrants and responded to the lobbying efforts of the immigrants themselves.

Senator William Dillingham of Vermont, who had headed the Immigration Commission of 1907–11, proposed a solution. He suggested that immigration quotas be tied to the proportion of a nationality group's representation in the census. He amended the House bill to limit immigration for the next year and proposed a quota based on 5 percent of a group's strength at the 1910 census. Dillingham's bill allowed some immigration and appeared equitable to all immigrants, yet it cut overall annual immigration to less than half a million. Further, the bill effectively discriminated against southern and eastern Europeans, since, as the most recently arriving groups, they had the smallest population base in the census. In this form the bill passed the Senate. The House cut the quota from 5 percent to 3 percent of a group's base, the Senate concurred, and the bill went to the president. Wilson vetoed it, but it was reintroduced days later in the first session of the Sixty-seventh Congress. Warren G. Harding signed the bill into law.

Though it was not immediately evident, the actions of this last session of the Sixty-sixth Congress signaled the beginning of a major realignment in American population policies. In the four short months of the winter of 1920–21, Congress had taken the first decisive step to end the historic American policy of open immigration. They had also balked at passing what had been in the past a fairly routine piece of legislative business: the reapportionment bill.

For cities, immigrants, and workers, such actions were truly ominous signs of what was to come. They signaled that Congress would try to prevent the shift of political power to the growing urban areas. And they would try to end the immigration policies that, they contended, fueled urban growth.

Nevertheless, supporters of open immigration and reapportionment were not immediately discouraged. The immigration restriction law was "emergency" legislation, authorized for one year only. Opponents of restriction felt it would be unworkable and would be repealed. Reapportionment legislation, others felt, could easily be passed in the Sixty-seventh Congress in time for the next congressional elections. Time would tell if Congress was really willing to violate the constitutional requirement for reapportionment, if Congress was willing to restrict immigration permanently.

In fact, Congress was willing. Immigration restriction and reapportionment remained on the legislative agenda of the Republican-controlled Congress throughout the 1920s. By 1929 a conservative antiurban majority had fashioned an immigration law that discriminated against immigrants from southern and eastern Europe. In the same period Congress rewrote the reapportionment rules to maintain rural and small town domination of the halls of Congress. To do so, however, was no easy task; the legislation clearly violated constitutional principles and the ideals of democracy and equality. Congress thus turned to the census and asked census statisticians to devise "scientific" rules and mechanisms to justify its antiurban, antidemocratic laws. The history of the passage and implementation of the permanent immigration restriction law and the 1929 reapportionment bill reveals these processes.

Albert Johnson was quite pleased with himself when the new immigration restriction law went into effect. After decades of unsuccessful effort, Congress had passed a severe restriction law. He and other supporters of restriction, however, were well aware that they would have to devise more elegant restriction legislation to stand the test of time. Restrictionists could justify "emergency" legislation in terms of the high unemployment of the postwar reconversion period, but they knew that when the economy improved and the traditional business lobbyists for immigrant labor came to town, Congress would hesitate to restrict immigration permanently. Further, once the supposed "national security" danger of immigrant revolutionary agitators passed, it would be harder to explain the openly discriminatory intent of the legislation to European diplomats. Accordingly, the House and Senate immigration committees immediately went to work to devise permanent legislation to replace the 1921 act when it expired.

Johnson and the House Immigration Committee wanted to suspend immigration altogether, but they knew that employers and representatives of the immigrant groups would probably block such a draconian bill. Short of suspension, they wanted to cut quotas further to limit overall immigration to around 150,000 a year. They also searched for a method that might split the immigrant lobbyists and permit immigration from northern and western Europe while closing the gates on southern and eastern Europe. Immigrants from northern and western Europe, the prevailing racial theorists agreed, were of Anglo-Saxon or Nordic stock and thus could be assimilated into American society. Southern and eastern Europeans, on the other hand, were from inferior races, "beaten men from beaten races," as Francis Amasa Walker put it, and thus would undermine American institutions and social values.[11]

The problem was to find a legitimate method of discrimination, one

11. Roy L. Garis, *Immigration Restriction* (New York: Macmillan, 1927); Francis Amasa Walker, *Discussions in Economics and Statistics*, vol. 2, ed. Davis R. Dewey (New York: Henry Holt, 1899), p. 447.

that would be logical, fair, understandable. The 1921 "emergency" law had employed the quota based on proportion of foreign-born in the 1910 census because these were the most recent data available on the proportion of foreign-born in the population. The 1920 census tabulations were not finished when the law was written. But the logic of apportionment implied that when more recent data became available the apportionment base would be shifted to the newer data—as was done with congressional apportionment. Unfortunately for the restrictionists, such a "reapportionment" would, over time, undermine the intentions of the 1921 law. Since southern and eastern Europeans were immigrating in greater numbers in the early twentieth century, their proportion of the foreign-born population was growing. Their proportion of the quotas would thus increase after each census if the principles of the 1921 law were embodied in permanent legislation.

These and other difficulties with the administration of the quota system made Congress reluctant to pass more comprehensive legislation. In May 1922, Congress extended the life of the 1921 law for two years to give itself breathing space. The ultimate fate of permanent restriction was unclear.

The restriction lobby was less concerned about the need for fairness and the niceties of democratic ideals. An extraordinarily virulent form of racialist thinking seeped into many sectors of American public opinion in the early twentieth century—including the new social science departments of elite universities and foundations. Eugenicists testified before Congress on the threats of the new immigrants to the nation's racial integrity. Psychologists developed their new IQ tests to prove the racial differences between natives and foreigners. Their work "confirmed" the conclusions of the prestigious Immigration Commission of 1907–11: indeed, a major change in the sources of immigration in the 1880s and 1890s had occurred. Before then, northern and western Europeans came to the United States. After 1890, the southern and eastern European migrations began in large numbers. Old and new immigrants, the commission asserted, following the major academic research of the time, were as different as night and day. The old immigrants were skilled, thrifty, hard-working, like native Americans; the new immigrants were unskilled, ignorant, predominantly Catholic or Jewish, and thus unfamiliar with and perhaps unassimilable to American institutions.

From this perspective, immigration restriction was no mere question of labor supply and economics. It was a question of preserving the American way of life from the "pollution" and "degradation" of racial mongrelization. As John R. Commons put it in his study, *Races and Immigrants in America,* "The race problem in the South is only one extreme of the same problem in the great cities of the North, where popular government, as our forefathers conceived it, has been displaced by one-man power."

Immigration had to be stopped to save the Republic from either a "class oligarchy" or a "race oligarchy."[12]

From this viewpoint, a good restriction law did not have to apportion quotas among the various sending nations equitably. It had to stop southern and eastern European immigration effectively while employing a simple allocation mechanism. In September 1922, Roy Garis, a professor of political science and economics at Vanderbilt University, devised such a mechanism in an article in *Scribner's*. He suggested that quotas be apportioned according to the proportion of the foreign-born enumerated at the 1890 census—before the massive influx of southern and eastern Europeans. This proposal struck a responsive chord among the restrictionist lobby. The *Saturday Evening Post* reprinted and publicized Garis's article. By late 1922 Johnson's committee had written a new quota law reducing the overall level of immigration and using the 1890 census as the apportionment base.[13]

At the end of 1922, however, the demand for labor tightened. Employers began to call for renewed immigration. The Sixty-seventh Congress did not act on Johnson's bill, and the whole matter was postponed until the Sixty-eighth Congress.

In December 1923, Johnson reintroduced his bill. By this time employer opposition had subsided. Outside of the immigrant groups themselves, few people raised serious opposition to the overtly racist rhetoric used to defend the bill. Nevertheless, to those not fully imbued with the assumptions of the Nordic supremacists, the bill was vulnerable to the attack that the use of the 1890 census for the quotas was clearly arbitrary. If the Sixty-eighth Congress could set the immigration quotas on the basis of the 1890 census, what would stop later Congresses from changing the census base to favor other ethnic groups?

The restrictionists found the answer to this dilemma in a special study published by the Census Bureau some fifteen years earlier. In 1909, William Rossiter, then chief clerk of the bureau, published *A Century of Population Growth*. This volume, designed to accompany the publication of the names of the heads of families enumerated in 1790, surveyed the growth and distribution of the population from 1790 to 1900. Rossiter was especially interested in measuring what he called the "vitality" of the

12. See, e.g., Allan Chase, *The Legacy of Malthus: The Social Costs of the New Scientific Racism* (New York: Knopf, 1976); Stephen Jay Gould, *The Mismeasure of Man* (New York: Norton, 1981); William Petersen, *The Politics of Population* (Garden City, N.J.: Doubleday, 1964); Higham, *History*; Oleson and Voss, *Organization of Knowledge*. See also James Reed, *The Birth Control Movement and American Society: From Private Vice to Public Virtue* (New York: Basic Books, 1978), pp. 197–210; John R. Commons, *Races and Immigrants in America* (New York: Macmillan, 1907), p. 4.

13. The Garis article is reprinted in House Committee on Immigration and Naturalization, *Hearings, Immigration and Labor*, 67th Cong., 4th sess., 1923, pp. 504–5, 586–89.

population, comparing the rates of population growth in the United States and western Europe to determine if the growth rate of the colonial stock population had surpassed that of their European cousins. To do so, Rossiter had to disaggregate the descendants of the colonists from those who immigrated after the Revolution. This was not an easy task, but Rossiter devised several methods that yielded similar results. He was downright ebullient about his findings. Thirty-seven million of the 67 million whites (56 percent) in the United States in 1900 were descendants of colonial stock. The 1900 American population was "twenty years in advance of what it would have been" had Americans reproduced at the fastest rate evident in Europe. Such growth "measured" "the wealth of opportunity in the young Republic and the unusual virility of the population."[14]

This volume became a stock reference for the Nordic supremacists, who believed, following Francis Amasa Walker, that the decline in the native white birth rate in the late nineteenth century was an "abnormal" and reversible condition that resulted from unhealthy competition with immigrants. In a kind of reverse of Social Darwinism, the racial thinkers had argued that the immigrants pulled the American standard of living down and that native white Americans responded by having smaller families to preserve their standard of living on a smaller income.

But what if one looked at Rossiter's figures from a positive perspective and recognized that the majority of white Americans of the 1920s were descended from the original "native stock"? Further, what if one continued Rossiter's logic further and determined the "national origins" of the white population? In 1922, Clinton Stoddard Burr, a great admirer of Madison Grant, took Rossiter's data and calculated estimates of the elements of the white race in the United States—that is, of the various nativities of members of the population. Burr demonstrated that the "Nordic" elements predominated. In early March 1924, John B. Trevor, the most influential lobbyist for restriction, used this logic in his defense of the 1890 census quota law. He provided a detailed table of the supposed "national origins" of the American population to the House Committee on Immigration.[15]

14. Bureau of the Census, *A Century of Population Growth*, comp. William Rossiter (Washington, D.C.: GPO, 1909), quotations on pp. 89–92. For a recent critique of Rossiter, see Henry Gemery, "European Emigration to North America, 1700–1820: Numbers and Quasi-Numbers," *Perspectives in American History*, n.s., 1 (1984): 283–342.

15. Solomon, *Ancestors and Immigrants*, pp. 71–81; Clinton Stoddard Burr, *America's Race Heritage: An Account of the Diffusion of Ancestral Stocks in the United States during Three Centuries of National Expansion and a Discussion of Its Significance* (New York: National Historical Society, 1922). For Trevor's statement, see *Congressional Record*, 68th Cong., 1st sess., 1924, pp. 5469–71.

Trevor explained why Congress was advised to use the 1890 census to apportion the immigration quotas. "Since it is an axiom . . ." he wrote,

> that a government not imposed by external force is the visible expression of the ideals, standards, and social viewpoint of the people over which it rules, it is obvious that a change in the character or composition of the population must inevitably result in the evolution of a form of government consonant with the base upon which it rests. If, therefore, the principle of individual liberty, guarded by constitutional government created on this continent nearly a century and a half ago, is to endure, the basic strain of our population must be maintained and our economic standards preserved.

Trevor continued:

> With full recognition of the material progress which we owe to the races from southern and eastern Europe, we are conscious not only that these people tended to depress our standard of living, unduly charge our institutions for the care of the socially inadequate and criminal, but also that they can not point during a period of seven centuries since Magna Charta to any conception of successful government other than a paternal autocracy.

Thus the true test of an immigration quota law was whether it maintained the current racial composition of the population. Under such a test, the 1910 quotas were too generous to southern and eastern Europeans. The bill using the 1890 census cut the Italian quota from 42,000 to 4,000, the Polish quota from 31,000 to 6,000. Accepting such logic, the House of Representatives passed the 1890 quota bill and sent it to the Senate.[16]

In the Senate, the Immigration Committee still worried over the use of the 1890 census as a quota base. As a solution Republican senator David Reed of Pennsylvania suggested using the principle of "national origins" directly and devising the quotas on the basis of the contribution of each nationality to the current white population. This would end the wrangling about which census was most appropriate and would settle the matter permanently, since future immigrants would only be admitted in the proportion they bore to the current racial composition of the population. Reed used Trevor's figures to prove that such a method was feasible. Joseph Hill, assistant director of the Census Bureau, testified that it would be technically feasible to calculate the national origins of the population, though he pointed out that Rossiter's figures were only a first approximation. The bureau had never undertaken such calculations.[17]

16. *Congressional Record*, 68th Cong., 1st sess., 1924, p. 5469.
17. Ibid. In January 1924, Vaile had asked Joseph Hill if the Census Bureau could reliably produce projections of the elements of the population as Burr proposed. See House Committee on Immigration and Naturalization, *Hearings, Restriction of Immigration*, 68th Cong., 1st sess., 1924, pp. 920–21. Hill replied by describing the mathematical method he would use to make such a calculation; he spoke neither to the question of the validity of the existing statistical sources he would have to use to make it nor to the question of the theoretical soundness of national origins.

Nevertheless, the Senate substituted a new immigration bill based squarely on the principles of "national origins." The law "temporarily" used the 1890 census as the basis for restriction until the Census Bureau could provide the official figures on the national origins of the white population. Opponents of restriction protested that the national origins mechanism was merely a device to sanitize the discriminatory intent of the restrictionists. Yet the new bill seemed to have the legitimacy of official statistics. As Congressman William N. Vaile, a Republican of Colorado, retorted to an opponent who charged that he did not agree with the principles embodied in the bill, "Then the gentleman does not agree with the census."[18]

Both houses passed the National Origins Act in the spring of 1924; Calvin Coolidge signed the bill in May. The act cut immigration to 165,000, using the 1890 census. By 1927 the Census Bureau was to provide official statistics on national origins for the full implementation of the law. The secretaries of State, Labor, and Commerce constituted a Quota Board to oversee the administration of the law and to certify the national origins figures.

There matters stood for about two years. Statisticians at the bureau went to work trying to determine the national origins data. Under the direction of Assistant Director Hill, officials worked to determine European boundary changes, researched nineteenth-century immigration patterns, and recalculated Rossiter's data in *A Century of Population Growth*. Early in 1925, Hill privately expressed his concerns about the validity of the concept of national origins; officially, though he continued to work on the problem. By mid-1926, though, Hill reported serious reservations about whether reliable figures on national origins could be determined. In particular, Hill discovered serious flaws in Rossiter's data. The problem boiled down to the fact that a minute error in apportioning the national origins of the colonial population would lead to a relatively large shift in the immigration quotas for the nations of western Europe.

A Century of Population Growth did not take into account the question of the anglicization of names. Rossiter had assumed that persons with English names were English, not Germans or Scots or Irish who had changed their names. Thus quotas based on his figures gave the overwhelming proportion of the immigration to Great Britain. Hill had discovered, as he wrote to Secretary of Commerce Herbert Hoover in June 1926, that Rossiter's "classification has been criticized adversely by one historian of high standing and I apprehend that there are others who share his views regarding it." "The general effect of the redistribution of immigration on the new basis after July 1, 1927," Hill continued, "will be to increase greatly the quota assigned to Great Britain and to diminish the quotas

18. *Congressional Record*, 68th Cong., 1st sess., 1924, p. 5647.

given to most other countries; and it is practically certain that as soon as the results of the apportionment based on national origin are announced, a storm of criticism will be aroused, and the validity of the figures will be attacked." Hill asked for direction from the Quota Board on how to proceed.[19]

Word of the trouble devising the national origins figures sent shock waves through the restriction lobby. Trevor in particular recognized that the whole restriction law could be undermined if the data proved unavailable or if the numbers were unreliable. The 1924 law had split the immigrant lobby because it favored northern and western European immigrants over southern and eastern European immigrants. But if the figures proved to discriminate against the Germans and the Irish, for example, opponents of national origins might be able to repeal the whole law. Trevor and other lobbyists thus renewed a campaign to shore up the national origins scheme in the press. Congress gave the bureau more time to work on the problems and postponed the 1927 implementation date first from 1927 to 1928 and then from 1928 to 1929.

Behind the scenes, activity to salvage the situation picked up. Trevor, for example, used his considerable charm directly on Joseph Hill. The two had met during the legislative debates on the 1924 legislation. Since Hill was in charge of the calculations of the quotas, Trevor made it a point to keep in contact with Hill, to visit him in Washington, to entertain him in New York. He thus made sure that progress was being made in producing the appropriate numbers. In addition, Walter Willcox of the Census Advisory Committee and the historian J. Franklin Jameson convinced the American Council of Learned Societies (ACLS) to fund a ten-thousand-dollar historical study of the issues. If historians had raised questions about the validity of the numbers, then historians would be asked to resolve the issues. Howard Barker, a genealogist, and Marcus Hansen, an immigration historian, were commissioned to do the work. Barker was charged with analyzing a sample of names from known areas of German and Irish colonial immigration. He was to decide how and when the names were anglicized and how much difference a recalculation of the names would make on Rossiter's data. Hansen studied "the minor stocks of the American population of 1790," and "the population of the American outlying regions in 1790."[20]

---

19. Joseph Hill to Niles Carpenter, Feb. 17, 1925, and Hill, memorandum for the secretary, June 21, 1926, Records of the Social and Economic Statistics Administration, box 1, file 15, NN374–63, RG 29, NA. The historian to whom Hill referred was J. Franklin Jameson, who, in an unpublished lecture, "American Blood in 1775," had made estimates of the size of the German and Irish colonial population that were double Rossiter's.

20. For the records of the Trevor-Hill correspondence, see Records of the Social and Economic Statistics Administration, box 1, files 15, 30, and 31, NN374–63, RG 29, NA. The results of the ACLS study were published in the *Annual Report of the American Historical*

For the next two years, the Census Bureau and the ACLS scholars worked on the figures. As a result of this work, the quotas for Germany and Ireland were adjusted upward slightly from the estimates made in 1924. The British quota was revised downward. Of course the quotas for southern and eastern Europe remained miniscule.

Opponents of restriction continued to lobby for repeal of national origins, but they lacked sufficient strength to combat either the shaky statistical base or the social theory that underpinned the law. Trevor and his associates pressed for implementation of the law. By early 1929, the Census Bureau had produced numbers acceptable to the academic community. All commentators at the time recognized that the numbers were estimates at best: "far from final," in the words of the ACLS study, "tainted" in the word of opponents of national origins. Nevertheless, after a congressional move to postpone implementation failed in the spring of 1929, Herbert Hoover announced the official, "scientific" national origins of the U.S. population. His action set U.S. immigration policy in a kind of racialist concrete for a generation and ended America's role as the haven for European immigrants. In the turbulent world of the 1930s and 1940s, this decision had major international repercussions as Jews and political refugees from southern and eastern Europe confronted the "paper walls" the United States erected in 1929. Not until the 1960s were the assumptions of the National Origins Act seriously challenged and immigration laws for Europeans rewritten on a less discriminatory basis.[21]

The fate of the reapportionment bill in the 1920s stood in stark contrast to that of immigration restriction. While the restriction lobby and Congress relentlessly overcame every practical and theoretical objection to restriction during the decade, Congress collapsed into confusion and

Association, 1931: Proceedings 1 (Washington, D.C.: GPO, 1932): 103–441. Jameson claimed to be the originator of this report some years later; see Jameson to Thomas A. Capek, Sept. 28, 1936, in *An Historian's World: Selections from the Correspondence of J. Franklin Jameson,* ed. Elizabeth Donnan and Leo F. Stock (Philadelphia: American Philosophical Society, 1956), p. 363. For the perspective of the Census Advisory Committee, see Records of the Social and Economic Statistics Administration, box 1, file 11, NN374–63, RG 29, NA. For a recent effort to rework the numbers and evaluate Jameson and Barker's efforts, see Forrest McDonald and Ellen Shapiro McDonald, "The Ethnic Origins of the American People, 1790," *William and Mary Quarterly,* 3d ser., 37 (1980): 179–99, and Thomas L. Purvis, "The European Ancestry of the United States Population, 1790," Donald H. Akenson, "Why the Accepted Estimates of the Ethnicity of the American People, 1790, Are Unacceptable," and Purvis, Akenson, and McDonald and McDonald, "Commentary," ibid. 41 (1984): 85–135.

21. In the *Legacy of Malthus,* Allan Chase points out the implications of national origins for Jews trying to immigrate to the United States to escape the Holocaust. See also David S. Wyman, *Paper Walls: America and the Refugee Crisis, 1938–1941* (Amherst, Mass.: University of Massachusetts Press, 1968), and Lionel Maldonado and Joan Moore, eds., *Urban Ethnicity in the United States: New Immigrants and Old Minorities* (Beverly Hills, Calif.: Sage Publications, 1985).

legislative stalemate every time opponents of the pending bill raised a technical objection to reapportionment. Because the political implications to reapportionment as usual were so unpalatable, Congress examined the reapportionment process particularly closely. They of course discovered that the seemingly objective and simple mathematical process of allocating House seats could be accomplished in many ways—all requiring political decisions about the character of the state.

Four basic issues emerged at the consideration of each bill. Throughout the 1920s, stalemate on one or another of these issues prevented passage of a bill. And, of course, the statistical experts at the Census Bureau were called on to explain the technical issues and suggest solutions.

First, Congress had to determine the size of the House. In the past, Congress had varied—primarily by increasing—the size of the House to ease political tensions resulting from reapportionment. Second, Congress had to determine the method of apportionment. As Balinski and Young have described, mathematically, there are many ways to apportion a legislative body, and the different methods favor one or another political constituency. In the 1920s, Congress debated whether to use "major fractions"—the new name for Webster's method—or "equal proportions"—a new method devised by Joseph Hill and championed by Edward Huntington. As the debate evolved, a prominent census statistician defended each method. Walter Willcox favored major fractions and Joseph Hill advocated equal proportions.[22]

22. Balinski and Young, *Fair Representation,* pp. 36–66. Webster's method, renamed "major fractions" by Walter Willcox, required that Congress first set the size of the House and then find a divisor "so that the whole numbers nearest to the quotients of the states sum" to the chosen total (p. 32). Fractions below 0.5 were rounded down, while those at or above 0.5 were rounded up. Hill's method of "equal proportions" required that Congress first set the size of the House and then allocate seats to the states "so that no transfer of any one seat can reduce the percentage difference in representation between those states." Hill argued that "the ratios of the number of inhabitants per Representative should be as nearly uniform as possible" (pp. 47–48).

The problem for all apportionments is the treatment of remainders. See chap. 1, above. Consider the following example of four states with a total population of 8,400 people; 84 seats are apportioned with a divisor of 100:

State	Population	Webster's apportionment	Inhabitants/ representative
1	145	1	145
2	160	2	80
3	4,040	40	101
4	4,055	41	99
Total	8,400	84	

For the states "entitled" to 1.45 or 40.4 representatives, Webster's method would drop the fraction and give the states 1 and 40 representatives, respectively. The other states,

Third, Congress had to decide if the census results were sufficiently accurate to provide an adequate population base for apportionment. In years past the bureau had struggled with fraudulent, inflated city counts or the zealous protests of city boosters who claimed that the bureau had undercounted their population. In 1920 congressional critics attacked the bureau for undercounting the rural population. The winter census date and the war had temporarily inflated city populations, critics charged. Census takers had missed rural households because of the bad weather. Had the census been taken in the spring, they claimed, the rural or farm population would have been significantly larger.

Finally, Congress again discussed the appropriate population base for apportionment. Was it to be the total population as in the past, or should Congress implement Section 2 of the Fourteenth Amendment to deny representation to southern states that barred black voting? Southerners countered these proposals and suggested that aliens should also be excluded from the apportionment base because northern states—and particularly northern cities—should not receive representation for an unenfranchised population. At the time, the census showed that many immigrants did not choose to become American citizens.

The technical difficulties of reapportionment emerged almost as soon as Congress began to consider a bill. As mentioned, Rep. Isaac Siegel initially proposed that the size of the House be increased to 483 so that no state would lose a seat. This bill was amended on the House floor to keep

---

entitled to 1.6 or 40.55 representatives, would receive 2 and 41 representatives, respectively. The number of inhabitants per representative ranges from 80 to 145. Hill found this discrepancy objectionable. Hill's method would ask a further question. If rounding leads to discrepancies between the number of inhabitants per representative that could be reduced by shifting a seat from one state to another, the shift should be made until no other shifts would reduce the percentage difference. Since the ratio difference between states 1 and 4 (1.46) could be reduced to 1.41 by moving a representative from state 4 to state 1, Hill would make the move:

State	Hill's apportionment	Inhabitants/ representative	Quotient with divisor of 102
1	2	72	1.42
2	2	80	1.56
3	40	101	39.60
4	40	101	39.80
Total	84		

Balinski and Young point out that, mathematically, Hill's method in this case is equivalent to using a divisor of 102 and rounding up any quotient that exceeded the geometric mean between the two numbers. The geometric mean of 1 and 2 equals 1.414, so state 1's quotient of 1.42 would be rounded up to 2. For small states in some circumstances, Hill's method grants a state an extra representative although the fraction is between 0.414 and 0.5.

the size of the House at 435 and in this form went to the Senate. The states that would lose representatives objected and killed the bill.

But there was also a second technical issue: the method of apportionment. From 1880 to 1900, Congress had noticed a recurring anomaly, the "Alabama paradox," in the then-used Vinton method of apportionment. The Census Bureau had pointed out to Congress that under certain circumstances, when the size of the House was increased, a state could lose a seat. Such an apportionment violated common sense; Congress had avoided the paradox by setting the House size to prevent the anomaly from occurring. By 1900, Census Bureau statisticians began to work seriously on the mathematics of the paradox to try to discover its cause. In 1911, Walter Willcox recommended that Congress use Webster's method of apportionment, or what he called "the method of major fractions," to avoid the Alabama paradox. Congress accepted Willcox's recommendation for the 1910 apportionment. At the same time, Joseph Hill, assistant director of the bureau, also worked on the issue. He had devised another method, which came to be called "equal proportions." And it turned out that these two methods gave results that paralleled the political splits in the apportionment debate. Willcox's method provided consistently better representation for the larger (urban) states; Hill's favored the smaller (rural) states. The question arose: Which was the most "scientific" or "unbiased"?

Congress had decided that it did not understand the mathematical niceties of the two methods. It had chosen Willcox's method because it had been used before 1850 and seemed to work. In January 1921, however, Harvard mathematics professor Edward V. Huntington, an old friend of Hill's, threw his professional weight behind Hill's method and wrote to Congress and the *New York Times* to endorse the method of equal proportions. The issue was no longer a mere academic debate. If Congress used Hill's 1920 apportionment rather than Willcox's, Huntington pointed out, they would take seats away from New York, North Carolina, and Virginia and give them to Rhode Island, Vermont, and New Mexico. How could one pass an apportionment bill if the methods of apportionment were so arbitrary?

The Sixty-sixth Congress adjourned in March 1921 without passing an apportionment bill. When the next Congress convened a few weeks later, the House Census Committee, hoping to break the stalemate, introduced a new bill. This bill set the size of the House at 460; only Maine and Missouri would lose a seat. On the House floor, members who wished to maintain the House at 435 members tried to amend the bill but failed. The bill was recommitted to the House Census Committee in October 1921. The issue continued to seethe within the House Census Committee, and the depth of the stalement slowly became evident. Citing Section 2 of the Fourteenth Amendment, Northerners proposed that southern representation be reduced in proportion to the disenfranchisement of blacks. Southern congressmen countered by proposing that aliens be excluded from the population base for apportionment. Republican George Tinkham of Massachusetts suggested a new census to break the stalemate. But no resolution to these conflicting proposals could be found. The committee did not report out a bill for the remainder of the Sixty-seventh Congress.[23]

Nor did the committee report a bill in the Sixty-eighth Congress. By the time the Sixty-ninth Congress convened in December 1925 the situation was approaching scandal. The House Census Committee held hearings on the issue in the winter of 1925–26, but again the committee could not report a bill. Supporters of reapportionment proposed moving a bill directly to the House floor without committee approval. The House voted this procedural motion down by a vote of 265 to 87 in April 1926.

This scenario repeated itself in the second session of the Sixty-ninth Congress with minor modifications. In hearings held during the winter of 1927, Edward Huntington, Joseph Hill, Walter Willcox, and Allyn Young testified on the merits of an apportionment based on major fractions or equal proportions. Congress remained thoroughly confused. Further, by the late 1920s, the 1930 census was fast approaching. Should Congress even bother to reapportion so late in the decade? Why not wait until the results of the 1930 census were in?[24]

Proponents of reapportionment found this argument even more dangerous. If Congress had failed to reapportion itself for the previous six years, they asked, why would a Congress in 1930 or after find the issue an easier one? Demographic trends revealed that urban areas continued to grow. Rapid urban population growth had not been merely an artifact of the war. Rather, the states that would benefit or lose from the 1920 apportionment would be the same ones that would benefit or lose from the 1930 apportionment. No, it would not do to postpone the issue.

Advocates of compromise recognized by the late 1920s that an innovative proposal was needed to break the logjam. Congress had rejected bills both to increase the size of the House and to maintain the size of the House. The House Census Committee could not decide on either Willcox's or Hill's methods of apportionment. A major constitutional crisis was brewing.

On March 3, 1927, the final day of the Sixty-ninth Congress, Republican representative E. Hart Fenn of Connecticut suggested a new pos-

23. *New York Times*, May 15, 1922, p. 4.

24. "Congressman Dodge Reapportionment," *Literary Digest* 89 (Apr. 24, 1926): 12; "Congress Evades Reapportionment," ibid. 92 (Feb. 19, 1927): 13; Joseph A. Hill, "Events Leading Up to the Present Situation in Congress as Regards Apportionment and the Census," Mar. 30, 1929, Records of the Census Advisory Committee, box 72, series 148, RG 29, NA.

sibility. He introduced a bill that had been discussed in the House Census Committee but had not received committee approval. He proposed to bypass the committee and introduce a ministerial apportionment based on the results of the 1930 census. He conceded that it was too late to reapportion according to the 1920 census and suggested that Congress return to a precedent set by the automatic features of the 1850 census law. Under Fenn's bill, the secretary of Commerce would report an apportionment based on the 1930 census results, and that apportionment would take effect in March 1933. Fenn's bill was defeated on a procedural vote of 187 to 199. Opponents objected that the Sixty-ninth Congress could not bind a future Congress.[25]

When the Seventieth Congress convened in December 1927, Fenn reintroduced the bill, and the debate began anew. Again the House Census Committee grappled with the methods to be used, and again Willcox, Huntington, Hill, and others confused the committee members in public hearings. But pressure for a solution was mounting; the press and the public were giving the issue closer attention. Critics pointed out that, regardless of the technical problems, the "reapportionment slackers" in Congress had to end their "brazen defiance" of the Constitution and pass a bill. By 1928, William Starr Myers pointed out in an article in the *North American Review* that the electoral college was so unrepresentative of the population that a majority of the electorate could vote for one candidate in 1928 but the electoral college could elect his opponent.[26]

And so key congressmen continued to work on the issue. The ministerial apportionment features of the Fenn bill seemed a promising approach, but its defenders had to meet the objections of opponents. One by one, the committee confronted these problems and amended the bill. One of the most crucial was offered by Democratic representative Meyer Jacobstein of New York. He proposed adding a clause to the ministerial apportionment features making them contingent on the inaction of Congress. In other words, the automatic apportionment would only go into effect if Congress took no action—as it had done in the 1920s. Thus a present Congress would not bind a future Congress, but neither would reapportionment be delayed. In this form, Fenn's bill went to the House floor in May 1928. It employed Willcox's method of apportionment. After two days of debate it was recommitted to the Census Committee.

In the second session of the Seventieth Congress, supporters of the bill tried again. The House speaker sought advice from the National Academy of Sciences on the relative merits of Hill's and Willcox's methods of

25. *Congressional Digest* 7, no. 2 (1928): 340–43.

26. "Congressmen Dodge Reapportionment"; "Congress Evades Reapportionment"; William Starr Myers, "An Unconstitutional President?" *North American Review* 226, no. 4 (1928): 385–89.

apportionment. The Census Committee made minor changes in the Fenn bill and reintroduced it in early January 1929. Debate on the House floor was again impassioned and complex. Again, southern representatives objected to the ministerial apportionment features of the bill. But time was finally beginning to work a subtle change in the tone of the debate. The 1930 census was only a year away. The enabling bill for the 1930 census had been placed on the legislative calendar. It was no longer easy simply to postpone the issue by raising either technical objections to this or that method of apportionment or doubts about the accuracy of the 1920 census.[27]

Further, supporters of reapportionment had learned from hard years of struggling with the issue that only compromise would break the stalemate. They were willing to jettison or change any objectionable features in the bill if that would facilitate its passage. And so, when Congressman Ralph Lozier of Missouri protested that any ministerial apportionment bill should not also contain language setting districting requirements or deadlines for state legislatures to reapportion, Fenn and his colleagues took notice. On January 11, he moved to delete Sections 3, 4, and 5 from the bill.[28]

These sections required that representatives be elected by single districts and that the districts "be composed of contiguous and compact territory and contain as nearly as practicable the same number of individuals." They also set rules for at-large elections of members if the state legislatures did not redistrict in time for the next election. In case a state received "an increased number of Representatives," such new members could temporarily be elected at large. If a state lost a congressman and did not redistrict, all members were to be elected at large until the state legislature redistricted. Similar language had been routinely included in reapportionment bills since 1840. At the time, little was said about the deletion of these sections. Some congressmen felt that the language was extraneous. Others argued that the language from old reapportionment bills not specifically repealed by the current bill would remain in force and thus that there was no need to repeat the language. Overall, passage of a viable reapportionment bill was the only question at hand. Districting seemed relatively unimportant.[29]

In this form H.R. 11725 passed the House on January 11, 1929. For the first time since January 1921, the full House had passed a reapportionment bill.

27. Hill, "Events Leading Up to the Present Situation . . . ," *Congressional Digest* 8, no. 2 (1929): 33–53, 57, 64.
28. *Congressional Record,* 70th Cong., 2d sess., 1929, pp. 1496, 1499, 1584, 1602, 1604, 1606.
29. H.R. 11725; the text of the original bill is in *Congressional Digest* 8, no. 2 (1929): 35.

The bill went immediately to the Senate, where things went badly. In February the National Academy of Sciences committee reported that it favored the method of equal proportions over the method of major fractions; H.R. 11725 employed major fractions as the method of apportionment. The rural interests, which opposed reapportionment, had much more power in the Senate. Fenn had estimated that seventeen states would lose congressional seats after 1930. Over a third of the senators thus could be expected to be unenthusiastic at best about reapportionment. The bill came up for debate in February, but it never came to a vote. One month later, the Seventieth Congress adjourned.[30]

The new president, Herbert Hoover, called Congress into special session in April 1929. On the agenda were farm relief, the tariff, reapportionment, a census bill, and repeal of the national origins provision of the immigration bill. Reapportionment bills traditionally originated in the House, but leaders demanded that the Senate pass a bill first. Since 1920, the House had sent two bills to the Senate, and the Senate had voted on neither of them. House leaders thus insisted that action start in the Senate.

Senator Arthur Vandenberg of Michigan led the debate; he reintroduced Fenn's bill as it had passed the House in January. Again opponents of reapportionment brought up the question of method; again they suggested that Congress should wait until after the 1930 census results were in to reapportion. Southerners proposed that aliens be excluded from the total population for apportionment purposes. Northerners responded and proposed a reduction in the representation for the southern states that prevented blacks from voting. Supporters of reapportionment had also combined the reapportionment bill and the census law. Planning for the 1930 census was held hostage to passage of the reapportionment bill.

Despite the obstacles, public opinion finally bore down with sufficient weight to move the Senate to pass the bill. The bill then passed the House again and went to conference. In the name of compromise, the conferees defeated amendments to change the apportionment base to exclude aliens or nonvoting blacks. They also amended the bill to include an official census report of an apportionment for 1930 based on both major fractions and equal proportions. On June 18, 1929, Herbert Hoover approved the bill, and the long ordeal of reapportionment was finally at an end.[31]

---

30. Hill, "Events." When the senators who opposed reapportionment killed the bill, supporters of reapportionment refused to act on the bill for the 1930 census.

31. Excluding nonvoting blacks or aliens from the apportionment base would have wrought major changes in the political balance in the House and would have fundamentally changed the nature of the apportionment system. Senator Coleman Blease (D–S.C.) produced data during the 1929 apportionment debate showing that the exclusion of un-

The Census Bureau reported the 1930 census results in December. The numbers were indeed stark. Twenty-one states would lose a combined total of twenty-seven seats in the House; eleven states would gain them. California's delegation grew from eleven to twenty, Michigan's from thirteen to seventeen. Texas gained three seats, New York, New Jersey, and Ohio, two each. Luckily, Hill's and Willcox's reapportionment methods produced identical results for the 1930 data. After twenty years Congress had been reapportioned.[32]

But the last word was not in. In 1932 Stewart Broom of Mississippi sued the state for violating the usual districting requirements of equality of size and contiguity and compactness of territory in its redistricting after the 1930 census. Broom claimed that the state had not followed Congressional guidelines in laying out the new districts. The case went to the United States Supreme Court. The court searched the legislative history of the reapportionment law and concluded that it "was manifestly the intention of the Congress not to re-enact the provision as to compactness, contiguity, and equality in population with respect to the districts to be created pursuant to the reapportionment under the act of 1929." It was, in short, perfectly legal to create gerrymandered and malapportioned congressional districts.

And so the ultimate "solution" to the reapportionment crisis created by the growing power of the urban population of the nation was to reapportion congressional seats among the states but to allow the states themselves to malapportion those seats within the states. By the early 1930s, Walter Willcox pointed out, the size of New York's congressional districts varied by a factor of 7.8. The largest district contained 799,407 people; the smallest 90,671. As with immigration restriction, Congress had found a conservative, backward-looking solution to the "problem" of the rise of new constituencies of the urban industrial society. They would cheat and change the rules of the apportionment game to preserve rural and small-town dominance of legislative halls for another generation. These actions eventually precipitated another reapportionment crisis, the "reapportionment revolution" of the 1960s.[33]

---

naturalized aliens from the apportionment base would shift 10 House seats away from California, Connecticut, Massachusetts, New Jersey, New York, and Pennsylvania. They would go to 10 rural states, 4 in the South (Arkansas, Georgia, Louisiana, and Mississippi), and Indiana, Kansas, Kentucky, Nebraska, Missouri, and Oklahoma.

Similarly, 79% of the black population lived in the South as of 1930. They made up 25% of the South's population. Thus, implementation of Section 2 of the Fourteenth Amendment would cost the South as many as 25 to 30 representatives (*Congressional Record*, 71st Cong., 1st sess., 1929, pp. 1711–14). See also the statement of Sen. Kenneth McKellar (D–Tenn.), who claimed that "the aliens would control" "any close division" "indirectly" (ibid., p. 1962). *Congressional Digest* 8, no. 5 (1929): 155.

32. *Congressional Digest* 9, no. 12 (1930): 314–15.

33. Wood v. Broom, 287 U.S. 1 at 7; Walter Willcox to W. L. Austin, Apr. 22, 1933,

Between the late 1920s and the 1960s, despite increasingly obvious malapportionment of Congress and state legislatures, reapportionment was not a burning political issue. Several factors drove it from the public agenda. First, and most obviously, the onset of the Great Depression in 1929–30 raised new, frightening questions about the viability of the modern American economy that pushed many of the pressing issues of the 1920s off the legislative agenda. Immigration restriction seemed unnecessary if a depressed economy no longer attracted European migrants. Prohibition appeared to be a foolish crusade. Government policymakers, like the general public, struggled to cope with mass unemployment, the collapse of the locally based social welfare system, the farm economy, and the most prosperous sectors of industry. In the face of the Depression, the census took on new functions. Malapportioned legislatures simply mattered less.

Second, census apportionment mechanisms are supposed to depoliticize the periodic allocation and transfer of power and resources among the elements of the population—in this case, among the states. They are designed to take these questions off the current policy agenda and consign them to "automatic" allocations. This is not to say that such census apportionment mechanisms are "fair" or politically "neutral." It is, though, to reiterate the conclusions that James Madison and Alexander Hamilton drew from their experience in developing the three-fifths compromise: An imperfect but workable apportionment rule is better than no rule at all and may endure for decades before it is again challenged.

Records of the Chief Statistician, entry 202, RG 29, NA; Calvert Dedrick, "Some Facts on Apportionment," Dec. 3, 1940, Records of the Geography Division, box 6, File: Apportionment, entry 160, RG 29, NA. See also P. J. Taylor and R. J. Johnston, *Geography of Elections* (London: Croom Helm, 1979); Robert Dixon, *Democratic Representation: Reapportionment in Law and Politics* (New York: Oxford, 1968); Robert McKay, *Reapportionment: The Law and Politics of Equal Representation* (New York: Twentieth Century Fund, 1965); and Congressional Quarterly, *Representation and Apportionment* (Washington, D.C.: Congressional Quarterly, 1966).

SEVEN | Counting the Unemployed and the Crisis of the Great Depression

Statistical method and statistical data are never ends in them-selves. They are always accessory to some purpose of control. We should then seek to catch the drift of events, to appraise the changing social issues, if we, as statisticians, are to foresee and understand the tasks to be imposed upon us.

—Stuart A. Rice, 1934

The June 1929 apportionment bill contained the enabling legislation for the 1930 census. Passage of that portion of the bill dealing with the administration of the census had been delayed by the turmoil surrounding reapportion-ment, but by and large the census bill had broad support. In keeping with long-term trends in census legislation, the bill ceded authority over many details of census taking to the Commerce Department and census director. For the first time, the bill did not specify in minute detail the questions to be asked, only the areas to be investigated. In 1930, these were to include population, agriculture, drain-age, distribution, mines, and unemployment. The exact form of the questions was left to the administrative discre-tion of the bureau. Congress changed the date of the enumeration to April 1 due to the dissatisfaction with the 1920 experience of a January enumeration. The decennial census period started in January 1930 and ran for three years.

During 1928 and 1929 the bureau solicited public in-put on questions for 1930. Many changes were suggested. The American Statistical Association and American Economic Association (ASA-AEA) Census Advisory Committee also considered in detail the questions for the various schedules. For the population schedule this resulted in a reduction of the number and complexity of questions dealing with immigration and the foreign-born. The bureau also asked new questions on consumer goods (radio sets), on unemployment, and on veteran status. None of these decisions were particularly controversial. The limited debate centered around the feasibility of particular inquiries—whether, for example, people could answer the questions as asked.[1]

Between the time that the schedules and the census tabulation procedures were planned and the census was actually taken, however, the 1929 stock market crash and the Great Depression had radically changed the economic situation of the country. By the late winter and early spring of 1930 rising unemployment began to put strains on local relief resources. Unemployment protests broke out in major cities. Nevertheless, the Hoover administration asserted that the unemployment situation was not deteriorating. "All the evidences indicate," Hoover stated in early March, "that the worst effects of the crash upon employment will have . . . passed during the next sixty days." He cautioned the country that statements about the severity of unemployment were not based on solid data. He quoted a memorandum from the secretaries of Commerce and Labor: "There are no detailed statistics as to the unemployed, and they can only be approximated." "The forthcoming census," they added, "will show the first real determination of unemployment."[2]

The public naturally looked to the responses to the inquiries on the 1930 census to clarify the unemployment situation. Was unemployment really becoming a serious problem? Was it general or merely concentrated in a few industrial cities? Was it the result of the stock crash or a function of the long-term technological changes affecting American industry? While the census was being taken in April, newspaper reports increasingly discussed such questions.

Unfortunately, despite Hoover's statement of March 1930, the decennial census was not planned to address such concerns. The census measured long-term trends, not short-term shifts in business conditions. It was a decennial enterprise that collected a wide variety of data. Years passed before all the data were cross-tabulated and reported. The only numbers that the bureau planned to report rapidly were the raw population counts for apportionment. Other data had to be coded on punch cards, verified, tabulated, analyzed for mistakes, corrected if necessary, and prepared for publication. Following past practices, the bureau had

1. W. Stull Holt, *The Bureau of the Census* (Washington, D.C.: Brookings Institution, 1929), p. 87; Minutes of the Census Advisory Committee, 1928–29, entry 148, RG 29, NA.

2. *New York Times*, Mar. 8, 1930, pp. 1–2.

already planned a schedule of tabulation. The unemployment data were a relatively low priority and were not scheduled for early release.

Census officials said this to the press in the spring of 1930, but explanations of the niceties of statistical processing did not satisfy those concerned with rising unemployment. Good data were needed, and the census bureau was the most respected of American data collection agencies. Should not procedures be changed to address the obvious policy questions?

These questions put the Census Bureau and the Hoover administration on the spot and began a controversy about the collection and reporting of unemployment and other population data that raged for the next ten years. In the process, the Census Bureau went through a crisis and an institutional restructuring that transformed it into an agency to serve Franklin D. Roosevelt's New Deal. By the early 1940s, despite the outward appearance of continuity, the major personnel, goals, and methods of the agency had changed. And so had the population policies of the federal government.

Symbolic of things to come, the beginning of the partisan controversy over depression unemployment statistics dates from rival press statements from Herbert Hoover and Frances Perkins in late January 1930. Hoover released a statement indicating that federal employment service data showed employment recovering from winter lows. Perkins, then Franklin Roosevelt's industrial commissioner in New York, knew that her own New York State data showed continued increasing unemployment. She challenged Hoover to reveal his data to the press. He declined to do so for technical reasons and charged that she was trying to make a party issue of the data. She charged that Hoover was deceiving the nation about the economic situation.[3]

Both were right in their own way, and both felt vindicated by the exchange. What was lost in this and later such exchanges was a serious nonpartisan estimate of the severity of unemployment. As the depression deepened, the securing of reputations overshadowed debate over the real problems with the statistics.

It is one of the deep ironies of the history of the 1930s that Herbert Hoover found himself attacked for the inadequacies of his economic statistical data. For the previous two decades, he had been one of the chief national exponents of the development of statistical reporting systems.

3. This story is recounted repeatedly in New Deal histories. See Frances Perkins, *The Roosevelt I Knew* (New York: Viking Press, 1946), pp. 93–96; Frank Freidel, *Franklin D. Roosevelt: The Triumph* (Boston: Little, Brown, 1956), pp. 133–34; and Joseph Duncan and William Shelton, *Revolution in United States Government Statistics, 1926–1976* (Washington, D.C.: GPO, 1976), pp. 23–24.

He had been the first secretary of Commerce to realize the potential of the department to provide businesses with the information they needed to operate in a modern bureaucratized economy. He had started the Survey of Current Business; he had encouraged the development of the Census Distribution. And perhaps most poignantly for the history of the 1930s, he had encouraged, sponsored, or organized the major research efforts on unemployment in the 1920s—both within government and among private scholars.

Specifically, when a severe postwar business recession hit the country in 1921, Hoover had convinced President Warren Harding to sponsor a national conference to address the unemployment crisis of the winter of 1921–22. The president's Conference on Unemployment conducted studies of unemployment and published several major volumes of economic analysis, most notably *Business Cycles and Unemployment* in 1923 and *Recent Economic Changes* in 1929. The conference office also monitored the local unemployment situation through the winter of 1921–22. A network of correspondents around the country reported the local situation in minute detail several times a month. These reports, covering several hundred cities, described who was unemployed, for how long, how the local business and political leaders were responding to the situation, and whether there had been hardship, protests, or other forms of social conflict. The reports were not quantified or subjected to any kind of formal analysis, but they were carefully filed and read for "trouble" spots and "improving" "conditions."

Hoover and his academic supporters felt they had made major gains in understanding the causes and cures of unemployment. In particular, they felt, as historian Carolyn Grin put it, that they had discovered the etiology of the business cycle. The unemployment and hardship of an economic downturn were merely the other side of the "waste, extravagance, speculation, inflation, and inefficiency that developed during a boom." Government and business had to develop new mechanisms to curb the extravagances of the boom periods and to foster economic activity during slumps. Hoover's experts recommended such measures as public works in times of downturns, restructuring of "sick" industries, and progressive leadership in industry.[4]

By the late 1920s, Hoover claimed that his policies and studies had "made a large contribution to our post-war stability and prosperity."[5] The economy did pull out of the 1921–22 slump; social unrest was minimized through the winter with judicious voluntary relief measures and enlightened national leadership. Hoover felt that his academic experts were well

4. Grin, "Herbert Hoover and the Social Responsibilities of the Expert: The Quantitatively Trained Idealist" (typescript, September 1971, HHPL), p. 19.

5. Ibid.

on their way to understanding how a modern economy functioned. Early in his presidency, he commissioned a second major study of American institutions—intended to be a companion effort to the earlier reports. *Recent Social Trends* appeared in 1932 and displayed a similar breadth and depth of analysis of contemporary American life.[6]

Nevertheless, from the perspective of the depression experience, this tradition of scholarship had serious deficiencies. In particular, none of Hoover's studies had ever developed a reliable, accurate, and continuous measure of unemployment. In late 1921, the Committee on Statistics of the Unemployment Conference was unable to develop a consensus on how to measure unemployment. Extrapolating from payroll data, they developed crude estimates of the number of people unemployed nationally. Different members of the committee calculated figures ranging from 3 million to 5.7 million unemployed. They also could not agree on a method to calculate an unemployment rate. Should the denominator be the total population, the total working population, or some subset thereof, such as the nonagricultural working population? The conference disbanded without reconciling the discrepancies; no new studies were commissioned to solve the problem.[7]

For the rest of the 1920s, the Bureau of Labor Statistics published monthly unemployment statistics by collecting information from most manufacturing and some nonmanufacturing industries. The American Federation of Labor published reports on the proportion of its members unemployed in various trades. Private business reporting services also reported payroll and employment data. No national statistic, however, was generally agreed upon for either the number of unemployed or the rate of unemployment.

Hoover's inattention to the question of unemployment statistics was a function of his and his supporters' notions of who should manage the economy and how it should be managed. Repeatedly, he and his advisers defined unemployment as "a production problem." Attention should be focused on wasteful and inefficient management practices. As he described his thinking to E. E. Hunt in preparation for the Unemployment

6. The literature on Hoover's sponsorship of academic scholarship is a rich and growing one. See, e.g., Grin, "Herbert Hoover"; Grin, "The Unemployment Conference of 1921: An Experiment in National Cooperative Planning," *Mid-America* 55 (April 1973): 83–107; Ellis Hawley, *The Great War and the Search for a Modern Order: A History of the American People and Their Institutions, 1917–1933* (New York: St. Martin's Press, 1979); Barry Karl, "Presidential Planning and Social Science Research: Mr. Hoover's Experts," *Perspectives in American History* 3 (1969): 347–409. The records of the Unemployment Conference are at HHPL. Included in the collection are 15 boxes of local reports from fall 1921 to spring 1922 with files identifying "trouble" or "improving" locations.

7. See "Progress Report of the Committee on Unemployment Statistics, September 30, 1921," box 638, Commerce Papers, HHPL.

Conference, Hoover wanted "to 'get over' the conception of the employers' obligation. The one who can do something now is the employer." Unemployment insurance, on the European model, was "neither desirable nor practicable in America." Hunt suggested that perhaps it might be necessary to "explain to workmen the necessity for reduction in hours and wages." Yet the major thrust of their work was "to bring home to the public mind the significance of the business cycle and enlist the individual enterprise of business managers . . . in this work of regularizing employment within their own establishments." There was to be no "palliation or tonic from the public treasury." From such a perspective, it was necessary to know which employers were not using their workers efficiently, where there was too much seasonal or part-time work. It was not important to know much about the situation of the individual workers and their families, the level of hardship they faced, the effects of unemployment on their lives.[8]

The Depression, however, raised precisely these issues of the impact of unemployment on the individual, the family, the community. Hence, when in March 1930 Hoover advised his critics to wait for the results of the 1930 census, he left himself vulnerable to continued attacks on his data and his credibility.

The census was taken in April, and the first reports of the results began to dribble out by midmonth. Meanwhile, Democratic senator Robert Wagner of New York held hearings on three bills he had introduced to cope with the worsening unemployment situation. One dealt with improving the Bureau of Labor Statistics unemployment data. The second called for the creation of a construction planning agency to authorize and fund countercyclical public works projects. The third would establish a national system of labor exchanges. Hoover disapproved of these measures but had no alternatives.[9]

In the face of this public debate, census officials thus found themselves pressured to present the results of the unemployment census as quickly as possible. They responded with bewilderment. From their perspective, the unemployment inquiry was one of the distinctly secondary inquiries in the count. The question had been dropped in the 1920 census because the statisticians had considered the data unreliable. In December 1928, the ASA-AEA Census Advisory Committee had recommended that the inquiry be omitted again in 1930. Senator Wagner, however, had amended

8. Memorandum, Hoover to Hunt and Hunt to Hoover, Sept. 1, 1921, box 654, Unemployment, Commerce Papers, HHPL; Hoover quoted in Daniel Nelson, *Unemployment Insurance: The American Experience, 1915–1935* (Madison, Wis.: University of Wisconsin Press, 1969), pp. 37–38.

9. Irving Bernstein, *The Lean Years: A History of the American Worker, 1920–1933* (Boston: Houghton Mifflin, 1960), pp. 267–69.

the census bill to include an unemployment question, so the data were collected.

They were collected, though, on a separate unemployment schedule. These had to be separately handled and tabulated. And, the unemployment schedule had to be matched to the responses on the population schedule so that the relevant background information on the unemployed, such as race, sex, age, and occupation, could be tallied with the unemployment data. It was, in short, a monumental bureaucratic problem to report the data.[10]

The pressure was so intense, however, that on May 27, 1930, Census Director William Mott Steuart agreed to release the unemployment results as quickly as they could be counted off the raw schedules. In late June, Commerce Secretary Robert P. Lamont reported that 2.3 million to 2.5 million Americans were unemployed in April 1930. The numbers were immediately challenged as too low. Critics charged that the true number of unemployed was between 4.0 million and 6.6 million. This wide discrepancy led to further inquiry into how the data were collected and what assumptions the census officials had made.[11]

The ensuing public discussions revealed that the officials had no clear conception of how to count the unemployed when they planned the census. They thus intended to cast as wide a net as possible—ultimately providing seven measures of the number of unemployed. When Steuart agreed to publish preliminary hand counts directly from the unemployment schedules, he chose the most conservative count possible. The administration data initially included neither the number of workers with a job but who were laid off nor new workers who were looking for jobs but had not yet found them. When those classes of the unemployed were added to the administration figures, the size of the unemployed population grew dramatically. As the controversy raged during the summer of 1930, the bureau statistician working on the data, Charles Persons, resigned and went to the press to protest the Hoover administration's figures. Wagner's statistics bill passed Congress in July. Hoover appointed an unemployment statistical commission to report on changes in Labor Department data.

Throughout these controversies, Hoover and his cabinet officials con-

10. For a copy of the schedules, see Bureau of the Census, *Population and Housing Inquiries in U.S. Decennial Censuses, 1790–1970*, working paper no. 39 (Washington, D.C.: GPO, 1973), pp. 145–49. In 1880, 1890, and 1900 the census had asked people declaring a gainful occupation the number of months they were unemployed during the previous year. In 1910, the census had asked employees if they were unemployed on the census day and how many weeks they were "out of work during the year 1909." Not much had been done with this data, because the statisticians could not decide how to interpret the answers, e.g., whether to separate those on voluntary or seasonal layoff from those wanting work.

11. See, e.g., *New York Times*, May 27, June 27, 28, 29, July 7, 10, 26, 27, Aug. 31, 1930.

tinued to assert that unemployment was not as bad as critics charged. Hoover, for example, claimed that the census figures were actually too high because some people listed as unemployed were not really looking for work. In August 1930, when the members of the unemployment statistical commission were appointed, Secretary of Labor James Davis commented that "he believed a study of statistics would reveal a steady decrease in unemployment." He predicted that "[m]uch of the unemployment which prevailed throughout the Winter and Spring and has been prevailing to some extent by reason of the drought, should vanish . . . with the revival of industry."[12]

By the fall, as most of the local reports were made, the census officials hoped that the issue would go away and that they could return to the business of tabulating the bulk of the census. To an extent it did, as public discussion shifted to the relief needs for the upcoming winter. In October, Hoover bowed to public pressure and appointed the President's Emergency Committee for Employment (PECE) to address the winter's needs. Modeled on the 1921 Unemployment Conference, PECE was to encourage employers to maintain employment, monitor local relief needs, and help coordinate "local responsibility and local initiative." PECE was set up as a temporary agency with no funds of its own to provide relief or sponsor public works. It was headed by Arthur Woods, World War I army colonel and official from the 1921 Unemployment Conference, former New York City Police commissioner, teacher, reporter, and businessman. PECE also addressed the question of the magnitude and size of the need. Hoover appointed an advisory committee of employment experts, including Bryce Stewart and Leo Wolman. Like the 1921 conference, the major thrust of the committee was to be on publicity and public relations—to alert employers of the special needs of the unemployed in the winter months. Once employment picked up in the spring, Hoover theorized, PECE would disband, and private initiative would resume.[13]

The administration expected unemployment to rise during the winter months, and PECE's efforts were designed to cushion the impact of the rise: by encouraging part-time employment and job sharing, by deporting illegal aliens, and by encouraging local relief efforts. Opponents of this approach, including the growing number of labor economists and social workers who supported some form of unemployment insurance and federalization of relief, kept pointing to the magnitude and duration of unemployment since the crash. For example, the American Statistical Association's Committee on Government Labor Statistics (CGLS), headed

12. *New York Times*, Aug. 21, 1930. See also Charles E. Persons, "Census Reports on Unemployment in April, 1930," *Annals of the American Academy of Political and Social Science* 154 (March 1931): 12–16.

13. Quoted in Irving Bernstein, *Lean Years*, p. 303.

by Mary Van Kleeck of the Russell Sage Foundation, was pressing for new data. Things were getting worse, they argued; the 1921–22 experience was not comparable to the winter of 1930–31.

Accordingly, both sides looked for reliable information and statistics to back their positions, and the debate about the quality of the data reopened. By late November, the Census Bureau began to release the state reports from the unemployment census. Administration critics, including members of PECE and CGLS, responded by calling for a second unemployment census. Extrapolating from Bureau of Labor Statistics reports and business statistics, the experts charged that the April data were inadequate to understand the situation.

At the same time, the ASA-AEA Census Advisory Committee met and discussed the issue. With the support of senior Census Bureau officials they advised against a second census of the unemployed. As word leaked out of their decision, however, intense political pressure on the secretary of Commerce reversed it. "The unemployment question keeps coming up," William Mott Steuart wrote to committee chair Walter Willcox on December 8. The secretary, Steuart continued, wanted to know if the committee would like to "help him by concurring in his efforts to meet the popular demand for this census by modifying its resolutions." Willcox telegraphed back that he did not think the committee should bow to political pressure and rescind the decision. The December 1930 issue of the *Journal of the American Statistical Association (JASA)* therefore recorded the Census Bureau's announcement of the January 1931 unemployment census, the ASA-AEA committee's disapproval of a special census, and the CGLS's endorsement of it. The statistical community was beginning to fracture along political lines.[14]

Meanwhile, Hoover administration officials discussed internally whether unemployment was becoming a serious problem. Statisticians and labor economists knew that vast seasonal differences in the number of unemployed existed; they knew also that workers in traditionally seasonal industries often had secondary occupations during the slack times of the year. The question was, as J. Frederick Dewhurst wrote confidentially to the Commerce secretary in November 1930, how much unemployment was "normal," how much a result of the crash. Using 1929 as a base year, Dewhurst determined that unemployment ranged from almost 2.5 million in the winter to a low of .5 million in the summer. He subtracted these figures from the 1930 numbers to assess the severity of the depression. By such calculations, unemployment did not "really" begin to grow sharply

14. Steuart to Willcox, Dec. 11, 1930, File: November 1930 Advisory Committee, entry 148, Records of the Census Advisory Committee, RG 29, NA. For the resolution of the advisory committee, see *JASA* 26 (1931): 272. See also Mary Van Kleeck, "The Federal Unemployment Census of 1930," *Proceedings of the American Statistical Association* (December 1930): 189–200.

until the summer of 1930, when the normal seasonal decline in unemployment did not occur. The April 1930 data indicated that 1.2 million more workers than normal were unemployed; the September 1930 data indicated 2.9 million more unemployed than normal. From such a perspective, the national response to the crisis was right on time; the winter of 1930–31, Dewhurst admitted, would be a hard one.

The Hoover administration expected the January 1931 special unemployment census to show dramatic figures for the number of unemployed. According to its analysis, the "unusual" unemployment generated by the stock crash would be compounded by the "normal" seasonal winter unemployment peak. Thus in March 1931, Secretary of Commerce Lamont could report with assurance that the administration was not surprised by the figure of 6.05 million unemployed workers counted in the January 1931 census. "Since the time of the census," Lamont continued, "there has been evidence of a slight but unmistakable improvement in the employment situation." He cited Bureau of Labor Statistics data and the reports collected by PECE. The worst was behind the nation. Lamont concluded that the "results of the unemployment census give definite evidence of the proportions of the great task which has been before the nation." Nevertheless, "effective relief activities" kept "distress at a minimum." Local community efforts would continue in order to cope with the problem. PECE concluded its activities in mid-1931 and waited for prosperity to return.[15]

In the spring of 1931, though, the worst was not yet behind the nation. Local relief efforts were edging toward the breaking point; the European banking crisis was about to send the economy into an even more serious decline. Further, Hoover alienated many of the experts in the labor and welfare fields who had supported him in the past when he vetoed the Wagner Employment Service bill in March. Hoover's Advisory Committee on Employment Statistics reported in February and provided a plan for improving the national system of employment and unemployment statistics, but the report fell on deaf ears. From mid-1931 on, discussion of the nation's unemployment statistics died as political opposition to Hooverism grew. As Daniel Nelson has shown, labor and relief reform efforts and analysis shifted to the state level.[16]

In such an atmosphere the census dropped from the public stage, and the bureau quietly proceeded to finish processing the 1930 count. Hoover

15. J. F. Dewhurst to the Secretary, Nov. 11, 1930, box 1136, Correspondence of Bryce M. Stewart, PECE/POUR Collection, HHPL; "Statement of Secretary Lamont on Special Unemployment Census," Mar. 21, 1931, box 337, Unemployment-Census Reports, Presidential Papers, HHPL.

16. "Report of the Advisory Committee on Employment Statistics," Feb. 9, 1931, box 337, Unemployment File, Presidential Papers, HHPL; Nelson, *Unemployment Insurance*, chaps. 7–8.

created another agency to coordinate unemployment relief during the winter of 1931–32, but the President's Organization on Unemployment Relief (POUR) made no effort to develop a systematic understanding of unemployment. The nation passed into a grimmer period of economic decline. By mid-1932, the gross national product had dropped almost 30 percent since 1929; unemployment rose above 10 million. Prices had fallen over 20 percent. Relief payments by state and local governments had quadrupled from 1929 levels. The banking system teetered on the verge of collapse. Hoover and Congress continued to feud over the propriety of federal antidepression efforts. Hoover vetoed or threatened to veto spending measures that would unbalance the federal budget or disrupt the historic division of responsibility between federal, state, and local governments. The Economy Act of 1932 cut federal expenditures to balance the budget. In November, Franklin D. Roosevelt was overwhelmingly elected president and pledged to offer a "new deal" to the American people.[17]

Census Bureau officials watched the unfolding political events and pondered their future. The bureau felt Hoover's budget cuts at the end of 1932 when the official decennial census period ended. Though no programs were canceled, the agency budget was 27 percent below the requested appropriation for the year. Longtime bureau officials such as Director Steuart and Assistant Director Joseph Hill had faced such cuts before. They remembered the fate of the bureau in 1912 when Wilson was elected, and they knew that they might face similar difficulties under the incoming Democrats.[18]

As many historians have documented, Franklin Roosevelt's election in November 1932 signaled a major shift in federal responsibility and philosophy toward the economy and the welfare of the population. Roosevelt would forge new institutions and new approaches to the problems of the Depression that fundamentally changed the character and reach of the federal government. To do so, he and his officials had to take hold of the existing federal institutions and mold or remake them to serve the new purposes. At the time, however, it was unclear how this process would develop. There was also an ambiguous four-month interregnum between Roosevelt's election in November and his assumption of power in March in which federal government policy making was on hold. During that time the Depression deepened; the banking system collapsed. Roosevelt said little about his concrete plans. Relations with the outgoing Hooverites were often barely cordial. Census Bureau officials watched and waited.

17. For POUR's role in measuring unemployment, see Bernstein, *Lean Years*, pp. 460–62.
18. Joseph Hill reported annually to *JASA* on the state of the bureau; see *JASA* 27 (December 1932): 436.

The Census Bureau was, as it turned out, one of those not very glamorous agencies whose smooth functioning was absolutely essential to the Roosevelt agenda. Roosevelt's advisers desperately needed to know where particular programs were to be targeted, how many people would need farm aid, how many work relief, how many general relief. By 1935 his aides were turning to the Census Bureau to determine the cost and scope of the new social security system. Many agencies collected pieces of these data, but it was the census bureau—as the closest agency to a central statistical bureau in the government—which always had as full a picture as there was.

Ironically, however, for the New Dealers, the Census Bureau was also a Republican bastion. As part of Hoover's favored Commerce Department and as a longtime Republican stronghold, the agency was targeted, like other Commerce Department offices, for political cutbacks. Seasoned politicians knew that the Commerce Department was the home of many a Republican loyalist. The agencies served business; their ambience was conservative. Their senior officials could be expected to resist or misunderstand New Deal initiatives.

Accordingly, in the months after Roosevelt's inauguration, the Census Bureau confronted two contradictory sets of pressures. On the one hand, officials throughout the new administration turned to the bureau for data to address the Depression crisis. On the other, bureau officials faced a new and much more severe round of budget cuts, as the New Deal Economy Act sought to reduce the size and power of the agencies that had traditionally had Hooverian Republican political leanings. New Dealers demanded that the bureau do more with fewer resources, and a new phase in the controversy about the character and quality of the statistical system began.[19]

Roosevelt took office in early March, and new leadership in the Commerce Department and the Census Bureau signaled the beginning of change in the American statistical system. William Mott Steuart, census director since 1921, retired. Daniel Roper, the initiator of the cotton statistics program in 1900 and longtime Democratic party activist, became secretary of Commerce. Roper had worked in related federal bureaucracies through the Wilson years and knew the inner workings of the agencies. In early April, he appointed William Lane Austin, a longtime official in the Census Bureau and a Democrat, to be the new census director.

Outside the Commerce Department even more dramatic changes were taking place. Shortly after she took her new post as secretary of Labor, Frances Perkins asked Stuart A. Rice (fig. 17), president of the American

19. Frank Freidel, *Franklin D. Roosevelt: Launching the New Deal* (Boston: Little, Brown, 1973), pp. 237–54.

17. Stuart A. Rice, Assistant Director, Census Bureau, and officials advertising census
products, 1930s. Stuart Rice, center, with Ralph C. Janoschka of the business division and
unidentified official, illustrate the role that census data could play for New Deal recovery
programs. Here, circa November 1933, they prepare a display in the anteroom outside the
office of the secretary of Commerce. The 1930 census volumes provided data for meeting
code requirements for the National Recovery Administration.

Statistical Association, to create "an advisory committee . . . to advise me
regarding the method, adequacy, usefulness, and general program of the
Bureau of Labor Statistics." Rice appointed the Advisory Committee to
the Secretary of Labor (ACSL) in April. It was chaired by Bryce M. Stewart;
Ewan Clague became secretary. Many of its members had been on the
ASA's Committee on Government Labor Statistics. Perkins's request effectively institutionalized the perspective of the CGLS within the New Deal.

But the ACSL was just the beginning. As the major figures from the
American Statistical Association, Social Science Research Council, and
new Roosevelt academic advisers discussed the statistical needs of the
nation in the spring of 1933, it became clear that the new programs—in
particular the National Recovery Administration—would require substantial amounts of data and coordination among statistical programs.
Thus in June of 1933, the ASA and the Social Science Research Council
officially created the Committee on Government Statistics and Informa-

tion Services (COGSIS) to serve the statistical needs of the Agriculture, Commerce, Labor, and Interior departments. Funding came from the Rockefeller Foundation. The committee was housed in the Commerce Department and was initially chaired by Stuart Rice. Edmund E. Day, director of the Rockefeller Foundation, and Frederick Mills of Columbia University served as chairs during its 2½-year existence. Meredith Givens of the Social Science Research Council was its secretary.

As Joseph Duncan and William Shelton have noted, in the "crisis atmosphere" of Washington, D.C., in the spring of 1933, the statisticians had a mandate to shake up the system. "We are facing fundamental changes in the social order," Stuart Rice wrote in his presidential address to the ASA in December 1933. Good statistics were absolutely necessary to "preserve the complexities and hence the standards of our civilization." Without the "social control of an economic mechanism that is no longer self-operating," the nation faced "drastically lowered population and living standards." The federal statistical system needed to be modernized, and it fell to COGSIS to seize the "statistical opportunities and responsibilities" that Rice described.[20]

COGSIS set and achieved some remarkable goals in the field of federal statistics. Many of its members and staff—for example, Bryce M. Stewart and J. Frederick Dewhurst—had worked for the Hoover administration. They were frustrated with the efforts there, but they had conducted many private studies in the 1920s and early 1930s and had come to a rough consensus on what was needed. They wanted new statistical programs— for example, to measure unemployment and address the needs of the unemployed and to institutionalize what we would call macroeconomic statistics. They wanted a coordinating agency to oversee all statistical programs, and they wanted to see statistical research and experimentation organized within the federal government.[21]

This was a tall order, but the ferment of the early New Deal opened many doors. Shortly after its initial meetings, COGSIS members saw their opportunity. The language of the National Industry Recovery Act (NIRA) and Title III of the Economy Act gave Roosevelt the authority to create through executive order institutions that he deemed necessary to the recovery program's success. COGSIS urged Roosevelt to use this authority to create a Central Statistical Board. In late July 1933 Roosevelt did so, naming Winfield Riefler as chair. Riefler had worked for the Federal Reserve Board in the 1920s and was also the economic adviser to the

20. Joseph W. Duncan and William C. Shelton, *Revolution in United States Government Statistics, 1926–1976* (Washington, D.C.: GPO, 1978), pp. 25*ff.*; Stuart A. Rice, "Statistical Opportunities and Responsibilities," *JASA* 29 (March 1934): 1–10.

21. Committee on Government Statistics and Information Services [COGSIS], *Government Statistics*, Social Science Research Council Bulletin 26 (April 1937).

National Emergency Council. The board had the authority "to formulate standards for and to effect coordination of the statistical services of the Federal government incident to the purposes of the National Industrial Recovery Act."[22]

By midsummer 1933 new personnel and new institutions were placed to tackle the problems with the statistical system. It remained to be seen what impact they would have on business as usual in the statistical agencies. The Census Bureau, "the only general-purpose statistical agency of the Federal Government," came in for immediate attention on two issues. First, the budget cuts from the Economy Act of 1933 compounded the cuts already made in 1932 and the natural shrinking of the bureau from the decennial census period. The printing budget was almost gone. Regular statistical programs—such as the collection of data on marriage and divorce—were suspended. Second, and related to the first, personnel decisions in light of the budget cuts seriously weakened the agency's overall strength. In particular, following past practice, senior bureau officials decided against a policy of major layoffs or dismissal of personnel. Instead work was shared; people were transferred among the divisions; salaries were cut. The effect of these policies, though, was to dilute expertise and reward seniority at precisely the point when the outside experts called for new blood and new ideas. As A. Ross Eckler, director of the Census Bureau in the 1960s, recalled, "In 1933, the Bureau had only three Ph.D.'s and only one professional man under forty-five years of age." A confrontation loomed between the bureau's staff and the New Dealers on COGSIS.[23]

The New Dealers resolved to begin their efforts to remake the bureau by installing a high-level official in the agency. In August 1933 Stuart A. Rice, president of the ASA and acting chair of COGSIS, sacrificed his career to become assistant director of the bureau. Joseph Hill, who had held this post during the decennial census period since 1910 and had been on the bureau staff since the 1900 census, became the head of the new Division of Statistical Research. Hill was in his seventies at the time. The new appointments served a dual purpose. Rice was able to exert direct control to remake the bureau, and Hill could use his considerable expertise to achieve another COGSIS goal: the creation of a research arm within the bureau. He was expected to hire younger statisticians who would then take his place when he retired.

Austin and Rice, with support from COGSIS, began a major effort to

22. Duncan and Shelton, *Revolution in Statistics,* pp. 146*ff.*; Freidel, *Franklin D. Roosevelt,* pp. 252*ff.*

23. COGSIS, *Government Statistics,* pp. 22, 60*ff.*; A. Ross Eckler, *The Bureau of the Census* (New York: Praeger, 1972), p. 19.

transform the bureau. It was a tall order. Their initial task was to rescind the 29 percent cut in the bureau's budget to restore morale and to prevent the agency from deteriorating further. Over the next few months, they convinced Budget Director Lewis Douglas to supply funds from emergency appropriations and to realize that the bureau was not an agency that wasted taxpayers' money.[24]

Reconstruction of the agency, though, was a much more difficult task and required a variety of complex changes involving administration, programs, and politics. For purposes of restructuring the nation's population statistics, Austin and Rice developed two long-term, related strategies: first, to hire a younger generation of professionally trained statisticians and social scientists to plan and administer the census; second, to expand the population statistics of the bureau beyond those collected in the decennial census to address current policy questions and to sponsor statistical research.

Just how they would implement these changes, however, was unclear in 1933 to any of the chief actors. Austin and Rice, with the help of the Central Statistical Board and the staff of cogsis, began a number of investigations of bureau policies and history to determine their next step. From mid-1933 until early 1935 bureau functions and policies came under careful scrutiny, and the experts found just how massive a task they had taken on. Things were as bad or even worse than they expected. As Rice put it in a memorandum to Austin in September 1934, "In reviewing my experience in the Bureau during the past year, I must confess to something like shock in the continuous discovery of our backwardness and unpreparedness." They discovered that the staff of the bureau was extraordinarily old and thus unlikely to change existing policies. "The average age of the 646 permanent employees of the Bureau on May 29, 1934, was 48.9 years," noted Calvert Dedrick and Morris Copeland in their report to the Central Statistical Board. The average age of the supervisory and official staff was 56; only five employees were ranked as professional statisticians. Dedrick and Copeland further documented disastrous personnel transfer policies that either "reduce[d] the efficiency of the division from which [the employee] was transferred" or resulted "in the transfer of misfits whom nobody wants." The cost accounting system was inadequate. Some bureau divisions—notably the Manufacturing Division—had no written instructions for editing schedules. There were no formal training programs, adequate job descriptions, or work incentives. And, probably most disturbing to the professionally trained men like Rice, bureau personnel were completely ignorant of the developments in

24. Duncan and Shelton, *Revolution in Statistics,* p. 28; Memorandum to the Census Advisory Committee, Sept. 22, 1933, Records of the Census Advisory Committee, box 72, series 148, RG 29, NA.

probability theory that had revolutionized the science of statistics since the turn of the century. Bureau officials did not understand or use sampling theory, correlation coefficients, or calculations of probable error. "Like the incompetent children of great men we are living off our past," concluded Rice.[25]

The studies discovered that previous generations of statisticians had complained about most of the same problems. There was never enough money. From senior to clerical positions, personnel practices had frequently been dictated by patronage needs. The wide swings in work load over the decade precluded carefully planned research efforts. Congress and departmental heads did not appreciate the technical difficulties with the statistics. Remedying these problems would not only require changing existing practices; they also would require restructuring the agency and its programs so that they would not be threatened once the initial glow had worn off the New Deal.[26]

Luckily for those involved, the somewhat messianic atmosphere in the administration insulated the reformers from the difficulties they faced. Stuart Rice saw himself responding to "the most superb leadership of our generation." The "American nation has broken from the moorings of its past," he wrote, and had "embarked upon a crucial national effort to reorganize its economic and social life." His task at the bureau was "to clear away from our cupboard the mouldy remains and dried bones" of a "past era," to "adapt ourselves to the spirit and the needs of the present."[27]

By late 1934, the New Dealers channeled a series of administrative reform proposals through the Central Statistical Board and to Department of Commerce officials. The proposals emphasized that bureau leadership had to be drawn from professional statisticians and social scientists and that new positions had to be created for such appointments. Existing employees had to be trained up to the level of current statistical knowledge. Programs to measure the costs and efficiency of bureau operations had to be created. These were adopted as department policy. By early 1935, the bureau began the slow process of restructuring its personnel.[28]

25. "Confidential Memorandum for the Director," Sept. 3, 1934; COGSIS, Census, 1932–34, Stuart Rice Papers, Harry S. Truman Presidential Library, Independence, Mo.; C. L. Dedrick and Morris A. Copeland to the Committee on Census Inquiries of the Central Statistical Board, Oct. 13, 1934, in Records of the Census Advisory Committee, box 73, series 148, RG 29, NA.

26. COGSIS, *Government Statistics*, Samuel A. Stouffer, "Problems of the Bureau of the Census in Their Relation to Social Science," in National Resources Committee, *Research: A National Resource* (Washington, D.C.: GPO, 1939).

27. Rice to William Lane Austin, Jan. 16, 1934, COGSIS, Census, 1932–34, Stuart Rice Papers, Harry S. Truman Presidential Library.

28. John Dickinson to Secretary Roper, Nov. 13, 1934, and Central Statistical Board attachments, Census Advisory Committee, box 73, series 148, RG 29, NA.

The other goal of the New Deal statisticians—instituting new data collection and analysis programs in the field of population statistics—was much more difficult to achieve. The Census Bureau was still, after all, the Census Bureau, and that meant that the bureau collected data on the population every ten years. In 1933 the bureau had just wound down the 1930 census effort and was not scheduled to take another population census until 1940. It had little statutory authority to conduct population studies in the interim. In fact, the agency was supposed to spend time during the intercensal period working on economic censuses, vital statistics, government statistics, and so on. Thus the New Deal statisticians who wished to create new statistical series on the unemployed, on the aged population, or on depression migrants found that they did not have the capacity to do so in the Census Bureau. In 1933 and 1934, appropriations from the emergency relief agency budgets allowed the statisticians to conduct some experimental new programs, most notably the Civil Works Administration (CWA) Trial Census of the Unemployed. But these programs formed only a temporary solution, since the bureau administration did not control the studies and they were often considered "relief" work for the statisticians themselves.[29]

What the bureau really needed was a special population census, one that would allow the statisticians to test new proposals for sample surveys and to prove to the country as a whole just what a revitalized Census Bureau could do. In late 1933 bureau officials and several congressmen proposed a special mid-decade census to satisfy the needs of the New Deal agencies for fresh data on the American population. Congressman Ralph Lozier of Missouri, a Democrat, introduced a bill for a November 1934 census in the second session of the Seventy-third Congress. The bill passed the House but died in the Senate in June 1934. In late 1934, the Central Statistical Board revived the idea, recommending that a census be taken in the summer or fall of 1935 and requesting a small appropriation to begin the planning work.

Such a census, Stuart Rice explained to the Census Advisory Committee, would provide data for such agencies as the Federal Emergency Relief Administration, the Labor Department, public health agencies, and the implementation of the Agricultural Adjustment Act. And, he continued, the census would be a major step in the research agenda for the bureau—in particular in the area of probability sampling. A subcommittee of the Central Statistical Board had been making "a very thoroughgoing analysis of the problems of sampling and estimating" and had concluded that "there were distinct possibilities of gaining information by sampling." The advantage of sampling studies of course was that infor-

29. Bonnie Fox Schwartz, *The Civil Works Administration, 1933–1934* (Princeton, N.J.: Princeton University Press, 1984), pp. 3–4; 138–39.

mation on the population could be collected at a fraction of the cost of a complete census. The drawback was that the statisticians had not yet developed either the statistical theory or the practical methodology necessary to evaluate the accuracy of the sample. They were unsure, in the mid-1930s, whether their results were representative of the population as a whole. They thus wanted to conduct sampling research in conjunction with a complete census to test their methods.

"Had the present demand been foreseen," Rice continued, "it might have been necessary in the 1930 census to get the data by different methods; a sample by blocks, one by enumeration districts, and so on, consideration being given to the different possibilities in urban and rural areas." Then the sample results could have been compared with the complete count to see which worked best. If a special census were taken in 1935, they could test the methods and have benchmark figures from which to take population samples for the rest of the decade.[30]

Two months later, however, senior administration officials killed the idea of a 1935 census for fiscal and political reasons. Such a census would be expensive; it was budgeted at $13.25 million. (The usual budget of the Census Bureau between decennial censuses was under $2.0 million a year.) Second, the major impetus for such a census came from a desire to get precise data on employment and unemployment. By early 1935, Franklin Roosevelt found himself in the same awkward position with respect to unemployment statistics that Hoover had been in. Unemployment was not declining sufficiently quickly; the number of people on relief was high. No good could be served in mounting an expensive national effort to produce data that would not reflect favorably on the administration. The statisticians' call for a census to test sampling methods was lost in the larger political arena.

For the next five years, this scenario repeated itself several times. Agency officials and sympathetic congressmen proposed an extraordinary census. Senior New Deal officials quashed the idea. Roosevelt himself and interested cabinet officials never quite understood what such a special census would mean for the improvement of the statistical system. When reporters suggested that his administration was not doing enough to reduce unemployment, Roosevelt obfuscated the discussion. He claimed that "nobody has been able to define an unemployed person" or "say what they mean by 'unemployed.'" He talked about girls who worked for "pin money" and carpenters who only worked in good weather. He suggested that an unemployment census would carelessly lump these "unemployed workers" together with the truly "needy."[31]

30. Minutes of the Census Advisory Committee, Dec. 14–15, 1934, box 73, series 148, RG 29, NA.

31. See, e.g., Roosevelt's comments at his press conferences of Oct. 30 and Dec. 23, 1935,

The Census Bureau and its chief officials thus found themselves facing a political stalemate. They could prove neither to themselves, to the politicians, nor to the nation at large that they were making major progress in statistical research on population until they conducted a census in conjunction with sample surveys. They also had little justification for beefing up the bureau's statistical research division until there was something to do. Thus, change in the late 1930s came at what seemed a glacial pace to those involved. Calvert Dedrick, who had worked for the Central Statistical Board and on the cwa Trial Census of Unemployment, joined the bureau staff as assistant chief of the Division of Statistical Research in early 1935. He became chief after Joseph Hill died in 1938. Stuart Rice left the bureau in early 1936 to head the Central Statistical Board. Morris Hansen, then a young economics graduate from the University of Wyoming and later a major innovator in sampling theory, joined the bureau in 1936. Bureau statisticians also tacked some of the other extraordinarily difficult methodological problems facing their work; they began, for example, to develop uniform federal classifications for occupation and industry statistics. But change came slowly.

Nevertheless, outside the bureau, the sheer growth of new welfare programs in the mid-1930s prompted continued study of "population problems," as they came to be called. This pressure had several aspects. First, legislators wanted simple information to determine, for example, who was unemployed, which industries were in trouble, where aid was needed. Second, the policymakers needed data to write legislative formulas to apportion federal funds to the state and local governments that administered the relief programs. In the frenetic days of the spring of 1933, the New Dealers had searched for precedents to enable them to distribute funds to relieve the worst forms of distress. They did not want the national government to do it directly. Political expediency and the basic character of American federalism indicated that the simplest, most effective, and least controversial route to distributing federal relief was to channel funds through existing state and local government agencies. The Federal Emergency Relief Administration operated in such a fashion, distributing $3 billion between May 1933 and the end of 1935. The mechanism it used was the "grant-in-aid."

Devised in the late nineteenth century, the money grant-in-aid was the successor to the land grant, which Congress had historically used to encourage and subsidize state government action and even private de-

---

Apr. 27, 1937, and Apr. 18, 1940, in the Franklin Delano Roosevelt Library, Hyde Park, N.Y. See also the Morgenthau diaries for July 10, 1935, and Apr. 13–14, 1936, Franklin Delano Roosevelt Library, or Corrington Gill: "Frankly no one knows exactly how many unemployed there are at the moment" (*Wasted Manpower: The Challenge of Unemployment* [New York: Norton, 1939], p. 14). Gill was assistant commissioner of the wpa and oversaw many of the research efforts to count the unemployed.

velopment. The grant-in-aid was first used in 1887, in the Hatch Act, to appropriate a small amount of funds to each state "to establish an agricultural experiment station in connection with the land-grant college." Proponents of such funding argued that the encouragement of agriculture, the provision of education, and certain welfare functions required uniform national policies and thus national funding. Without national coordination, the states were either incapable or unwilling to perform these functions.

Over the next thirty-five years, Congress quietly expanded the grant-in-aid system to promote specific programs. By the early 1920s, grants covered vocational education, agricultural extension work, conservation programs, a national highway system, and public health measures. The amount of money allocated was relatively small; by 1930 grants amounted to about 3 percent of the federal budget (about $100 million); 60 percent of that went for highway aid. Nevertheless, it was this disparate set of laws that laid the foundation for the grant-in-aid system and that first made use of census allocation formulas for distributing federal funds to the states.[32]

Needless to say, when these grants-in-aid grew to $2 billion and one-third of the federal budget in 1936, there was a flurry of interest in the allocation methods themselves. Were the population figures adequate to devise good formulas? Could better ones be devised? Just as public attention focused on the legislative apportionment mechanisms during the reapportionment crisis of the 1920s, so now did Congress and the public question the formulas used to make federal grants to the states.

The passage of the Social Security Act in 1935 brought the issue into sharp focus. This act appropriated funds for public health, maternal and child health, old age assistance, aid to the blind, aid to families with dependent children, and old age pensions and unemployment insurance. All the programs, with the exception of the old age pensions, were administered through the states. The federal government had thus taken a major step toward creating a permanent, broad-based, and comprehensive grant-in-aid system in the social welfare field. Census data would be used in the formulas to make the grants.

Finally, despite the increasingly systematic efforts to reduce unemployment and counteract the effects of the Depression, an unacceptably high number of people still remained on relief. In universities, in private foundations, and in government agencies, social scientists and statisti-

32. V. O. Key, *The Administration of Federal Grants to States* (Chicago: Public Administration Service, 1937), pp. 5–16, quotation on p. 7; Committee on Federal Grants-in-Aid of the Council of State Governments, *Federal Grants in Aid* (n.p.: Council of State Governments, 1949); William Anderson, *The Nation and the States, Rivals or Partners?* (Minneapolis, Minn.: University of Minnesota Press, 1955); Jane Perry Clark, *The Rise of a New Federalism* (1938; reprint, New York: Russell & Russell, 1965).

cians grappled with the questions raised by the collapse of the economic system. They developed new statistical methods and a new conceptualization of the meaning of population growth and change and its relationship to the failure of the larger economic system. These new ideas and methods ultimately provided the scientific and intellectual underpinnings of much New Deal social welfare policy. Although, as the historians of New Deal policy have shown, social science research was used to define and support the legislation, much of the basic research was done after the laws themselves were passed. Good unemployment statistics, the housing census, and the improvements in the vital statistics system, for example, were all developed after the major New Deal legislation on these matters was in place. The programs fostered the development of the statistics; the data in turn made it possible for federal officials to determine if the programs were meeting their goals, if they should be extended, and how the federal government was functioning in its new role. By the late 1930s, the new generation of New Deal social scientists and statisticians had defined a dramatic new approach to the study of population in the United States. They had indeed responded to the "statistical opportunities and responsibilities" that Rice defined in 1933.

The search for a new concept of population study is best exemplified in the 1938 National Resources Committee publication *The Problems of a Changing Population*. In 1934, the committee's predecessor, the National Resources Board, noted in its report that the study of "natural resources" was the means to furthering "human resources and human values." "The application of engineering and technological knowledge to the reorganization of the natural resources of the Nation," the board wrote, "is to be conceived as a means of progressively decreasing the burdens imposed upon labor, raising the standard of living, and enhancing the well-being of the masses of the people." The committee recommended a study of "population problems," "by persons competent by training and point of view to appraise the human values involved." They appointed a Committee on Population Problems, chaired by Edwin B. Wilson of the Harvard School of Public Health. The technical work was directed by Frank Lorimer of the Population Association of America.

The report summarized the state of knowledge on population issues. It provided a basic compilation of information on historical population trends, on migration and regional differences in the United States, and on the racial, ethnic, class, and industrial distributions of the population. It reported on the state of knowledge about differential fertility and mortality patterns, the "biological inheritance" of physical and mental defects, and of differential educational opportunity among the various regions and economic groups in the country. Throughout, the report displayed an extraordinarily open, liberal view of the diverse ways of life in Depression America. Unlike the narrow racist thinking that characterized such research in the 1920s, the National Resources Committee could find no firm evidence that ethnic or racial minorities had lowered the American standard of living, that mental defects were inherited and concentrated in particular racial stocks, that the migrations that had characterized American social life over the past three centuries resulting in undermining the vitality of the Republic. While not formally dissociating from the population theories of Francis Walker, the eugenicists, or the immigration restriction lobby, the committee nevertheless stressed the positive aspects of the "cultural diversity" and "traditions" of immigrants, blacks, and Indians. And the committee asserted that the "problems" facing the poor communities of America were the results of inadequate educational opportunities, of improper exploitation of land and mineral resources, of inadequate planning for technological change. It was thus a federal responsibility to provide leadership and funds to insure educational opportunity and minimum health standards to all Americans, to restore forests and agricultural land that had been wastefully exploited by previous generations, and to anticipate technological change through planning for growth. "It cannot be too strongly emphasized," the Committee concluded,

> that this report deals not merely with problems regarding the quantity, quality, and distribution of population, important as they are, but also with the widening of opportunities for the individuals making up this population, no matter how many or where they are. In our democratic system, we must progressively make available to all groups what we assume to be American standards of life. The gains of the Nation are essentially mass gains, and the birthright of the American citizen should not be lost by indifference or neglect.[33]

No longer would the major figures in population research deplore the "degradation" or "pollution" of the original colonial stock, and hence no longer would they worry about the growth of urban America or the decline in the native white American birthrate. Rather these statisticians asked what it would take to provide "American standards of life" to everyone, to reduce regional, racial, and ethnic inequality. To do so, these statisticians recognized that they needed a new set of statistical tools to conceptualize and measure "levels of living" and socioeconomic status.

Thus the new grants-in-aid and the new concept of population policy resulted in a historic shift in the purpose of the decennial census. No longer would the statisticians be concerned primarily with providing

---

33. Report of the Committee on Population Problems to the National Resources Committee, *The Problems of a Changing Population* (Washington, D.C.: GPO, 1938), esp. pp. 4–5. For the context of the report, see Otis Graham, *Toward a Planned Society: From Roosevelt to Nixon* (New York: Oxford University Press, 1976), and Marion Clawson, *New Deal Planning: The National Resources Planning Board* (Baltimore: Johns Hopkins University Press, 1981), pp. 125*ff.*

apportionment data for reallocating political power to the growing areas of society. Rather, they would stress measures that might be used to "balance" or "equalize" social conditions, to provide uniform national standards despite differential rates of population growth and change. The new measures used in *The Problems of a Changing Population* illustrate these concerns.

In particular, the population study searched for new measures to describe per capita income by region, differential fertility rates among poor and better-off populations, and regional productivity. The data and methods were gleaned from a variety of private and small government studies and were clearly suggestive of the need for systematic government efforts in collecting these data. Rough per capita income measures for states, for example, were calculated using Bureau of Labor Statistics "entrance wage rate" data, retail sales data, and such. Industrial area data was available from the census of manufacturing, but there was no direct information on income for individuals. Thus the study could define regions or geographic areas that were richer or poorer but could not capture rich people in poor areas or vice versa.

The study pointed to the need for the collection of more national, individual-level socioeconomic data; the statisticians naturally looked to the decennial census to do it. But adding new questions to an already complex census reduced public cooperation with the census and clogged the bureau tabulation facilities. By the 1930s, though, as we have seen, the new generation of statisticians had developed another solution—namely, adding a sample census to the complete count. Despite the lack of a mid-decade census, the New Deal statisticians hoped to employ sampling in the 1940 census.

On one level, "sampling" a population to learn about some aspect of it is simple common sense. If one is interested, for example, in knowing the proportional distribution of a characteristic in a population, not the total number in each category, then sampling the population is sufficient to answer one's research question. If a politician wants to know if he will win an election, he simply needs to know if he will get the majority of the votes, not what the total vote count will be. The problem is that, practically, it is difficult to collect accurate information about proportional strength without also knowing something about the whole population. The famous 1936 *Literary Digest* presidential election poll illustrated this dilemma nicely. That poll predicted that Landon would carry thirty-two states and defeat FDR. In fact, Landon won only two states. The poll did not predict Roosevelt's overwhelming reelection victory because the "sample" poll was biased. Landon supporters responded and sent in the mail ballot more frequently than did Roosevelt supporters. Thus the poll did not represent voter behavior on election day. The census takers who wanted to employ sampling in the decennial census had to solve this problem of guaranteeing the "representativeness" of their sample before they could use such a technique.

Broadly speaking, there were then two solutions proposed to this dilemma. Some statisticians proposed what came to be called "purposive selection," or conscious collection of information from "typical" respondents or individuals. The other group of statisticians relied on the branch of mathematics known as probability theory and argued that populations should be sampled at "random." Then the statistician should calculate the "probable error" of the estimates derived from the sample to determine if the results were sufficiently representative of the population. The first method had the advantage of being intuitively obvious to the layperson—and to many in the older generation of the statistical community. The second method had the advantage of being rigorous and of proving itself, since the turn of the century, in applications in genetic improvement in crop yields, in medicine and epidemiology, and in industrial quality control.[34]

Theoretically, however, until the mid-1930s the mathematics of sampling presumed "a normally distributed infinite population." The classic example used in the textbooks was the dice thrower or card player. If one continued to roll a pair of fair dice an infinite number of times, the distribution of the numbers would approximate the normal curve. The number seven would, on average, appear six times more frequently than either a two or a twelve. Statisticians dubious about the applicability of sampling theory to socioeconomic questions pointed out that "human populations" were not "normally distributed," as were, presumably, pea plants. Nor was the "human population" infinite. The statisticians knew what the total number of people was.

Sampling theory also presumed an understanding of mathematics beyond that of the average government official—including statisticians—as well as the average American at the time. Thus the general discussion of the applicability of sampling to census taking was muddled both by theoretical difficulties and by ignorance among the decision makers. Throughout the mid-1930s, therefore, the professional statistical community engaged in an impassioned but muted debate and finally began to resolve the issue. Breakthroughs were made on two fronts.

Practically speaking, the small experimental studies sponsored by COG-SIS, university statisticians, and the Central Statistical Board began to provide concrete experience on methods. In the winter of 1933–34, the CWA sponsored a Trial Census of Unemployment in three cities to determine if sampling was feasible, what the best unit for sampling was, and what kind of practical difficulties the statisticians would face. Calvert Dedrick, Frederick F. Stephan, and Samuel A. Stouffer worked on the

34. Duncan and Shelton, *Revolution in Statistics,* pp. 32–50.

project. They reported that sampling was feasible for such studies; that the smaller the sampling unit, the more accurate the sample results; and, probably most importantly, that the preparatory work for a sample survey was critical for the accuracy of the results. The statisticians had to know in advance the characteristics of what was later called the "sampling frame." If one was going to take a sample of households by city blocks, for example, one had to have accurate information on all city blocks and on how many households there were in all city blocks, so that the survey would not inadvertently miss whole blocks or collect too few cases from crowded blocks.[35]

The decennial census had of course faced similar issues, but, because the goal of the data collection was a complete count, enumerators were told simply to keep collecting data until they had counted everyone. An error in a census map could be corrected in the field. A sample, on the other hand, by definition counts only a small number of the total. Thus if the researcher designing the sample does not have accurate data on the "sampling frame" to determine how to draw the sample, the results generally are unreliable.

The statisticians took away from this experience a deeper understanding of the need for good preparatory work for sample surveys and lobbied for a mid-decade census. When this effort failed, they continued to build small studies into other projects. Works Progress Administration (WPA) statisticians used the periodic counts of the relief population to conduct sample surveys. Agencies also cooperated on these efforts. In 1935–36, the Bureau of Labor Statistics, the WPA, the Bureau of Home Economics, and the National Resources Planning Board jointly conducted *The Study of Consumer Purchases* to measure differential family expenditure patterns around the country.[36]

Finally, by mid-1937, political pressure had mounted sufficiently that the Roosevelt administration could no longer prevent Congress from mandating a national unemployment survey. The unemployment census as legislated was not what the statisticians wanted—Stuart Rice lobbied against the legislation, for example—but it did provide the statisticians with the opportunity to try out their new methods in a highly publicized national survey. The "census" was a voluntary registration. Postal carriers delivered a form to all residential addresses. The unemployed worker was supposed to fill it out and mail it in. The statisticians had objected to this method because they felt that many people would not admit they were unemployed or would not consider themselves unemployed or underemployed. Calvert Dedrick, Morris Hansen, Samuel Stouffer, and Frederick Stephan thus convinced John Biggers, the temporary administrator of the registration, to add a sample household enumeration project to the

35. Ibid., pp. 37–38.
36. Ibid., p. 39.

effort to evaluate the accuracy of the registration. Biggers agreed, and the postal carriers enumerated a 2 percent sample of households in "nonbusiness postal routes" with a separate form in late 1937.[37]

The results justified the statisticians' methods and concerns about self-registration. Seven million eight-hundred thousand unemployed workers registered, but this was only 71.4 percent of the unemployed, according to the sample survey. The true number of unemployed was 11 million. Biggers and the statisticians reported the sample results first in early January 1938; the press treated these as the official results. Even Roosevelt admitted afterward in a press conference that his skepticism about the possibility of an efficient, inexpensive survey of employment and unemployment was unjustified. The results looked promising for plans for the 1940 census.[38]

While the New Deal statisticians were achieving practical gains in sampling methods, other statisticians made mathematical breakthroughs in sampling theory. In particular, for our purposes, Jerzy Neyman, a Polish-born statistician who had immigrated to the United States in the mid-1930s, contributed directly to the theoretical underpinnings of much of the work being done by Dedrick, Hansen, and others. In 1934 Neyman had published an article in the *Journal of the Royal Statistical Society* showing that it was possible to draw rigorous samples from non-normal finite populations and that "purposive selection" of samples would give biased results. In April 1937, W. Edwards Deming, then head of the Department of Agriculture Graduate School, organized a Conference on Sampling Human Populations in Washington. Neyman spoke and related both his practical experience in conducting sampling surveys in Poland and his broad theoretical understanding of the mathematics of these efforts. In the March 1938 issue of the *Journal of the American Statistical Association*, Neyman published an article responding directly to the concerns of the government statisticians at the 1937 conference. His "Contribution to the Theory of Sampling Human Populations" provided a theoretical justification of double sampling and continued his interest in stratified sampling as a means to solve the peculiar problems of sampling "human populations." Neyman's work showed the statisticians how they could "stratify" a population to collect more accurate sample data—for example, by race, income, or some other characteristic. He also indicated how accurate samples could be taken in stages—for example, first a sample of cities or regions, then of subunits within those cities and regions—and then how to calculate sampling error for the whole survey.[39]

37. Ibid., pp. 44*ff.*

38. Presidential Press Conference, May 13, 1938, Franklin Delano Roosevelt Library.

39. For these and other related papers, see Jerzy Neyman, *Lectures and Conferences on Mathematical Statistics and Probability*, 2d ed. (Washington, D.C.: Department of Agriculture Graduate School, 1952).

By the late 1930s, then, both the practical and the theoretical work necessary for broadening the decennial census to include sample inquiries into socioeconomic questions had been done. It remained to convince the older generation of census statisticians, Congress, and the public that the changes should be made.

The final chapter of the story in the revitalization of the national census revolves around the plans for the 1940 census. In 1937 the bureau began formal preparatory work. The Geography Division increased its staff to update census maps, draw enumeration district lines, and create new geographic divisions for tabulating the census—the metropolitan areas and census tracts for cities. Technicians in the mechanical laboratory updated the bureau tabulating equipment to handle a forty-five-column punch card; the bureau contracted with IBM to use a "printer-tabulator" to compile the data. The Population Division began formal discussion of the questionnaire design; the statisticians asked other government agencies and private groups which questions they wanted on the 1940 form and which ones could be eliminated. By early 1938 it was clear that there was great pressure to add a large battery of questions on socioeconomic status to assess the effects of the Depression on the population. And there was a growing consensus in the Roosevelt administration to add a new set of questions to the population census to measure the adequacy and capacity of the nation's housing stock.[40]

Through 1938 and into 1939 the statisticians discussed how to fit new questions onto the schedule, how to word such questions, and whether the questions would provide the needed information. As the discussions continued, the statisticians separated what became the housing census questions from the population census. In August 1939, Congress passed legislation authorizing a census of housing. The new schedule, administered simultaneously with the population schedule, asked questions on the value, condition, rent, or mortgage of all occupied dwellings. It also included questions on water supplies, bathroom facilities, lighting, heating, and appliances. For the first time, the federal government would collect data to provide a full picture of the nation's housing stock.[41]

For the population schedule, the officials agreed to add questions on income, migration, fertility, educational attainment, social security status, and usual occupation. They also agreed to put the unemployment inquiry on the main schedule. This added seven questions to the schedule. As the planning continued, it became increasingly clear that it would be impossible to include these new inquiries without deleting others. The chief

40. Robert Jenkins, *1940 Census of Population and Housing: Procedural History* (Madison, Wis.: University of Wisconsin Center for Demography and Ecology, 1983; University of Wisconsin Press, 1985).

41. For the reports of these discussions, see Files of the Census Advisory Committee, 1938–40, series 148, RG 29, NA.

candidates for omission were those dealing with mother tongue, place of parents' birth, and veterans' status. Yet many statisticians—within and outside the government—wanted the information to make historical comparisons with past censuses. The young New Deal statisticians thus lobbied their older colleagues to accept a sample census along with the complete count. The questions crowded off the main schedule could thus be asked on a sample basis. More data could be collected without greatly increased additional costs, and the sample results could be tabulated quickly for summary public presentations. Director William Lane Austin and other old-timers were dubious about such claims, but they were willing to be convinced by the Dedricks, and Hansens, and Stephans of the younger generation.

The 1940 census took a major step forward in statistical method by including "supplementary questions," as they were euphemistically called, for two people on each side of the forty-line population schedule. The questions on parents' birthplace, mother tongue, veterans' status, usual occupation, social security status, and fertility were asked on the sample schedule. The bureau hired a number of statisticians to administer the sample census and the other new features of the 1940 count. Among the most prominent was Philip Hauser, the assistant chief statistician for population, W. Edwards Deming, sampling expert in the Population Division, and William Hurwitz, of the Statistical Research Division. These men supported the work begun by Stuart Rice, Calvert Dedrick, and Morris Hansen in the mid-1930s.

As planning continued, the statisticians struggled with a number of thorny technical issues. They had to define the sample and they had to perfect the wording of the new questions. Neither was particularly easy, but the statisticians drew from their now broad experience with population surveys of the previous ten years. For example, a new concept of occupational status—the labor force concept—replaced that of the gainful worker to improve the measurement of unemployment. Now workers were first asked if they were working or looking for work the week the census was taken. If they were, the enumerator recorded their occupation; if not, they were not included in the labor force. For the first time, the bureau pretested the schedule. In August 1939, the bureau conducted a special census using the 1940 questions in Saint Joseph and Marshall counties in Indiana. The experience of this test was used to modify some questions and finalize the schedule design. The bureau debated various approaches to the sampling design. Finally they printed five schedules with different sample lines to prevent line bias from vitiating the results.[42]

42. Frederick F. Stephan, W. Edwards Deming, and Morris H. Hansen, "The Sampling Procedure of the 1940 Population Census," *JASA* 35 (December 1940): 615–30.

With such ambitious new plans in the works, the bureau naturally anticipated a good deal of public scrutiny and criticism. From their experience with the Indiana pretests and general knowledge of resistance to survey questionnaires, they were especially ready to field criticisms from people opposed to the new socioeconomic questions—particularly those on income, home value, plumbing, and so on. While government officials and most politicians agreed that such information would be extremely useful to plan legislative initiatives and evaluate programs, they also worried that such questions were an invasion of privacy and that it might be difficult to keep the answers confidential. (To put the issue in context, one should remember that until World War II, relatively few Americans reported any financial information to the federal government. Few, for example, filed federal income tax returns. In 1940, in a population of over 130 million, only 15 million income tax returns were filed. At the end of World War II, the federal government received 50 million tax returns.)

Nevertheless, the officials felt that the new initiatives were worth the political risk, and they went ahead with their plans. They also knew from the Indiana pretest that most opposition to the income question came from upper-income groups; the statistical interest in the question arose from the need to know the distribution of income in lower- to middle-income groups. The question was thus worded to request specific wage or salary income for amounts under $5,000. Seventy-five percent of American families then made under $5,000 a year. Further, if the individual did not wish to answer the enumerator, he or she could send in a confidential card with the income information. In January 1940, therefore, when Republican senator Charles Tobey of New Hampshire announced a campaign to force the administration to delete the income questions, the statisticians were ready to respond. They mobilized a lobby of business, labor, and academic experts to endorse the questions, and they pointed out that the question had been worded to protect privacy. Tobey and his allies continued their attacks until the census date, but they were unsuccessful in reducing compliance with either the question or the census as a whole. Two percent of the population did not answer the question. The bureau was pleased with the results.[43]

Perhaps most ironically, the flurry of criticism over the income question overshadowed criticism of other aspects of the 1940 census. The sample census went smoothly. The 1940 census counted a population of almost 132 million. The predictions that the Depression had had a dramatic effect on the character and trajectory of the population proved correct. Population growth between 1930 and 1940 dropped to the historically low rate of 7.2 percent. Cities stopped growing. The 1941 congressional apportionment redistributed nine House seats. Six seats went

43. Eckler, *Bureau of the Census*, pp. 192*ff.*; Jenkins, *1940 Census*, pp. 17*ff.*

to the western states of California, Arizona, New Mexico, and Oregon; three went to the southern states of Florida, Tennessee, and North Carolina. Massachusetts, Pennsylvania, Ohio, and Illinois each lost a seat. So did the agricultural states hard hit by the Depression: Oklahoma, Nebraska, Iowa, Kansas, and Indiana. The new migration questions allowed the statisticians to trace these changes directly. The data for the people who answered the additional questions was tabulated separately to provide earlier summary results for all the questions as well as to provide the answers on the additional questions. As in the 1937 unemployment census, the public soon accepted the sample results as official. The New Deal census takers had proved to themselves and the public that their new efforts worked.[44]

As the year 1940 wore on, the sixteenth decennial census was quickly swept off the front pages of the nation's newspapers by more dramatic events. The deepening war in Europe and the upcoming presidential election drew national attention elsewhere and even lessened interest in the results of the new socioeconomic inquiries of the census. Unemployment was still at historic levels in 1940. It stood at 15 percent of the labor force and totaled 8 million. Yet economists and government officials could see that the war mobilization was beginning to provide a push to the American economy. In September 1940 the United States instituted the first peacetime military draft in its history. By the end of the year the Census Bureau had begun to take on defense work.

There is a final footnote to this story of New Deal census taking, which permitted the bureau to consolidate its achievements and to plan even more ambitious statistical efforts during the war years and beyond. In 1939, as the bureau geared up for the 1940 census, the Works Progress Administration initiated a new Sample Survey of Unemployment, designed to provide current estimates of the nation's rate of unemployment. The survey was national, monthly, and used WPA workers as the field force. Twenty thousand households were surveyed using a complex system to select counties to sample and then to select households within the counties. The sample changed every six months to keep the data current. This effort was expensive; whether it would work was unclear at the time. Designed as it was to overlap with the decennial census, however, the survey provided the statisticians with a unique opportunity to check their results.

High-quality planning characterized the survey. It was conceived by Howard Myers, director of the WPA Division of Research, and John Webb,

---

44. There was also a controversy of apportionment methods which resulted in the use of Hill's method of equal proportions. See Michel L. Balinski and H. Peyton Young, *Fair Representation: Meeting the Ideal of One Man, One Vote* (New Haven and London: Yale University Press, 1982), pp. 57–59.

chief of the Social Research Section. They hired mathematical statisticians J. Stevens Stock and Lester Frankel to design the survey. As the survey developed, the statisticians learned much from the work, and by the end of 1940 they confirmed their hopes that such a current reporting system was both feasible and accurate. The survey continued to operate as the war began, but, ironically, as prosperity returned, its continued existence was threatened by the abolition of the WPA. In 1942, therefore, a government statistical commission convinced the Budget Bureau to maintain the survey and transfer it to an existing government agency. Several agencies were interested in taking it over—especially the Bureau of Labor Statistics and the Census Bureau. The Census Bureau won. The survey was transferred to the bureau in August 1942 and was renamed the Monthly Report on the Labor Force. In 1947, the Monthly Report on the Labor Force was broadened again in scope and technique and called the Current Population Survey. With the integration of this survey into the official statistical system, the New Deal statisticians had solved the problem of measuring unemployment that had discredited Hoover's Census Bureau.[45]

By the early 1940s, then, the Census Bureau had achieved most of the goals set forth in the early days of the Roosevelt administration for the nation's population statistics. Its personnel had changed, and the Statistical Research Division of the bureau stood at the cutting edge of probability sampling and survey research. Broad new initiatives had been made in the decennial census. A protean system of current surveys had been started, and the bureau had a current surveys division for population research. It would be the task of this generation of statisticians to direct the bureau for the next quarter-century or more and bring the American census into the age of computers and the information revolution.

45. Duncan and Shelton, *Revolution in Statistics,* pp. 47*ff.*; Judith I. deNeufville, *Social Indicators and Public Policy* (New York: American Elsevier Publishing, 1975), pp. 70–86.

EIGHT || The High-Tech Census and the Growth of the Welfare State

Statistics, then, both in the sense of numbers and the sense of methods, clearly pervade our national government. . . . Nearly all of the federal statistics program deals with important, interesting problems, and conscientious federal statisticians, in dealing with these problems, do battle with a host of methodological demons—ambiguity of definition (for example, unemployment), nonresponsiveness in surveys, difficulties in estimating error, problems of cooperation and comparability among the states of the union—and among the countries of the world.
—Report of the President's Commission on Federal Statistics, *1971*

Two contradictory trends characterize the American census experience since World War II. The Census Bureau has built on the innovations and accomplishments of the 1930s and has continued to be praised for its high-quality survey research. Since the late 1960s, however, the bureau has faced increasing public criticism. A wide variety of public and private officials have demanded more from the bureau and its data than it could deliver. At the height of the controversies during the 1980 census period, the bureau faced fifty-four lawsuits charging it with improper and unconstitutional methods of counting. Why the bureau has come under attack, when by all accounts it is at the forefront of survey research techniques, is a paradox. To solve the paradox one must interweave the history of the bureau since World War II with the new demographic trends that again made census apportionment mechanisms and methods problematic. In this chapter I trace that history to the early 1970s. In the following, I examine the planning and controversies surrounding the 1980 census.

Many historians and contemporary political commentators have pointed out that until World War II, the Roosevelt administration did not fully embrace Keynesian economic policies or understand the power of the new state institutions it had built. During the worst years of the Depression, the New Deal employed a variety of measures; sometimes the efforts to ameliorate the conditions of one group of Americans worsened those of others. For example, farm policies aimed at raising prices paid to farmers also increased the cost of food to consumers. During the 1930s, the Democrats could never quite muster the all-out enthusiasm and political strength necessary to use federal fiscal power and authority to pull the nation out of depression. The historical consensus has been that the New Dealers were by and large developing the appropriate policies but that they did not put enough money behind them.

The coming of World War II changed all this. Political opposition to federal spending disappeared when that spending was going for national defense instead of relief for the unemployed. As the threat of war grew, federal policymakers found themselves asking new questions about the capacities of the national government. Could the nation mount a sufficiently powerful counterattack against the Nazis? If the nation had to go to war, would there be sufficient manpower and productive capacity to prosecute the war?[1]

In the Census Bureau, such questions prompted the statisticians to look at the new tools and methods they had developed in the 1930s and to redirect them toward questions of national defense. The Sample Survey of Unemployment was a survey both of employment and of unemployment. It could be used to project sources of manpower for the army and the defense industries just as effectively as it could identify idle capacity. The 1940 census contained detailed information to calculate draft quotas. On a more sinister note, the population census also identified alien populations who might post a security threat to the nation.

The mobilization of the nation for total war provided the census bureau with the opportunity to consolidate the achievements of the 1930s and to prove to the larger policy-making community just what the revitalized bureau could do. It also provided the bureau with the oppor-

---

1. For a discussion of similar debates of the potential of the National Income and Products Accounts for war planning, see John Kenneth Galbraith, "The National Accounts: Arrival and Impact," in Bureau of the Census, *Reflections of America: Commemorating the Statistical Abstract Centennial* (Washington, D.C.: GPO, 1980), and Joseph Duncan and William Shelton, *Revolution in United States Government Statistics, 1926–1976* (Washington, D.C.: GPO, 1978), pp. 83*ff.*

tunity and funds to pursue further innovations in census taking and data processing—most notably in the development of the first UNIVAC computer. These wartime achievements in turn encouraged a kind of momentum that propelled the bureau to become a permanent innovator in survey research techniques.

The initial buildup for national defense did not immediately provide new resources of the bureau. Rather, by late 1940 the bureau was being asked to loan staff to the new defense agencies and to trim its budget at the same time that it was trying to publish the 1940 census results. The housing census was particularly squeezed. Through 1940 the bureau juggled plans and staff to get the most from its limited resources. In early 1941, William Lane Austin retired. J. C. Capt, an assistant to the director since 1939 and a former official of both the Texas Relief Commission and the WPA, became director. Capt, another Southerner, served until his death in 1949. He was not a professional statistician; he devoted most of his efforts to working with Congress and in bureau relations with other government agencies and the public.

In the months before Pearl Harbor, the prognosis for the bureau was clouded. At a particularly contentious meeting of the ASA-AEA Census Advisory Committee in September 1941, for example, Fred Stephan spoke for academic statisticians and pressed the bureau to complete the planned analytical studies in the census monograph series; bureau officials disagreed. Philip Hauser testily responded that there was "no way" that the bureau could "come within ten percent of meeting the kind of a program" Stephan expected. The bureau had a responsibility, as Vergil Reed put it, to the "Joneses and the Smiths" among census users who "don't give a damn for this analytical stuff." "I don't feel," he continued, "we are justified in holding up," the routine tabulations to satisfy "the Cabots and the Lodges in the statistical field." The advisory committee members, though, continued to press the point, and the matter was left unresolved.[2]

The Japanese attack on Pearl Harbor in December, however, shifted the terms of the discussion. Bureau officials turned their attention to the question of how they could most effectively participate in the war effort and promote the general position of the bureau within the executive branch. The motives were both patriotic and somewhat self-serving, for the statisticians knew that if they did not seize the initiative, rival statisticians in one of the temporary war agencies would. If the bureau was to come out of World War II with more prestige and resources than it had in World War I, the officials noted, it had to play an aggressive role in mobilizing the government for the war.

2. Minutes of the Census Advisory Committee, pp. 134–41, Sept. 12–13, 1941, Records of the Census Advisory Committee, box 76, series 148, RG 29, NA. These studies were canceled during the war.

And so it did—initially by providing detailed hand tabulations on the Japanese population for the internment program. Calvert Dedrick, head of the Statistical Research Division, was sent to California in February 1942 to supervise the statistical efforts necessary to round up the Japanese. The Japanese were readily identified in the 1940 population census because they were a small, highly concentrated ethnic minority. Though the bureau claims it did not release individual names and addresses from the 1940 census schedules, as prescribed by law, it did prepare detailed counts of the Japanese for small geographic areas. These provided the parameters for finding and interning the population.[3]

Later actions have proved less controversial, though they were perhaps more important to the war effort and the development of the bureau. The bureau provided tabulations for projecting draft quotas. It also provided population data for the location of military installations and the impact of defense industries. The sample of the Monthly Report of the Labor Force was expanded and redesigned when it became clear that it did not accurately capture the characteristics of the farm population.

Further, bureau statisticians moved into key statistical roles in other government agencies. Calvert Dedrick continued to work "on problems of alien registration and control" for the provost marshal general's office. W. Edwards Deming worked for the Division of Statistical Standards of the Bureau of the Budget in an effort to help other federal agencies adopt probability sampling methods. Samuel Stouffer ran a major survey research effort on the attitudes and behavior of the American army, which was published as *The American Soldier* in 1949.[4]

Moreover, the generation of officials who had taken the 1940 census—later called "the class of 1940" because they had such a lasting impact on the bureau—evaluated their own planning and performance in the sixteenth census and strove for new ways to improve their work. In particular, as the collection and tabulation of the data proceeded, the statisticians noticed that errors crept into the data at a variety of points. Because some answers were obviously inconsistent, the statisticians knew that enumerators made errors in reporting information. An example of such an error was a worker who reported he was working but had no income listed. They noticed that coders entered the wrong codes for particular answers and that keypunchers might punch the wrong code on the population card. And the statisticians knew that some of the tabulations they made

3. See Minutes of the Census Advisory Committee, January 9–10, 1942, Records of the Census Advisory Committee, box 76, series 148, RG 29, NA; Roger Daniels, "The Bureau of the Census and the Relocation of Japanese Americans: A Note and Document," *Amerasia Journal* 9, no. 1 (1982): 101–5.

4. Daniels, "Bureau of the Census," p. 105; Duncan and Shelton, *Revolution in Statistics*, p. 66; Samuel Stouffer, *The American Soldier* (Princeton, N.J.: Princeton University Press, 1949).

were obviously flawed because other sources of information on the same question reported very different numbers. For example, the census count of public emergency workers came in with an undercount of almost 31 percent, according to administrative records. A comparison of the 1940 draft registration figures and the equivalent population in the 1940 census indicated a census undercount of 13 percent for black men.[5]

Previous generations of census officials had known of these problems, but, since the substitution of enumerators for the assistant marshals and the introduction of machine tabulation, little effort had been placed in trying to solve them. They were seen as unfortunate but intractable problems in taking a census in a large, diverse country.

The class of 1940 did not see it that way. Morris Hansen, joined in late 1940 by William Hurwitz, W. Edwards Deming, and others, saw these problems of accuracy and error as problems to be solved, not faults to be lived with. If certain census methods were prone to error, then better census methods would have to be devised. The initial steps along these lines were taken by introducing quality control tests in the coding and punching processes at the bureau. In a further application of probability sampling, Deming applied Walter Shewhart's theories of industrial quality control to coders to find out just who made the best coders and punchers. The statisticians systematically analyzed the errors, trying to find the sources and the correlates of the mistakes.

Finally, during the war years, Hansen and Hurwitz, along with William Madow and others, pushed ahead with the mathematical theory of sampling and by 1942–43 had developed the finite population approach. They showed—both mathematically and practically—that it was not necessary to assume a normally distributed infinite population to calculate precise sampling errors for population surveys. They published their results in a series of seminal articles in the *Journal of the American Statistical Association*. Hansen, Hurwitz, and Madow also began work on a textbook that would collect and summarize their practical and theoretical experience. The two-volume *Sample Survey Methods and Theory* was published in 1953 and became the standard textbook for large-scale survey research techniques.[6]

Other events of the war years affected the bureau in some less obvious ways. The first was the relocation of the bureau offices to the Washington, D.C., suburb of Suitland, Maryland, then quite far from the population center of the capital. Since the first central office had been set up to

5. A. Ross Eckler, *The Bureau of the Census* (New York: Praeger, 1972), pp. 95*ff.*; Robert Jenkins, *The 1940 Census of Population and Housing: Procedural History* (Madison, Wis.: University of Wisconsin Press, 1985), pp. 96–104.

6. Duncan and Shelton, *Revolution in Statistics*, pp. 50–66; Morris Hansen, William Hurwitz, and William Madow, *Sample Survey Methods and Theory*, 2 vols. (New York: John Wiley & Sons, 1953).

process the census in Washington in 1850, the bureau had always been housed within walking distance of the major downtown government offices. For the first third of twentieth century, the offices had been located in the Commerce Department building itself, which was centrally located on the Mall. Thus placed, the bureau had always been a prominent part of the Washington scene. With the growth of the federal government in the 1930s, though, many new agencies competed for prime Washington space. The number of federal employees working in Washington rose from 70,000 in 1933 to 191,000 in 1941 and to 276,000 in 1942. The bureau contained relatively few major officials who needed to be at the center of things and a relatively large number of clerks. The bureau also required massive amounts of space for schedules, processing equipment, and so forth. By the 1940s, therefore, it seemed logical to relocate the agency to less cramped quarters. The bureau thus built a new facility for the 1940 census at Second and D streets, SW. When the war broke out, war agencies took over the new building. The bureau was moved again to the large sprawling facility in Suitland that it still occupies. The move had several drawbacks. Symbolically, the bureau was no longer at the center of the Washington action; the research statisticians were isolated from their colleagues. Practically, the bureau also faced problems in recruiting good clerks to travel to the no man's land of suburban Maryland of the 1940s.[7]

The decentralization process continued in later years. By the time of the 1950 census, major processing of the census was relocated to other parts of the country. In 1950, 74 percent of the processing of the population data was performed at a Philadelphia Decennial Tabulation Office. In July 1958 an Army Quartermaster Corps Depot was converted into a permanent processing facility in Jeffersonville, Indiana; old census records were relocated to Pittsburgh, Kansas.[8]

The other major innovation of the war years was the entry of the bureau into the infant world of electronic computing. During the war years, the federal government sponsored several projects to build what we would call today electronic computers; ENIAC, "the first electronic digital computer to function dependably," was built by John Mauchly and J. Presper Eckert of the Moore School of Electrical Engineering of the University of Pennsylvania. The machine, ordered in 1943 and completed in early 1946, calculated ballistics tables for the Ordnance Department of the War

7. The data on federal employment are from Bureau of the Census, *Historical Statistics of the United States, Colonial Times to 1970* (Washington, D.C.: GPO, 1975), pt. 2:1102. For contemporary impressions of Suitland, see Minutes of the Census Advisory Committee, November 1945, p. 11, box 78, series 148, RG 29, NA.

8. Bureau of the Census, *The 1950 Censuses—How They Were Taken* (Washington, D.C.: GPO, 1955), pp. 29*ff.*; Bureau of the Census, *1960 Censuses of Population and Housing: Procedural History* (Washington, D.C.: GPO, 1966), p. 36; Eckler, *Bureau of the Census,* p. 34.

Department. In 1944, while the machine was still under construction—shrouded in a confidential security classification—Mauchly met Lillian Madow, a mathematician at the Ordnance Department. She was the wife of William Madow of the Census Bureau; the three discussed the broader implications of new technology. Madow introduced Mauchly to Morris Hansen, and Hansen naturally recognized the phenomenal savings that computers could bring to census processing. If the data could be recorded and tabulated as electrical impulses rather than as mechanical holes in punch cards, fantastic improvements in tabulating speed would be possible. The figures could be tabulated one thousand to one million times faster than on existing equipment. The statisticians saw that the savings from such technological innovations would enable the bureau to process more data, at a lower cost, with more accuracy. The savings could also be plowed back into further improvements in the statistics—to improve survey methods, to analyze errors, to try experimental new techniques.[9]

At the time, the project appeared both visionary and a bit "harebrained," as Duncan and Shelton put it. The mainstream data processing companies—and most notably IBM—were uninterested in developing computers. Over the next year, though, Hansen worked with the Department of Commerce Science Committee and the National Bureau of Standards to plan a computer project. In 1946, the bureau contracted with the recently created Eckert-Mauchly Computer Corporation to design a machine for statistical purposes. Eckert-Mauchly produced the plans for UNIVAC, the Universal Automatic Computer, in 1947. In June 1948, the Bureau of Standards and the Census Bureau ordered a machine for processing the 1950 census; the machine was delivered in March 1951. Functionally, UNIVAC was a system of machines. It included a card reader, which converted the information on the traditional census punch cards to magnetic tape. The tapes then became the input to the central processing unit, which was made up of some eighteen thousand vacuum tubes. This was programmed to tabulate the data. The results were printed out on a Uniprinter, initially a rather slow device. The machine arrived too late for much of the decennial census processing, but it did fulfill the hopes of the statisticians. It was the first nonmilitary computer; it proved the feasibility of electronic computing for tabulating and analyzing large amounts of information (see fig. 18).

In the 1880s, the bureau had sponsored the development of punch card tabulation equipment. In the 1940s and 1950s, the bureau again led the way in data processing for the rest of the government and the private sector. Most of the secondary literature on the history of computing indicates that the industry giants were slow to see the possibilities in the new electronic technology. As in the 1880s, it took government encour-

9. Duncan and Shelton, *Revolution in Statistics,* pp. 120–29.

18. Walter Cronkite, J. Presper Eckert, and Harold Sweeny with UNIVAC, 1952. Inventor J. Presper Eckert explains the new UNIVAC computer system to Walter Cronkite and how it could be used to monitor the results of the 1952 election campaign. Harold Sweeny operates the console.

agement and sponsorship, and government money, to provide the impetus for the development of this dramatic new technology.[10]

As World War II ended in mid-1945, officials in the Census Bureau, as in other government agencies, looked back at the difficult and hectic days of the Depression and war years and pondered the future. So much had changed in the previous ten years. Total war had followed the massive domestic crisis of the Depression. Franklin Roosevelt was dead and a less well known man, Harry Truman, was president. An era was over, and most hoped that the days of depression and war would not return.

Despite the hardship of those years, however, the officials knew that the crises had fostered innovation. They had accomplished a great deal, and they were optimistic about the future. Across the federal statistical

10. Ibid.; Nancy Stern, "From ENIAC to UNIVAC: A Case Study in the History of Technology" (Ph.D. diss., SUNY Stony Brook, 1978); Herman Goldstine, *The Computer from Pascal to Von Neumann* (Princeton, N.J.: Princeton University Press, 1972); Eckler, *Bureau of the Census,* pp. 116*ff.*

system, major new data collection efforts and analytical tools had been developed in the previous fifteen years. The National Income and Products Accounts had proved themselves to be supple planning tools during the war. The Full Employment Act of 1946 pointed the way to further efforts at the measurement and control of the economy to guarantee prosperity. In the Census Advisory Committee meetings at war's end, there was much enthusiastic talk of new initiatives. Secretary of Commerce Henry Wallace looked favorably on bureau proposals for new efforts. The Agriculture Census was proceeding well; the statisticians had also introduced probability sampling methods for this census. And, of course, the statisticians were already thinking about 1950. The methods introduced in 1940 had been so successful that they would be pursued further.

Hansen, Hurwitz, and their staff were confident that they could both increase the accuracy of the decennial census and reduce its costs. Some cost reductions in turn would be used to expand the kinds of data collected and sponsor further methodological research. The statisticians took two broad approaches. They wanted to expand the scope of sampling techniques in taking the decennial census. Further, they wanted to root out the sources of census errors by systematically analyzing the census-taking process from the respondent's doorstep to the publication of the final data.

The initial concern with census errors was a function of the new sampling methods. Since the mid-1930s, the statisticians had repeatedly had to prove to themselves and to the public that their samples were as accurate as the complete counts. They became accustomed to calculating and reporting precise sampling errors to prove the quality of their work. As they did so, however, they recognized that sampling error was merely one part of a much broader issue: total survey error. By the mid-1940s, Hansen, Hurwitz, Deming, and others were reconceptualizing the question of census error to include, as they put it, "the control of total survey error." This included measuring not only sampling variability but also errors caused by sloppy or biased work by enumerators, errors in transcribing data to the punch cards, or miscoded answers.

In the 1950 census, therefore, the statisticians increased the size of the sample census to 20 percent from 5 percent. For every fifth person whose name fell on a sample line, the enumerator asked an additional eighteen questions. They also built into the census-taking process an elaborate set of research and evaluation studies designed to measure enumerator variability and other census errors. They wrote a procedural history of the decennial census process to guide their own and their users' interpretations of the data.[11]

11. *1950 Censuses*, pp. 1–8.

"It's OK Boys. You can tell him everything... He's the Census Man!"

You're right, Rafe! The Census-Taker hasn't got any connection with the "Revenooers." Anything anybody tells him is strictly confidential. By law, Census facts and figures can't be shown to the tax people, the police, or anybody else.

Everything the Census-Taker asks is important to you and your family. Your answers will help leaders in industry, business, labor and civic groups to plan such things as better schools, better roads, better housing; better distribution of such services as telephones, gas, water, and electricity.

What's more, if you want to have a voice in the government you have to be counted in the Census. According to the Constitution, the number of Representatives your state is entitled to send to Congress is determined by the Census taken every ten years.

The Census man will come around to your house some time after April 1. Be ready to answer all his questions accurately, and honestly, and *quickly*. (Remember, it's a big job to count upwards of a hundred and fifty million noses!)

Radio and newspapers will do their best to tell you beforehand what most of the questions are. Watch for them and have your answers ready.

Like other American business firms, we believe that business has a responsibility to contribute to the public welfare. This advertisement is therefore sponsored by

NAME OF SPONSOR

Public service advertisement prepared by the Advertising Council, Inc. as part of the 1950 Censuses information campaign.

19. Advertising the Census, 1950. This Census Bureau cartoon was part of the 1950 census publicity campaign. Rural hillbillies are urged to cooperate with the enumerator. They are assured that their answers are confidential and that the data serves the society as a whole. The text raises many of the problems of counting a large, diverse population quickly and accurately.

The results of these studies confirmed the statisticians' fears. As all census officials since the nineteenth century had known, it was extraordinarily difficult to recruit in a number of months a reliable, competent staff of census enumerators and to guarantee uniform application of census procedures in the field. The 1950 evaluation studies indicated that on simple census questions, such as age and sex, the enumerators performed well. But in recording the answers to such complex questions as occupation and industry, two different interviewers recorded the answers differently in a sufficient number of cases to render the data suspect.

The census takers concluded from these studies that a decennial census would be more accurate if the enumerators could be eliminated altogether—that is, if the population could enumerate themselves. At the time, though, it was unclear if self-enumeration could be achieved. The statisticians also concluded that the errors introduced by the enumerators were of the same magnitude as the sampling error of a 25 percent sample. Thus, from the perspective of the total census, more accurate results could probably be achieved in a carefully taken sample than from a complete census.[12]

In line with these conclusions, therefore, the 1960 census design differed radically from its predecessors. For the first time, the sample census contained the majority of the questions. The bureau asked only five questions of the total population: the respondent's relationship to the household head, sex, color or race, marital status, and month and year of birth. The remaining population questions, containing thirty-one inquiries, were included on a 25 percent sample form. Further, the sampling unit was changed from the individual to the household "so that statistics on population characteristics such as education and employment status could be obtained from the sample for all members of families and households."[13]

The bureau also moved toward self-enumeration. In most urban areas—containing "80 percent of the population and housing units"—the post office delivered an "advance census report form" containing the complete count questions. Respondents were to fill out the form and wait for an enumerator to pick it up. If the individual filled it out correctly, the enumerator merely picked up the form, and, for every fourth household, left the longer sample form and made sure it was returned. If the individual did not fill out the advance form, the enumerator administered the questionnaire as he or she had in the past.[14]

Two other major innovations were also introduced in 1960. The first dealt with the census undercount. The 1950 evaluation studies had con-

12. Duncan and Shelton, *Revolution in Statistics*, pp. 60–65.
13. *1960 Censuses of Population and Housing: Procedural History*, p. 7.
14. Ibid., p. 6.

firmed work done in the 1940s documenting the differential census undercount. The officials estimated that they had missed 2 to 3 percent of the population in 1950, in particular, minorities, young men, and people living in poor, urban areas. In 1960, therefore, the bureau developed procedures to find hard-to-enumerate groups. They provided formal procedures for enumerators for filling out the forms when no one was home and for supervisors to assess if the enumerators were missing people.[15]

The other major innovation was the introduction of FOSDIC processing of the schedule data. FOSDIC, which stood for Film Optical Sensing Device for Input to Computers, eliminated the punch cards that had been used to transfer the data from the schedule to machine-readable form. The enumerators transferred the answers on the census form to the appropriate circles on a paper form. The forms were then microfilmed. FOSDIC then "read" the data according to the position of the marked circles and transformed the answers to computer-readable magnetic tape.[16]

These changes had considerable effects. In 1940 the decennial census had cost 51 cents per capita. By 1950 it cost 60 cents per capita, an 18 percent increase. At the same time, though, inflation, as measured by the consumer price index or the gross national product deflator, rose 70 to 80 percent. Despite this increase in efficiency, the coding, punching, and tabulating of the data took roughly the same amount of time in 1940 and 1950. Between 1950 and 1960, the gains were even greater. Again the per capita cost of the census rose considerably less than inflation (15 percent for the census and 25 to 30 percent for inflation). Even more dramatic evidence of the new methods are evident in the size of the census clerical and office staff. In 1950 an office staff of 9,233 worked on processing the census; in 1960 that number dropped to 2,960. In 1950, 3,000 key punchers transferred the data from the schedules to the machine-readable punch cards. In 1960, 100 "operators" accomplished the same task running the FOSDIC equipment. In 1950, all the data was ready for tabulation by July 1951; in 1960, it was ready two months earlier, in May 1961.[17] All these gains in processing efficiency freed up funds for additional tabulations and publications. The bureau published 58,400 pages of published reports in 1940, 61,700 in 1950, and 103,000 in 1960.

As the 1960s dawned, then, the bureau planned to build on the innovations of the 1940s and 1950s. Research and development of new methods had been built into the ongoing census work, and the bureau staff consistently looked for methods to try on the next census or survey. The census

15. Ibid., pp. 51–66.

16. Ibid., pp. 72–74; Duncan and Shelton, *Revolution in Statistics*, pp. 129–33.

17. *Historical Statistics*, pt. 1:197, 198, 210; Eckler, *Bureau of the Census*, p. 24; *1960 Censuses of Population and Housing: Procedural History*, pp. 73–74.

monograph series was revived in the 1950s, a working papers and technical papers series of publications was added to the occasional publications of the bureau, and the procedural histories were expanded.

Generally speaking, the continued upgrading of census data was prompted by demands for more and better data from other public officials. As the bureau developed more and better census statistics in the late 1940s, 1950s, and 1960s, legislators and officials in other government agencies learned to make increased use of them. Census data was being used for increasingly detailed analyses of the social and economic condition of American society. Further, Congress expanded federal aid to state and local governments through the grant-in-aid system. Congress enacted programs that used statistically based funding formulas to cover federal support to states and localities for school lunch programs, airport construction, and hospital construction in 1946, and for water pollution control in 1948. In the 1950s and 1960s, the grant-in-aid was used to supply federal funds for the interstate highway system, housing assistance, antipoverty programs, employment and training programs, urban redevelopment, and water and sewer projects.[18]

As the programs proliferated, so did concern about how the money was being spent, whether it was being distributed equitably, and whether the funding formulas worked adequately. Scholars began to explore the impact of the grants on the fiscal policies of American government and created the new field of intergovernmental relations. One aspect of this scholarly tradition examined the funding formulas and their statistical data bases. In particular, as the types of federal aid proliferated, so also did the types of allocation formulas used in particular pieces of legislation. The pre-Depression grant programs had used very simple formulas based on such measures as population, area, or road mileage. The agricultural extension and the vocational education grants had employed slightly more complicated measures: the Census Bureau's rural population, urban population, or farm or nonfarm population. These measures had sometimes proved troublesome in practice, since, for example, not all rural populations were farm populations. Nevertheless, they functioned well enough, given the small amounts of money being allocated.[19]

With the New Deal and postwar programs, though, Congress began to allocate funds on the basis of such measures as per capita income, mater-

18. The Committee on Federal Grants-in-Aid of the Council of State Governments, *Federal Grants-in-Aid* (n.p.: Council of State Governments, 1949), pp. 31*ff.*, chaps. 14–16; Paul Dommel, *The Politics of Revenue Sharing* (Bloomington, Ind.: Indiana University Press, 1974), pp. 19, 127*ff.*; Herrington Bryce, "The Impact of the Undercount on State and Local Government Transfers," in Bureau of the Census, *Conference on Census Undercount: Proceedings of the 1980 Conference* (Washington, D.C.: GPO, 1980), p. 112.

19. V. O. Key, *The Administration of Federal Grants to States* (Chicago: Public Administration Service, 1937), pp. 322*ff.*

nal mortality rates, or population density. Congress introduced these indicators because it recognized the differential fiscal capacity or wealth of the various states and wanted to equalize the national impact of the programs. As it did so, the grant programs shifted from simple mechanisms for delivering money to another, more appropriate administrative level of government and became more controversial methods of national income redistribution. A new set of census apportionment mechanisms— this time designed to distribute economic power—were being born. As they developed, it became obvious that they were designed to have a markedly different impact from the census political apportionment mechanisms.

The somewhat jerry-built character of American intergovernmental relations gives the impression that many of the effects of these measures were unintentional. Yet, if anything, the record of intent of the major policymakers concerned with these matters in the Roosevelt and later administrations indicates that they had much grander schemes for income redistribution and social equalization than they achieved in actual legislation. In particular, the rich literature on population policy that harks back to the census studies of urban congestion, rural depopulation, and migration played a major role in convincing both lawmakers and the public that policies promoting income redistribution were absolutely essential to prevent further depressions and guarantee national prosperity. We have already seen an early formulation of this concern in the National Resources Committee's study *The Problems of a Changing Population*.[20]

Economists Alvin Hansen and Harvey Perloff went even further in their 1944 study, *State and Local Finance in the National Economy*. They suggested that the federal government should "underwrite" "minimum service standards" in such matters as education, urban redevelopment, public health, national health insurance, and welfare. And they argued that the absence of such national standards already amounted to subsidies from one part of the nation to another. By way of example they suggested that the long-term migration pattern of youth from poorer, rural areas into the cities in effect constituted an educational subsidy to the cities. It was only fair, therefore, that the declining population region receive aid to equalize the educational burden. In short, Hansen and Perloff envisioned a kind of Keynesian countercyclical grant-in-aid policy. They advocated a streamlined, coordinated federal grant system that would both provide effective services and equalize the delivery of the services

20. National Resources Committee, *The Problems of a Changing Population* (Washington, D.C.: GPO, 1938), p. 5. For the context of the report, see Otis Graham, *Toward a Planned Society: From Roosevelt to Nixon* (New York: Oxford University Press, 1976), and Marion Clawson, *New Deal Planning: The National Resources Planning Board* (Baltimore: Johns Hopkins University Press, 1981), pp. 125*ff.*

nationwide. This would become a mechanism for smoothing out the ups and downs of the business cycle by preventing the kinds of fiscal crises that state and local governments faced in the early 1930s.[21]

The theories developed by the National Resources Committee staff and such economists as Alvin Hansen provided some of the basic philosophical principles that prompted the increased uses of grants to state and local governments in the 1940s, 1950s, and 1960s. Moreover, in the postwar period, since state governments remained in control of rural interests, the cities came to demand their own place in the intergovernmental sun. They developed direct relationships with Washington; by 1967, thirty-eight grant programs dealt directly with cities. Federal aid paid for 15 percent of total state and local government spending in 1960. The money involved in the programs amounted to $10 billion in 1964.[22]

There was much academic debate about whether these grants had the kind of "equalization" effect that Hansen and Perloff wanted them to, but it is clear from the indicators used in many of the grant formulas that Congress aimed at such an intent. In various laws, Congress used the unemployment rate, poverty level, per capita income, growth lag, or proportion of substandard housing of a geographic area to distribute funds. Overall, 83 of the 146 programs analyzed in a late 1970s study employed population or a derivative of population as a factor for distributing funds. Clearly, the census numbers had become critical to American fiscal life.[23]

By the early 1960s, then, census data were being used in a variety of new federal grant programs. Until this point statistical innovations and

21. Alvin Hansen and Harvey S. Perloff, *State and Local Finance in the National Economy* (New York: Norton, 1944); see also Hansen's discussion of the implications of the slowing national population growth rate in his *Fiscal Policy and Business Cycles* (New York: Norton, 1941), pp. 42*ff.* Hansen had been using census population statistics to analyze the changes in the American economy as early as 1920. See Margo Anderson Conk, *The United States Census and Labor Force Change* (Ann Arbor, Mich.: UMI Research Press, 1980), pp. 77*ff.* For a broader discussion of Keynes and population theory, see William Petersen, "John Maynard Keynes' Theories of Population and the Concept of the 'Optimum,'" in his *The Politics of Population* (Garden City, N.Y.: Doubleday, 1964), pp. 46–71.

22. Dommel, *Politics of Revenue Sharing*, pp. 127*ff.*; Bryce, "Impact of Undercount"; Claude E. Barfield, *Rethinking Federalism: Block Grants and Federal, State, and Local Responsibilities* (Washington, D.C.: American Enterprise Institute, 1981), p. 13.

23. See, e.g., Key, *Administration of Federal Grants*, pp. 3–5; U.S. Advisory Commission on Intergovernmental Relations, *The Role of Equalization in Federal Grants* (Washington, D.C.: GPO, 1964); Richard Nathan, Allen Manvel, and Susannah Calkins, *Monitoring Revenue Sharing* (Washington, D.C.: Brookings Institution, 1975), pp. 37–177; Roy Bahl, *Financing State and Local Government in the 1980s* (New York: Oxford University Press, 1984), pp. 19*ff.*; Lawrence Gelfand and Robert J. Neymeyer, eds., *Changing Patterns in American Federal-State Relations during the 1950's, 1960's and 1970's* (Iowa City, Iowa: University of Iowa Press, 1985).

legislative innovations had developed in tandem. Congress and the agencies looked for new types of data; the bureau responded and produced it. The Census Bureau increased the amount of detail in its publications, and it added and refined the questions. By the 1950s and 1960s, the bureau aimed at providing data for smaller and smaller geographic areas—census tracts and blocks—to target programs and analyses. The answers from the income question allowed statisticians to calculate per capita income distributions for local areas. The data on educational attainment—persons enrolled in school and number of years of school completed—improved steadily in the postwar period. In 1960 the bureau added questions on place of work and means of transportation to work to provide data on commuting.

As the processing of the 1960 census neared completion, the future looked good both for creating new methods and in providing higher-quality data to the general public. In particular, the statisticians hoped to completely dispense with one layer of bureaucracy—the enumerators—by going directly to the respondent's house by mail in 1970. They could finally then eliminate enumerator error as well as the increasing problem of dwellings with no one home during the day. And they could save money at the same time.[24]

Things for the rest of the decade did not turn out as planned, however. Significant demographic changes in the American population, political changes in the federal statistical system, and a spate of Supreme Court decisions, civil rights laws, and Great Society measures all placed new demands on the census. The Census Bureau again became embroiled in controversy.

Between the late 1920s and the 1960s, the American population was as heterogeneous and the growth patterns as volatile as they had been in the past. Nevertheless, as we have seen, Americans did not attribute social problems to population change itself. Urban society was no longer something to be dismantled. Immigrants and ethnic or regional minorities brought diversity, not racial "pollution." In fact, many of the most dramatic demographic trends of the mid-twentieth century were hailed as remedies to long-term population imbalances. Thus, for example, the postwar suburban migration and housing boom relieved the historic congestion of the old industrial cities and symbolized the prosperity of a new middle class. The dramatic black migration out of the South into the urban areas of the North and West indicated new employment possibilities in heavy industry and perhaps even a weakening of discriminatory practices. The postwar baby boom signaled a return of good economic

24. *1950 Censuses*; *1960 Censuses of Population and Housing: Procedural History*, esp. p. 9; Bureau of the Census, *1970 Census of Population and Housing: Procedural History* (Washington, D.C.: GPO, 1976).

times and a family-oriented society. By the 1950s, urban industrial society was not seen as the seedbed of class conflict and inequality. Rather, a well-managed capitalist economy could produce "the affluent society" and "the end of ideology."

Nevertheless, the future was not completely rosy. Postwar prosperity had not reached all Americans; it was not clear that the "natural" patterns of social mobility and population change would bring what Michael Harrington called "the other Americans" into the mainstream. In particular, while white migrants moved to the new desirable housing in the suburbs, black migrants were legally and economically barred from the suburban housing market. The result was that the old central cities became increasingly black and poor in the postwar years, while the suburbs stayed white and relatively affluent. Between 1950 and 1960, for example, the black population of inner cities grew by 3.3 million while the white population declined by 2 million. Relatedly, new forms of job discrimination in northern industry and new patterns of de facto segregation in the large public school systems of the North presaged not a decline in racial antagonisms but a nationalization of America's racial problems.

Harrington and the federal government further documented the existence of almost 40 million poor Americans in 1959. Over half the black population was poor; over one-third of the persons over 65 were poor. Large pockets of poverty still existed in the remote rural areas of the nation. The nation had not yet fulfilled its ideal of providing opportunity and an equitable allocation of society's resources to all Americans. By the mid-1960s, the Johnson administration called for a war on poverty. The legislative initiatives of the Great Society—Medicare, Medicaid, aid to education, food stamps, Job Corps, Legal Services—expanded both the scope and cost of federal social welfare programs. Civil rights activists called for national legislation to end the historic patterns of discrimination against black Americans. The Civil Rights Act of 1964 barred discrimination in employment on the basis of race, religion, sex, or national origin; it banned discrimination in public accommodations and in the allocation of federal funds; and it empowered the Justice Department to defend individuals whose rights had been violated. The Voting Rights of 1965 guaranteed blacks and other minorities access to the vote and created strict federal enforcement mechanisms. The Civil Rights Act of 1968 banned discrimination in the sale and rental of housing.[25]

The implications of the demographic changes in the population were

25. John Kenneth Galbraith, *The Affluent Society* (New York: Houghton Mifflin, 1958); Daniel Bell, *The End of Ideology* (Glencoe, Ill.: Free Press, 1960); Michael Harrington, *The Other Americans: Poverty in the United States* (New York: Macmillan, 1962); August Meier and Elliott Rudwick, *From Plantation to Ghetto* (New York: Hill and Wang, 1966); Richard Polenberg, *One Nation Divisible: Class, Race, and Ethnicity in the United States since 1938* (New York: Penguin Books, 1980).

also being felt in the political realm. In 1962 the Supreme Court ruled that malapportioned state legislatures were unconstitutional and opened the way for the decade of lawsuits that led to the "reapportionment revolution" of the 1960s. The effect of these suits on the census was profound and unexpected.

For forty years the federal courts, and particularly the Supreme Court, had refused to rule on apportionment cases. The courts had argued that legislative apportionment was strictly a legislative matter. The remedy for a group of people underrepresented in a malapportioned legislature was through that legislature itself. In the most important case on the issue, Colegrove v. Green (1946), Justice Frankfurter had ruled that congressional apportionment was a "political thicket" that the courts had no right to enter. The effect of the decision was to uphold the constitutionality of the Illinois congressional delegation. Illinois's largest district encompassed 914,053 people and the smallest only 112,116.[26]

Throughout the country, congressional districts represented radically different-sized populations. For example, as mentioned earlier, under the 1930 apportionment, the largest congressional district in New York contained 799,407 people, the smallest 90,671. In 1960, 14 of Michigan's 19 districts were malapportioned, 14 of Ohio's 24, 20 of Texas's 23. On the state level, many legislatures simply stopped reapportioning altogether. Illinois and Tennessee did not reapportion after 1901, despite massive population growth, until forced by the federal court decisions. These malapportioned legislatures overrepresented the rural areas of the country and underrepresented the urban and suburban areas.[27]

In the 1950s, however, the malapportionment issue reemerged in the federal courts, and slowly a series of carefully designed test cases made their way to the Supreme Court. Perhaps the relative political calm of the 1950s compared with the upheavals of Depression and World War II allowed Americans to take a look at their representative institutions and see the anomalies of malapportionment. Certainly reformers pressing the issue said as much. They pointed to two cogent reasons for reversing the trend toward malapportionment. First, they pointed out that by the 1950s, malapportionment was not simply a rural versus urban issue. The exploding suburban populations of middle-class whites were also under-

26. Colegrove v. Green, 328 U.S. 549 (1946) at 557–59. The first notation of the need to tailor census data to apportionment needs in an official census bureau history occurred in the *1970 Census of Population and Housing: Procedural History* (pp. 1–13).

27. See, e.g., Congressional Quarterly, "History of Reapportionment and Redistricting," *Guide to U.S. Elections* (Washington, D.C.: Congressional Quarterly, 1975), pp. 519–41; Gene Graham, *One Man, One Vote* (Boston: Little, Brown, 1972); Robert Dixon, *Democratic Representation: Reapportionment in Law and Politics* (New York: Oxford University Press, 1968); and Robert McKay, *Reapportionment: The Law and Politics of Equal Representation* (New York: Twentieth Century Fund, 1965).

represented in congress and their state legislatures, and the discrepancies were widening. Further, commentators in the 1960s suggested that the problems of the cities were at least partly the result of decades of systematic underrepresentation and underfunding.[28]

The Supreme Court accepted these arguments and in 1962 ruled in Baker v. Carr that the Tennessee legislature had to be reapportioned. A series of cases that overthrew apportionments in other legislatures and in Congress followed. By 1964 the phrase "one man one vote" had entered the nation's political vocabulary to define the new principle of legislative apportionment. Suddenly, accurate census data for small geographic areas became more important. Not only were the grants-in-aid of the Great Society programs of the mid-1960s prompting increased use of census data. The apportionment cases suggested that the Census Bureau had a strict constitutional duty under the equal protection clause of the Fourteenth Amendment to count everyone.[29]

By the 1960s, then, the new constitutional requirements for apportionment and expansion the federal grant system led to major new pressures on the census. In particular, the bureau was required to provide detailed cross-tabulations of the census information for smaller and smaller geographic areas to make sure that the apportionments were fair and equitable.

Further, the civil rights legislation also relied on high-quality census data for administration and implementation. For the Census Bureau, the most immediately controversial law was the Voting Rights Act of 1965. This law enforced the Fifteenth Amendment to the Constitution, which stated that the "right . . . to vote shall not be denied or abridged by the United States or by any State on account of race, color, or previous condition of servitude." In the 1870s, of course, though the effort had failed, Congress had also tried to use the Census Bureau and census data to enforce black voting rights. In the mid-1960s, Congress created clear numerical tests of compliance with the constitutional goals of voting rights. As written in the original 1965 provision, if a state used a literacy test for voter registration and if voter registration or turnout was less than 50 percent of the voting age population of a jurisdiction, then the law presumed a violation of the Fifteenth Amendment. In such a case, the literacy tests were suspended, and the Justice Department could send

28. Paul David and Ralph Eisenberg, *Devaluation of the Urban and Suburban Vote: A Statistical Investigation of Long-term Trends in State Legislative Representation* (Charlottesville, Va.: Bureau of Public Administration, 1961), pp. 10*ff.*; Andrew Hacker, *Congressional Districting: The Issue of Equal Representation* (Washington, D.C.: Brookings Institution, 1964); Graham, *One Man, One Vote.*

29. Graham, *One Man, One Vote*; Dixon, *Democratic Representation*; Baker v. Carr, 369 U.S. 182 (1962); Reynolds v. Sims, 377 U.S. 533 (1964); Wesberry v. Sanders, 376 U.S. 1 (1964), was the major congressional districting case.

federal registrars and election observers to monitor elections. Such jurisdictions also had to "preclear" any new voting qualifications with the
attorney general of the United States. Six southern states came under
these rules; counties in several other states were also affected. Again,
census data would have a direct impact on a highly charged political
issue.[30]

During the planning phase for the 1970 count, census officials and
policymakers generally began to recognize just how much they had come
to rely on adequate, accurate census data. They further recognized that
the differential census undercount of certain segments of the population—especially minorities and the urban poor—was not merely a technical question. Once the Supreme Court had invalidated the massive legislative malapportionments of the past, the census undercount could also
have the effect of denying representation to the uncounted. The undercount ceased to be simply a technical problem of census field procedures;
it became an explosive political issue. The 1967 Conference on Social
Statistics and the City marked the change. At that conference, census
officials and prominent social scientists met in Washington to discuss the
extent and cause of the undercounts and to propose remedies. They
articulated the constitutional principle that made eliminating the differential undercount imperative. "Where a group defined by racial or
ethnic terms, and concentrated in special political jurisdictions," wrote
David Heer in the conference report, "is significantly undercounted in
relation to other groups, then individual members of that group are
thereby deprived of the constitutional right to equal representation in the
House of Representatives and, by inference, in other legislative bodies."
They are also "deprived of their entitlement to partake in federal and
other programs designed for areas and populations with their characteristics." In other words, miscounting the population could unconstitu-
tionally deny minorities political representation or protection under the
Voting Rights Act. It could also deny local jurisdictions grant funds from
federal programs.[31]

By the time the conference was held, the Census Bureau was well into
its planning phase for the 1970 census. The bureau had decided to use a
mail census for 60 percent of the country—primarily the large metropolitan areas. As in 1960, most of the detailed questions were placed on
the sample questionnaire. Two samples were planned, one of 5 percent of

30. Eckler, *Bureau of the Census*, pp. 157*ff*.; Abigail Thernstrom, "Statistics and Politics:
The 1965 Voting Rights Act," in *The Politics of Numbers*, ed. William Alonzo and Paul Starr
(New York: Russell Sage, 1987).

31. David Heer, ed., *Social Statistics and the City* (Cambridge, Mass.: Joint Center for
Urban Studies, 1968), quotation on p. 11.

the households and one of 15 percent. Some questions were on both and thus effectively constituted a 20 percent sample. The bureau was also in the process of developing complex geographic coding systems to facilitate the mail census. The calls for detailed information on blacks and other minorities had prompted efforts to increase the publication of data on minorities in the 1970 census. Officials expressed guarded optimism about their ability both to move toward a mail census and to improve overall coverage of the population. After all, the technical studies of census procedures and special test censuses had provided the bureau with a great deal of information about what did and did not work, where errors crept into the data, which methods were most efficient, and so on.[32]

Nevertheless, some troubling signs had appeared on the horizon. First, although the bureau had known the magnitude of the differential under-count for almost twenty years, they had not been very successful in reducing it. In 1950, 11.5 percent of blacks were missed; in 1960, 9.5 percent. Only 2.2 percent of whites were missed in 1960. Eli Marks and Joseph Waksberg concluded in 1966 that the techniques designed to improve coverage in 1960 "were not sufficient to deal with the extraordi-nary difficulties that were encountered in the slum areas." Further, social scientists worried that mail enumeration procedures would even worsen coverage if address lists were incomplete, if the local population did not read English, or if people lacked that middle-class attribute of civic-mindedness that would make them voluntarily fill out and mail in a census schedule. The bureau assured its critics that it would develop major new publicity programs to advertise the census and that it would work closely with local leaders and officials to make sure that everyone was counted.[33]

At the same time, other pressures also bore down on the bureau. Some congressmen objected to particular questions on the census on the grounds of invasion of privacy, as had occurred in previous decades. In 1940, as we have seen, the income question became the focus of an attack on the Roosevelt administration for promoting Big Government and violating the privacy of the individual. In the late 1960s, the questions on the number of children ever born to a woman and on bathroom facilities prompted similar types of objections. There were proposals to drop the penalties for refusing to answer the census. These efforts were not suc-cessful, but they did consume precious official time and effort. The bureau found itself condemned both for collecting too much information

32. *1970 Census of Population and Housing: Procedural History*; see also the papers pre-sented at the American Statistical Association meeting in August 1966, published as the *Proceedings of the Social Statistics Section of the American Statistical Association* (1966): 1–42.

33. Eli Marks and Joseph Waksberg, "Evaluation of Coverage in the 1960 Census of Population Through Case-By-Case Checking," in *Proceedings . . . of the American Statistical Association* (1966): 64.

and for not collecting enough. As the census year approached, the pressure increased.[34]

Overall, the 1970 census proceeded according to plans. The bureau counted 203 million people and came extremely close to its own estimate of the 1970 population. Eleven seats in Congress were reapportioned. The census showed dramatic population shifts out of cities and toward the suburbs and away from the North and East and toward the South and West. California outstripped New York to become the most populous state.

Nevertheless, there were complaints about the count. Several federal lawsuits were filed against the Census Bureau charging that the mail census would fail to reach the non-English speaking urban populations and Hispanic Americans. The courts dismissed the suits on the grounds that the bureau had the authority and the expertise to determine the method of enumeration and that there was no evidence to indicate that the mail census would produce an undercount. Mayors of large cities were worried that their cities would show population declines. And a coalition of civil rights groups had formed a Coalition for a Black Count to encourage people to cooperate with the census and then to make sure the Census Bureau counted black Americans. As the bureau finished processing the data in the early 1970s, congressional committees and civil rights organizations began to look ever more closely into the internal workings of the census. The bureau would soon face major new challenges.[35]

34. Jenkins, *1940 Census*, pp. 15*ff.*; *1970 Census of Population and Housing: Procedural History*, chap. 1, pp. 16–17; Conrad Taeuber, "Invasion of Privacy: The Case of the United States Census," and William Petersen, "The Protection of Privacy and the United States Census," both in Martin Bulmer, ed., *Censuses, Surveys and Privacy* (London: Macmillan, 1979), pp. 170–83.

35. *1970 Census of Population and Housing: Procedural History*, pp. 1–13*ff.*; Quon v. Stans, 309 F. Supp. 604 (1970); Prieto v. Stans, 321 F. Supp. 1420 (1970); *New York Times*, Feb. 11, 1970.

NINE | The 1980 Census and
the Politics of Counting

*No issue figured as prominently in planning the 1980 census as
the undercount of minority groups in 1970.*
—*Bureau of the Census*, 1980 Census History, *1984*

During the 1960s, the expanded federal grants-in-aid, the
civil rights laws, and the reapportionment decisions had
gradually placed new burdens on the federal census and
on population statistics generally. Congress, federal court
judges, and public officials had turned to census data to create and apply standards of equitable distribution of political
and fiscal resources. They had done so because a census apportionment mechanism was simple, automatic, and part of
the long-standing traditions of American constitutional law.
In many cases, Congress and the Supreme Court couched
their new rules in terms of the historic role of the census in
the American constitutional system. After all, Americans
had allocated political power to geographic areas "according to their respective numbers" for almost two hundred
years. Federal grants to states and local areas were eighty
years old.

Despite these continuities, the new entitlements and apportionments were not uncontroversial and spawned debates about the propriety, justice, and effectiveness of the
new mechanisms. On the right, racists continued to oppose
the dismantling of the Jim Crow system. Politicians from
sparsely settled areas opposed the one-man-one-vote principle and continued to litigate legislative apportionment in
the courts. Conservatives opposed the expansion of the
welfare state. On the left, leaders of the newly active com-

munity groups in the cities pressed for more federal funding to end poverty. Radical civil rights activists doubted that the new laws would be effective in ending minority poverty and institutional racism and called for compensatory treatment to hurry up the process of equalization. By the late 1960s, within this increasingly contentious arena, federal officials began to implement much of the new Great Society and civil rights legislation and thus to define what they meant in practice.

In the area of civil rights, judges and government officials quickly discovered that ending school segregation or guaranteeing blacks (and soon other minorities and women) access to jobs was not as easy as opening public accommodations. Slowly, therefore, these judges and officials began to articulate standards for "affirmative action" by school districts and employers to end discrimination. By 1970 the courts endorsed a "very limited use of mathematical ratios" to determine the racial balance of a school system. In 1971 the Office of Federal Contract Compliance required employers to set "goals and timetables" for levels of minority hiring in firms with federal contracts. Census numbers would be used to set the "quotas."[1]

Implementing the new procedures generated new controversy. While the federal officials and judges who set the rules claimed that they were simply doing what had to be done to implement the intent of Congress and guarantee the victims of discrimination "equal protection of the laws," critics of the new procedures found the quotas and preferences a dangerous violation of traditional American values. "Are the members of the minority groups to be found in employment, at every level," asked Daniel Bell rhetorically in 1972, "in numbers equal to their proportion in the population?" He could not believe that Americans intended to embrace such a position. He suggested that "an entirely new principle of rights has been introduced into the polity"—"without public debate." The new affirmative action rules meant that "*the principle has changed from discrimination to 'representation.'*" Thus, he continued, meritocratic ideals would suffer: "Women, blacks, and Chicanos now are to be employed, as a matter of right, in proportion to their number, and the principle of professional qualification or individual achievement is subordinated to the new ascriptive principle of corporate identity."[2]

1. See Richard Polenberg, *One Nation Divisible: Class, Race, and Ethnicity in the United States since 1938* (New York: Penguin Books, 1980), pp. 237–41. The "mathematical ratios" quotation is from Swann v. Charlotte-Mecklenburg Board of Education, 402 U.S. 1 (1971) at 25.

2. Daniel Bell, "On Meritocracy and Equality," in *The New Egalitarianism: Questions and Challenges*, ed. David Lewis Schaefer, (Port Washington, N.Y.: Kennikat Press, 1979), pp. 25–26, emphasis in original. The article initially appeared in the *Public Interest* 29 (Fall 1972): 29–68. See also Terry Eastland and William J. Bennett, *Counting by Race: Equality from the Founding Fathers to Bakke and Weber* (New York: Basic Books, 1979).

Here are the QUESTIONS ↓	These are the columns for ANSWERS ➡ Please fill one column for each person listed in Question 1.	PERSON in column 1	PERSON in column 2
		Last name	Last name
		First name — Middle initial	First name — Middle initial
2. How is this person related to the person in column 1? Fill one circle. If "Other relative" of person in column 1, give exact relationship, such as mother-in-law, niece, grandson, etc.		_START_ in this column with the household member (or one of the members) in whose name the home is owned or rented. If there is no such person, start in this column with any adult household member.	If relative of person in column 1: ○ Husband/wife ○ Father/mother ○ Son/daughter ○ Other relative ○ Brother/sister — If not related to person in column 1: ○ Roomer, boarder ○ Other nonrelative ○ Partner, roommate ○ Paid employee
3. Sex Fill one circle.		○ Male ■ ○ Female	○ Male ■ ○ Female
4. Is this person — Fill one circle.		○ White ○ Asian Indian ○ Black or Negro ○ Hawaiian ○ Japanese ○ Guamanian ○ Chinese ○ Samoan ○ Filipino ○ Eskimo ○ Korean ○ Aleut ○ Vietnamese ○ Other — Specify ○ Indian (Amer.) Print tribe →	○ White ○ Asian Indian ○ Black or Negro ○ Hawaiian ○ Japanese ○ Guamanian ○ Chinese ○ Samoan ○ Filipino ○ Eskimo ○ Korean ○ Aleut ○ Vietnamese ○ Other — Specify ○ Indian (Amer.) Print tribe →
5. Age, and month and year of birth a. Print age at last birthday. b. Print month and fill one circle. c. Print year in the spaces, and fill one circle below each number.		a. Age at last birthday / c. Year of birth / b. Month of birth / ○ Jan.—Mar. ○ Apr.—June ○ July—Sept. ○ Oct.—Dec.	a. Age at last birthday / c. Year of birth / b. Month of birth / ○ Jan.—Mar. ○ Apr.—June ○ July—Sept. ○ Oct.—Dec.
6. Marital status Fill one circle.		○ Now married ○ Separated ○ Widowed ○ Never married ○ Divorced	○ Now married ○ Separated ○ Widowed ○ Never married ○ Divorced
7. Is this person of Spanish/Hispanic origin or descent? Fill one circle.		○ No (not Spanish/Hispanic) ○ Yes, Mexican, Mexican-Amer., Chicano ○ Yes, Puerto Rican ■ ○ Yes, Cuban ○ Yes, other Spanish/Hispanic	○ No (not Spanish/Hispanic) ○ Yes, Mexican, Mexican-Amer., Chicano ○ Yes, Puerto Rican ■ ○ Yes, Cuban ○ Yes, other Spanish/Hispanic
8. Since February 1, 1980, has this person attended regular school or college at any time? Fill one circle. Count nursery school, kindergarten, elementary school, and schooling which leads to a high school diploma or college degree.		○ No, has not attended since February 1 ○ Yes, public school, public college ○ Yes, private, church-related ○ Yes, private, not church-related	○ No, has not attended since February 1 ○ Yes, public school, public college ○ Yes, private, church-related ○ Yes, private, not church-related
9. What is the highest grade (or year) of regular school this person has ever attended? Fill one circle. If now attending school, mark grade person is in. If high school was finished by equivalency test (GED), mark "12."		Highest grade attended: ○ Nursery school ○ Kindergarten Elementary through high school (grade or year) 1 2 3 4 5 6 7 8 9 10 11 12 ○○○○○○ ○○ ○○○ ○ College (academic year) ■ 1 2 3 4 5 6 7 8 or more ○○○○○○○○ ○ Never attended school — Skip question 10	Highest grade attended: ○ Nursery school ○ Kindergarten Elementary through high school (grade or year) 1 2 3 4 5 6 7 8 9 10 11 12 ○○○○○○ ○○ ○○○ ○ College (academic year) ■ 1 2 3 4 5 6 7 8 or more ○○○○○○○○ ○ Never attended school — Skip question 10
10. Did this person finish the highest grade (or year) attended? Fill one circle.		○ Now attending this grade (or year) ○ Finished this grade (or year) ○ Did not finish this grade (or year)	○ Now attending this grade (or year) ○ Finished this grade (or year) ○ Did not finish this grade (or year)
		CENSUS USE ONLY **A.** ○ I ○ N ○○	CENSUS USE ONLY **A.** ○ I ○ N ○○

20. 1980 Census of Population Inquiries. The 1980 schedule (with the sample questions) was filled in by the respondent and mailed back. The questions are very detailed. The schedule is designed so that the FOSDIC system could "read" the answers and transfer them to magnetic tape.

Name of Person 1 on page 2:

Last name   First name   Middle initial

11. In what State or foreign country was this person born?
Print the State where this person's mother was living when this person was born. Do not give the location of the hospital unless the mother's home and the hospital were in the same State.

_____
Name of State or foreign country; or Puerto Rico, Guam, etc.

12. If this person was born in a foreign country —
a. Is this person a naturalized citizen of the United States?
- ○ Yes, a naturalized citizen
- ○ No, not a citizen
- ○ Born abroad of American parents

b. When did this person come to the United States to stay?
- ○ 1975 to 1980 ○ 1965 to 1969 ○ 1950 to 1959
- ○ 1970 to 1974 ○ 1960 to 1964 ○ Before 1950

13a. Does this person speak a language other than English at home?
- ○ Yes   ○ No, only speaks English — *Skip to 14*

b. What is this language?
_____
(For example — Chinese, Italian, Spanish, etc.)

c. How well does this person speak English?
- ○ Very well   ○ Not well
- ○ Well   ○ Not at all

14. What is this person's ancestry? *If uncertain about how to report ancestry, see instruction guide.*
_____
(For example — Afro-Amer., English, French, German, Honduran, Hungarian, Irish, Italian, Jamaican, Korean, Lebanese, Mexican, Nigerian, Polish, Ukrainian, Venezuelan, etc.)

15a. Did this person live in this house five years ago (April 1, 1975)?
If in college or Armed Forces in April 1975, report place of residence there.
- ○ Born April 1975 or later — *Turn to next page for next person*
- ○ Yes, this house — *Skip to 16*
- ○ No, different house

b. Where did this person live five years ago (April 1, 1975)?
(1) State, foreign country, Puerto Rico, Guam, etc.: _____
(2) County: _____
(3) City, town, village, etc.: _____
(4) Inside the incorporated (legal) limits of that city, town, village, etc.?
- ○ Yes   ○ No, in unincorporated area

16. When was this person born?
- ○ Born before April 1965 — *Please go on with questions 17-33*
- ○ Born April 1965 or later — *Turn to next page for next person*

17. In April 1975 (five years ago) was this person —
a. On active duty in the Armed Forces?
- ○ Yes   ○ No
b. Attending college?
- ○ Yes   ○ No
c. Working at a job or business?
- ○ Yes, full time   ○ No
- ○ Yes, part time

18a. Is this person a veteran of active-duty military service in the Armed Forces of the United States?
If service was in National Guard or Reserves only, see instruction guide.
- ○ Yes   ○ No — *Skip to 19*

b. Was active-duty military service during —
Fill a circle for each period in which this person served.
- ○ May 1975 or later
- ○ Vietnam era *(August 1964–April 1975)*
- ○ February 1955—July 1964
- ○ Korean conflict *(June 1950–January 1955)*
- ○ World War II *(September 1940–July 1947)*
- ○ World War I *(April 1917–November 1918)*
- ○ Any other time

19. Does this person have a physical, mental, or other health condition which has lasted for 6 or more months and which . . .

	Yes	No
a. **Limits** the kind or amount of work this person can do at a job?	○	○
b. **Prevents** this person from working at a job?	○	○
c. **Limits or prevents** this person from using public transportation?	○	○

20. If this person is a female —
How many babies has she ever had, not counting stillbirths?
Do not count her stepchildren or children she has adopted.
- None 1 2 3 4 5 6 ○ ○○○○○○
- 7 8 9 10 11 12 or more ○○○○○○

21. If this person has ever been married —
a. Has this person been married more than once?
- ○ Once   ○ More than once
b. Month and year of marriage? / **Month and year of first marriage?**
(Month) _(Year)_   _(Month)_ _(Year)_
c. If married more than once — Did the first marriage end because of the death of the husband (or wife)?
- ○ Yes   ○ No

22a. Did this person work at any time last week?
- ○ Yes — *Fill this circle if this person worked full time or part time. (Count part-time work such as delivering papers, or helping without pay in a family business or farm. Also count active duty in the Armed Forces.)*
- ○ No — *Fill this circle if this person did not work, or did only own housework, school work, or volunteer work.* Skip to 25

b. How many hours did this person work last week (at all jobs)?
Subtract any time off; add overtime or extra hours worked.
_____ Hours

23. At what location did this person work last week?
If this person worked at more than one location, print where he or she worked most last week.
If one location cannot be specified, see instruction guide.
a. Address (Number and street) _____
If street address is not known, enter the building name, shopping center, or other physical location description.
b. Name of city, town, village, borough, etc. _____
c. Is the place of work inside the incorporated (legal) limits of that city, town, village, borough, etc.?
- ○ Yes   ○ No, in unincorporated area
d. County _____
e. State _____   **f. ZIP Code** _____

24a. Last week, how long did it usually take this person to get from home to work (one way)?
_____ Minutes

b. How did this person usually get to work last week?
If this person used more than one method, give the one usually used for most of the distance.
- ○ Car   ○ Taxicab
- ○ Truck   ○ Motorcycle
- ○ Van   ○ Bicycle
- ○ Bus or streetcar   ○ Walked only
- ○ Railroad   ○ Worked at home
- ○ Subway or elevated   ○ Other — *Specify*
If car, truck, or van in 24b, go to 24c. Otherwise, skip to 28.

c. When going to work last week, did this person usually —
○ Drive alone — *Skip to 28*   ○ Drive others only
○ Share driving   ○ Ride as passenger only

d. How many people, including this person, usually rode to work in the car, truck, or van last week?
○ 2   ■ 4   ○ 6
○ 3   ○ 5   ○ 7 or more ■
After answering 24d, skip to 28.

25. Was this person temporarily absent or on layoff from a job or business last week?
○ Yes, on layoff
○ Yes, on vacation, temporary illness, labor dispute, etc.
○ No

26a. Has this person been looking for work during the last 4 weeks?
○ Yes   ○ No — *Skip to 27*

b. Could this person have taken a job last week?
○ No, already has a job ■
○ No, temporarily ill
○ No, other reasons *(in school, etc.)*
○ Yes, could have taken a job ■

27. When did this person last work, even for a few days?
○ 1980   ○ 1978   ○ 1970 to 1974
○ 1979   ○ 1975 to 1977   ○ 1969 or earlier   } Skip to 31d
○ Never worked

28 – 30. Current or most recent job activity
Describe clearly this person's chief job activity or business last week. If this person had more than one job, describe the one at which this person worked the most hours. If this person had no job or business last week, give information for last job or business since 1975.

28. Industry
a. For whom did this person work? *If now on active duty in the Armed Forces, print "AF" and skip to question 31.*

(Name of company, business, organization, or other employer)

b. What kind of business or industry was this?
Describe the activity at location where employed.

(For example: Hospital, newspaper publishing, mail order house, auto engine manufacturing, breakfast cereal manufacturing) ■

c. Is this mainly — (Fill one circle)
○ Manufacturing ■   ○ Retail trade
○ Wholesale trade   ○ Other — *(agriculture, construction, service, government, etc.)*

29. Occupation
a. What kind of work was this person doing?

(For example: Registered nurse, personnel manager, supervisor of order department, gasoline engine assembler, grinder operator)

b. What were this person's most important activities or duties?

(For example: Patient care, directing hiring policies, supervising order clerks, assembling engines, operating grinding mill)

30. Was this person — (Fill one circle)
Employee of private company, business, or individual, for wages, salary, or commissions ..... ○
Federal government employee .... ○
State government employee .... ○
Local government employee *(city, county, etc.)* ...... ○
Self-employed in own business, professional practice, or farm —
Own business not incorporated .... ○
Own business incorporated .... ○
Working without pay in family business or farm ..... ○

31a. Last year (1979), did this person work, even for a few days, at a paid job or in a business or farm?
○ Yes ■   ○ No — *Skip to 31d*

b. How many weeks did this person work in 1979?
Count paid vacation, paid sick leave, and military service.
_____ Weeks

c. During the weeks worked in 1979, how many hours did this person usually work each week?
_____ Hours

d. Of the weeks not worked in 1979 (if any), how many weeks was this person looking for work or on layoff from a job?
_____ Weeks

32. Income in 1979 —
Fill circles and print dollar amounts. If net income was a loss, write "Loss" above the dollar amount. If exact amount is not known, give best estimate. For income received jointly by household members, see instruction guide.

During 1979 did this person receive any income from the following sources?
If "Yes" to any of the sources below — How much did this person receive for the entire year?

a. Wages, salary, commissions, bonuses, or tips from all jobs ... *Report amount before deductions for taxes, bonds, dues, or other items.*
○ Yes → $ _____ .00
○ No   *(Annual amount – Dollars)*

b. Own nonfarm business, partnership, or professional practice ... *Report net income after business expenses.*
○ Yes → $ _____ .00
○ No   *(Annual amount – Dollars)*

c. Own farm... *Report net income after operating expenses. Include earnings as a tenant farmer or sharecropper.*
○ Yes → $ _____ .00
○ No   *(Annual amount – Dollars)*

d. Interest, dividends, royalties, or net rental income ... *Report even small amounts credited to an account.*
○ Yes → $ _____ .00
○ No   *(Annual amount – Dollars)*

e. Social Security or Railroad Retirement ...
○ Yes → $ _____ .00
○ No   *(Annual amount – Dollars)*

f. Supplemental Security (SSI), Aid to Families with Dependent Children (AFDC), or other public assistance or public welfare payments ...
○ Yes → $ _____ .00
○ No   *(Annual amount – Dollars)*

g. Unemployment compensation, veterans' payments, pensions, alimony or child support, or any other sources of income received regularly ... *Exclude lump-sum payments such as money from an inheritance or the sale of a home.*
■ Yes → $ _____ .00
○ No   *(Annual amount – Dollars)*

33. What was this person's total income in 1979?
Add entries in questions 32a through g; subtract any losses.
$ _____ .00   *(Annual amount – Dollars)*
If total amount was a loss, write "Loss" above amount.   OR ○ None

By the mid-1970s, neoconservatives had defined such "group rights" claims for preferential treatment as "reverse discrimination" against white males. The courts wrestled with the implications of the "timetables" and "quota" systems and handed down a series of ambiguous rulings that neither endorsed group rights arguments nor banned quotas to end discrimination.[3]

The history of census apportionments provides insight into the reasons for these ambiguous rulings. The Constitution and American law clearly have not been color-blind and have used numerical rules to define both equality and inequality. The Constitution numerically defined slaves as three-fifths of a free person for apportionment purposes. Congress wrote the Wartime Amendments to guarantee freed slaves formal equality after emancipation and attempted to define a numerical rule to penalize states that did not enfranchise the freed slaves. And Congress legislated immigration quotas to exclude immigrants from southern and eastern Europe because of their racial characteristics. However, neither the Constitution nor Congress has explicitly accorded apportionment benefits or penalties to groups. Census apportionments were always accorded to geographic areas—states or local areas—even when these were proxies for particular interests or social groups. What did ring true to many Americans in the new efforts to create "group rights" apportionments was the ideal of equitable and fair apportionment of society's benefits—particularly in remedying the maldistributive effects of previous discriminatory practices. Like the countercyclical grants-in-aid developed during the New Deal years, the affirmative action quotas sought to counteract the bad effects of America's racist past. Whether they have succeeded or have created more social conflict than they eliminated is still at issue. What is clear is that they have made accurate statistical descriptions of the population and its subgroups extraordinarily important for social policy.[4]

Relatedly, as the 1970s dawned, Congress and the more conservative Nixon administration wrestled with the propriety and effectiveness of the Great Society measures. Conservatives continued to oppose the new categorical social welfare measures and moved to trim and redirect these

3. See, e.g., Nathan Glazer, *Affirmative Discrimination: Ethnic Inequality and Public Policy* (New York: Basic Books, 1975); Barry Gross, ed., *Reverse Discrimination* (Buffalo, N.Y.: Prometheus Books, 1977); Timothy J. O'Neill, *Bakke and the Politics of Equality: Friends and Foes in the Classroom of Litigation* (Middletown, Conn.: Wesleyan University Press, 1985); Bernard Boxill, *Blacks and Social Justice* (Totowa, N.J.: Rowman & Allanheld, 1984); and Daniel C. Maguire, *A New American Justice: Ending the White Male Monopolies* (Garden City, N.Y.: Doubleday, 1980).

4. For the frustrations of the statisticians concerned with civil rights enforcement, see the chapter on "Civil Rights Data" in Department of Commerce, Office of Federal Statistical Policy and Standards, *A Framework for Planning U.S. Federal Statistics for the 1980's* (Washington, D.C.: GPO, 1978), pp. 214–53.

programs. Liberals wanted to expand federal domestic spending into new areas. Out of this peculiar mix of priorities came perhaps the culmination of the grant-in-aid allocation system: the revenue sharing legislation of 1972. Recognizing the superior tax capacity of the federal government, Congress and the Nixon administration agreed to the legislation for very different reasons. Republicans hoped to end the targeted grant programs to state and local governments and give money to the more conservative majority of local officials. Liberals saw a general expansion in the grant-in-aid system and hence the possibility of an equitable and nationally based set of state and local services. Everyone aimed at developing uniform, national, automatic, and precise mechanisms for allocating federal funds to all fifty states and 39,000 local governments. The formulas again employed census data.[5]

Advocates of general revenue sharing hoped that this legislation would signal a fundamental new relationship between the national and the state governments. In the eighteenth century, as we noted, the census was designed to allocate the tax burden as well as political representation among the states. As we have seen, Congress tried and rejected this facet of the census apportionment system, since the tariff and land sales made for "an overflowing Treasury" for much of the nineteenth century and since a direct tax apportioned on the basis of population did not adequately measure the differential tax capacities of urban and rural areas. In 1913 the Sixteenth Amendment repealed the provision and permitted a federal income tax without apportionment among the states on the basis of population. Over the course of the twentieth century, the share of federal revenues from the income tax grew, as did the proportion of federal tax revenue to all government revenue. Policymakers suggested that it was possible to use the revenue-sharing mechanism to provide financial resources to all the states and local governments in the country and still preserve the principles of a federal governmental system. In a sense, Congress recreated the census revenue apportionment system in a late twentieth-century form—reversing the roles played by the respective taxpayer and recipients.[6]

By the early 1970s, then, census-based quotas, apportionments, and grants were very much a part of business as usual in national politics, and Census Bureau officials found themselves called on to provide more numbers on the population and more information on the numbers to Congress and the general public. The bureau, and many of the top

5. Paul Dommel, *The Politics of Revenue Sharing* (Bloomington, Ind.: Indiana University Press, 1974), pp. 175*ff.*; Richard Nathan, Allen Manvel, and Susannah Calkins, *Monitoring Revenue Sharing* (Washington, D.C.: Brookings Institution, 1975), pp. 344–72.

6. Nathan, Manvel, and Calkins noted the precedent of the distribution of the surplus in 1837 (*Monitoring Revenue Sharing*, pp. 344–45). See also chaps. 1, 3, 4, above.

officials in the federal statistical system, were not, however, initially attuned to the demands that were about to be made on them.

In the postwar period, the federal statistical system had continued to grow dramatically. The government produced population statistics, economic statistics, health and vital statistics, government statistics, international statistics. Sample surveys proliferated. New groups of data users—most notably the Association of Public Data Use (APDU) and the Federal Statistics Users' Conference—organized to support innovation and to lobby for the data they wanted to see developed. As in the 1930s, the statistical system was decentralized; many agencies produced and analyzed the data. Coordination and general policy making for the statistical system remained the function of the assistant director for statistical standards in the Bureau of the Budget. In the postwar period, leadership of the federal statistical system had shifted to experts in economic statistics. When Stuart Rice retired in 1954, Raymond Bowman replaced him as assistant director for statistical standards in the Bureau of the Budget. Bowman, who served until 1969, "advanced the idea of using the national economic accounts as a guiding principle for the integration and coordination of economic statistics." Social statistics—and population statistics—were not then considered problematic. The men who served as census directors in the Eisenhower and Nixon administrations had backgrounds in marketing and economic statistics. In the 1960s, government and private statisticians began to work on the development of "social indicators" to parallel the highly successful "economic indicators" derived from the National Income and Products Accounts and related series. The impetus for the "social indicator" movement came from professional statisticians and some government officials rather than from Congress or an organized political constituency. Further, as the census experience with unemployment statistics documented, major new initiatives in population statistics can take a decade—if not a generation—of work before appropriate numbers are developed. Since so many initiatives were underway, the administrators in the statistical system had not focused major attention on the flaws in the population data and their impact on grants or apportionments. Yet the data from the decennial census—in particular the 1970 census—still constituted the baseline statistics for both.[7]

As Congress and the public debated just what the new apportionments meant and how they worked, they discovered that what had seemed a

7. Joseph Duncan and William Shelton, *Revolution in United States Government Statistics, 1926–1976* (Washington, D.C.: GPO, 1978), pp. 154–56, 206–8, quotation on p. 154; Department of Health, Education, and Welfare, *Toward a Social Report* (Washington, D.C.: GPO, 1969); Office of Management and Budget, Statistical Policy Division, *Social Indicators, 1973* (Washington, D.C.: GPO, 1973). For an overview of the development and progress of the "social indicators" movement, see special issue, Social Science Research Council, "The Council's Program in Social Indicators," *Items* 37 (December 1983).

simple matter of legal or fiscal rule making was not nearly so clear-cut. Census data contained errors—overcounts, undercounts, miscounts. People fibbed about their ages; they reported their incomes inaccurately. They did not understand the census questions. All of this became painfully obvious in the 1970s as the census takers tried to explain to Congress and the public just how good the data were. For the rest of the decade the census and the Census Bureau came under increasing scrutiny by Congress and the public. Since the laws and Supreme Court decisions were already on the books, the data had to be improved.[8]

As in the past, changing census methods to serve the new needs was no small task. As the decade wore on, the evaluations of the 1970 census continued. Both the bureau and its critics acknowledged that little could be done to improve the 1970 census once it had been taken. All the interested parties refocused their attention to 1980, and a new round of controversies emerged.

Discussion of the form and content of the 1980 census thus began before the 1970 census was completed. But unlike previous decades, the planning effort did not take place primarily in the quiet offices of the bureau. In the press and in congressional hearings, critics attacked existing bureau policies. For the first time since the Census Bureau had been organized as a government agency, a broad-based coalition of local officials, civil rights activists, academics, and congressmen demanded to be included in the planning process for the 1980 census.

The groups asking for change in the census had a diverse agenda, but some common themes kept coming up. First, they felt that their concerns were not addressed through existing bureau policy channels. Representatives of black and Hispanic civil rights groups felt that the 1970 census results confirmed their fears on the differential undercount of minorities. They had voiced reservations about the accuracy and adequacy of the count before the census. By late 1971 the *New York Times* reported that its demographic analysis of the published census results indicated that the bureau had again undercounted the black population. The bureau responded by saying that the 1970 count was the most accurate ever taken. In April 1973 the bureau announced the results of its analysis of the coverage of the census and admitted that the bureau had missed 2.5 percent of the population, some 5.3 million people. Again the undercount differed sharply by race. Of whites, 1.9 percent were missed; of

8. Ian Mitroff, Richard O. Mason, and Vincent Barabba, *The 1980 Census: Policymaking amid Turbulence* (Lexington, Mass.: Lexington Books, 1983), pp. 20*ff.* See also Congressional Research Service, Library of Congress, "The Decennial Census: An Analysis and Review," prepared for the Subcommittee on Energy, Nuclear Proliferation, and Federal Services of the Senate Committee on Governmental Affairs (Washington, D.C.: GPO, 1980), and Daniel Melnick, "The 1980 Census: Recalculating the Federal Equation," *Publius* 11 (Summer 1981): 39–65.

blacks, 7.7 percent. In July 1973, Dr. Robert Hill of the Urban League reported that the largest number of blacks missed were in New York City. In New York and California alone over a million people were missed in the 1970 census.[9]

A second source of irritation was the enormous intellectual gulf that separated the official statisticians and the public clamoring for better data. Since the 1940s, the bureau had developed policies in tune with the increasing technical capabilities of the fields of survey research and statistics. The statisticians leaned toward using more sampling to collect their data and more computers and increasingly sophisticated programming to tabulate and evaluate the data. In 1980 the basic output of the decennial census was to be the computer tapes themselves, not the long shelves of bound volumes that had represented the census to the average American since the nineteenth century. The printed volumes would only cover a small proportion of the information available on the tapes. The bureau also intended to increase the scope of the mail census, from 86 percent of the households served in 1970 to 96 percent in 1980. Computers had replaced the enumerators, the punchers, and many of the routine clerical jobs. Increasingly, the people who could make best use of the census were highly trained statisticians and social scientists—either in academe or the burgeoning private "demographics industry"—who had access to computers and who knew how to use the data.[10]

The city officials, congressmen, and minority representatives who complained about the undercount at the outset had neither the knowledge nor the technology to fathom—much less suggest improvements in—the methods of the late twentieth-century Census Bureau. Like most Americans, they thought of the bureau as it was in its folksier past—as the lumbering institution that sent out legions of enumerators to ask a few questions, add up and publish the answers. They knew little of editing and imputation rules, probability proportionate to size, sampling theory, or FOSDIC. They kept returning to the basic problem they saw with census methods: minorities and the poor were missed or misclassified in the census. And they attacked the bureau's high-tech methods for causing the problems in the first place. If it was hard to take a census by mail in poor, urban areas, then the bureau should not try to take a census by mail in poor urban areas. It was as simple as that.

The professionals in the bureau responded with increasing dismay at these criticisms, because they knew that the old methods were even less

9. *New York Times*, Dec. 26, 1971, Apr. 26, July 24, 1973; Bureau of the Census, "United States of America, 1980," in *Censuses of Asia and the Pacific: 1980 Round*, ed. Lee-Jay Cho and Robert L. Hearn (Honolulu, Hawaii: East-West Population Institute, 1984), chap. 19.

10. See, e.g., *American Demographics* and *The Numbers News*, both published by Dow Jones, and Bureau of the Census, *The Census Bureau: A Numerator and Denominator for Measuring Change* (Washington, D.C.: GPO, 1975).

accurate than the ones then in use. They also knew, though, that suggesting that the bureau could not reduce the undercount any further was both impolitic and probably untrue. But many statisticians harbored a sense that the undercount controversy was consuming too much official time and money that could be better spent on other data improvements. Neither side convinced or trusted the other.

A third source of contention arose when new constituencies mobilized and demanded recognition in census statistics. In the early 1970s Hispanic and Asian Americans called for better coverage from the census. The demands followed on the heels of changes in immigration law in the 1960s and subsequent significant changes in the character of the foreign-born population. Until 1965 the National Origins Act officially governed immigration quotas to the United States. After World War II, however, Congress had quietly legislated many exemptions to the law to admit refugees from southern and eastern Europe and to increase the number of immigrants admitted. In 1965 Congress finally disavowed the racialist logic of the 1924 law and voted to admit immigrants from all over the world according to their order of application. For Asia, Africa, and Europe, 170,000 were to be admitted a year; no one nation could send more than 20,000. Preference would be given to people with professional training or skills. The 1965 law also set a quota of 120,000 a year for immigrants from the Americas; this measure would primarily affect Canadian and Mexican immigration.

The law coincided with a major shift in the sources of immigrants. Between 1961 and 1965, 42 percent of the 290,000 legal immigrants to the United States came from Europe; 41 percent came from North America—primarily Canada, Mexico, and Cuba. Between 1978 and 1981, 43 percent of the 547,000 legal immigrants came from Asia. Twelve percent came from Europe and 34 percent from North America. Relatedly, an increasing number of Hispanic migrants—primarily from Mexico—who had been outside the quotas altogether were turned into "undocumented" or "illegal" immigrants as the quota for the Americas turned out to be too low to accommodate the demand for their labor in the United States. In 1970 the Immigration and Naturalization Service reported 219,000 Mexican "deportable aliens located." After 1974, the numbers rose to between 579,000 and 866,000 per year. As the new immigrant communities grew and government officials debated the implications for social policy, demands emerged for data on the new minorities.[11]

Hispanic Americans were the largest of the new pressure groups.

11. Polenberg, *One Nation Divisible*, pp. 202–7; Morrison G. Wong, "Post-1965 Immigrants: Demographic and Socioeconomic Profile," in *The New Urban Ethnicity*, ed. Lionel Maldonado and Joan Moore (Beverly Hills, Calif.: Sage Publications, 1985), pp. 51–71; Bureau of the Census, *Statistical Abstract of the United States, 1982–83* (Washington, D.C.: GPO, 1982), p. 94.

Before the 1970 census the federal Inter-Agency Committee on Mexican American Affairs had requested that the 1970 census contain a question on Spanish origin. The bureau responded that most of the schedules had already been printed and that Hispanics would be identified by the questions on language, birthplace, and on surname in the five southwestern states. The committee pressed further, and a Spanish origin question was added to the 5 percent sample questionnaire. The results of these efforts did not satisfy Hispanic Americans, and scholars charged that the 1970 census undercounted Hispanics. The bureau did mail "instruction sheets in Spanish" along with the English questionnaires in "selected areas," but there were no official Spanish language questionnaires. Critics charged the bureau did not put sufficient manpower into solving the problems of counting a non-English speaking population. At the same time, though, good administration of such laws as the Voting Rights Act and the Civil Rights Act of 1964 required data on the Hispanic population to determine, for example, if election ballots should be printed in Spanish or if a company was fulfilling its affirmative action plans.[12]

In 1974 the U.S. Commission on Civil Rights focused many of these complaints in its report *Counting the Forgotten: The 1970 Census Count of Persons of Spanish Speaking Background in the United States*. This report was a major indictment of the Census Bureau and its methods. Calling the efforts of the bureau to count Hispanics in 1970 "disastrous," "confusing," and "not well thought out," the commission also accused the bureau of stonewalling when pressed on what it would do in 1980. The commission recommended a Spanish origin question for the 100 percent schedule and called on the bureau to "take steps to ensure that all aspects of its program, including questionnaire design and data collection, tabulation, and publication, are responsive to the needs of the Spanish speaking background population."[13]

Additional adverse publicity focused on the census when the allocations of the $5 billion to $7 billion in revenue-sharing funds were made in the early 1970s. The revenue sharing allocation formulas relied on population and per capita income measures. It thus seemed to be a relatively simple matter to calculate the allocations. Yet the numbers seemed less reliable after Congress and local officials learned that revisions in the 1970 census data had changed the final allocations for thirteen thousand communities from those used by Congress to write the legislation some months earlier.[14]

12. Bureau of the Census, 1970 Census of Population and Housing, Series PHC(R)–2, *Data Collection Forms and Procedures* (Washington, D.C.: GPO, 1971), esp. p. 7.

13. Commission on Civil Rights, *Counting the Forgotten: The 1970 Census Count of Persons of Spanish-Speaking Background in the United States* (Washington, D.C.: GPO, 1974), quotations on pp. 99, 100, 106.

14. Dommel, *Politics of Revenue Sharing*; Nathan, Manvel, and Calkins, *Monitoring Reve-*

Needless to say, this controversy unnerved the officials of the Census Bureau. Bureau statisticians were proud of their achievements in producing a professional, objective census, and they responded somewhat defensively to the charges of outright bias or neglect of coverage issues. They continued to point to their accomplishments and to suggest that they were doing the best job of counting the population, given their technical and financial capabilities.[15]

The Census Bureau responded to its critics by creating several advisory committees of experts involved with minority statistics. The Census Advisory Committee on the Black Population for the 1980 Census was organized in 1974. The initial meetings between black leaders and Census Director Vincent Barabba were described by the *New York Times* as "tense." In 1975 the bureau activated a similar committee on the Spanish origin population; an Asian and Pacific Americans Population Committee was convened in 1976. All three were designed to improve communications between the bureau and the affected community and to decide on plans for the 1980 census. The power and scope of the committees themselves soon became a further source of dispute.[16]

The bureau had had a system of advisory committees on particular phases of census work since the end of World War I. Usually membership for these committees has been drawn from professional groups interested in using census data or from retired bureau officials whose expertise the bureau still wished to use from time to time. The American Statistical

---

nue Sharing; For Nathan's estimates of the impact of the undercounts on the allocations, see Arthur J. Maurice and Richard P. Nathan, "The Census Undercount: Effects on Federal Aid to Cities," *Urban Affairs Quarterly* 17 (March 1982), pp. 251–84, and Nathan, "Clarifying the Census Mess," *Wall Street Journal*, Jan. 2, 1981. See also Courtenay Slater, "The Impact of Census Undercoverage on Federal Programs," in Bureau of the Census, *Conference on Census Undercount: Proceedings of the 1980 Conference* (Washington, D.C.: GPO, 1980), pp. 107*ff*. Slater points out that "income undercoverage has a far greater impact on the distribution of revenue-sharing funds than does population undercoverage" (p. 108). Because the formulas are so complicated, it is hard to predict the impact of census undercounts on the allocations. See also Robert Strauss and Peter Harkins, *The 1970 Census Undercount and Revenue Sharing: Effect on Allocations in New Jersey and Virginia* (Washington, D.C.: Joint Center for Political Studies, 1974).

15. For the Census Bureau's responses to criticism, see *New York Times*, Dec. 16, 1971; testimony of George H. Brown, census director, at the hearings on the "Accuracy of the 1970 Census Enumeration and Related Matters," in House Committee on Post Office and Civil Service, Subcommittee on Census and Statistics, *Hearings*, 91st Cong., 2d sess., Sept. 15, 1970, pp. 3*ff*.; *Counting the Forgotten, passim*; Bureau of the Census, *1970 Census of Population and Housing: Procedural History* (Washington, D.C.: GPO, 1976), pp. 1–17.

16. *New York Times*, Sept. 26, 1974. For a description of the bureau's efforts to reach out to minority representatives in the mid-1970s, see the Mar. 9, 1977, memorandum on the "Minority Statistics Program of the Bureau of the Census," reprinted as part of the testimony of Manuel Plotkin, census director, before the House Committee on Post Office and Civil Service, Subcommittee on Census and Population, *Hearings on the 1980 Census*, 95th Cong., 1st sess., June 1977, pp. 83*ff*.

Association and the American Economic Association contributed members to the original committee. By the 1970s, there were additional committees on such areas as marketing statistics, agricultural statistics, or government statistics, as well as on the general question of privacy and confidentiality of data. The minority advisory committees were in one sense logical extensions of the traditional advisory system, but their functioning soon proved to be different.[17]

In particular, these committees were strong advocates for changing census procedures to correct what the groups saw as inadequate coverage in the past. When they felt that the bureau did not respond sufficiently to their suggestions, they went to Congress and the media to press their proposals further. For example, in June 1977, Luz E. Cuadrado, chair of the Spanish Origin Advisory Committee appeared before the House Subcommittee on Census and Population. She testified that the advisory committee felt that the Census Bureau had not accepted their recommendation to include a question on Spanish origin on the 100 percent schedule. In their view, the bureau planned to repeat the mistakes of the 1970 questions. Nor were the proposed field procedures adequate to guarantee good coverage of Hispanics.[18]

By the time Jimmy Carter took office in 1977, the planning phase for the 1980 census was on in earnest; public disclosures of the internal battling in the Census Bureau did not assure Congress that the problems of the 1970 census would be solved. At the same time, the cost estimates for the coverage improvements began to escalate sharply. The 1970 census had cost $221.6 million. By 1977, the bureau predicted the 1980 cost at $500 million. In 1977, Carter's Census Director Manuel Plotkin predicted the bureau would spend $75 million for coverage improvements—up from the $11 million in 1970. The final cost of the 1980 census came to almost $1.1 billion, of which $406 million were devoted to upgrading the census. Of this $203 million was spent on "obtaining a better population count."[19]

In the late 1970s, the bureau and its critics made accommodations

17. For a discussion of the role of census advisory committees and their memberships from the 1960s through 1976, see *1970 Census of Population and Housing: Procedural History*, chap. 1, pp. 56–73. Until 1960, the only standing advisory committees were those sponsored by the ASA (and the AEA from 1919 to 1937) and the American Marketing Association (founded in 1946).

18. *Hearings on the 1980 Census*, pp. 174*ff.*

19. For the 1977 estimates, see David Kaplan's figures in the *New York Times*, Nov. 25, 1977; Plotkin's estimates are in his testimony at the June 1977 *Hearings on the 1980 Census*, p. 82. For an analysis of the costs of the 1980 census, see the 1982 GAO study, *A Four Billion Dollar Census in 1990?* (Washington, D.C.: GAO, 1982), pp. 4–6. For additional discussion on the plans for the 1980 census, see House Committee on Post Office and Civil Service, Subcommittee on Census and Population, *Hearings on the 1980 Census*, 94th Cong., 2d sess., June 1976.

about the form and content of the 1980 count. In 1978 the bureau "bowed" to the pressure of minorities and changed the race and ethnic questions for the 100 percent schedule. They expanded the list of possible responses to the race question, and they added a separate Spanish/Hispanic origin question. The bureau also included a question on "ancestry" on the sample questionnaires; this question replaced the birthplace of parents questions initiated during the period of major European immigration in the nineteenth century. Representatives of minority groups were pleased with these changes; demographers were not so sure of their advisability. Nevertheless, they calmed some of the major fears about the 1980 census, though at the time it seemed that the only effect was to prompt attention to shift to the adequacy of the field enumeration itself.[20]

As the time for the census drew near, the results of the pretests added fuel to the controversies about an undercount. New York City, for example, complained that the bureau's intercensal estimate of its population was too low. City officials testified before Congress that the dress rehearsal conducted in the city indicated that the 1980 methods would miss people. In early 1979, Carter's census director Manuel Plotkin resigned after criticisms of his handling of the bureau. Several high-level career officials of the bureau also took early retirement. David Kaplan, associate director for Demographic Censuses, had worked at the bureau since 1940. When he resigned in February 1979, he explained why he did not wish to continue with the bureau through the completion of the 1980 census. "The question was," he asked rhetorically, "did I want to go through another several years of mounting pressure." The long years of experience that men like Kaplan had no longer seemed to serve them well in conducting the census.[21]

In April 1979 President Carter replaced Plotkin with Vincent Barabba, who had been census director during the second Nixon and the Ford administrations. A Republican, Barabba had initially not been a popular appointment with the academic community, but he had proved himself to be an effective administrator of the bureau during his tenure. It was clear by 1979 that the bureau needed a leader who could handle the "mounting pressure" on the census in such a way as to calm outside critics, build internal morale, and conduct the census efficiently and effectively.[22]

By the time Barabba was appointed, most of the crucial plans for the 1980 census had been made. In the year before the count, the bureau turned its attention to publicizing the census effort and minimizing bar-

20. *New York Times*, May 14, 1978.

21. *Washington Post*, Feb. 6, 1979; *New York Times*, Feb. 2, 6, 1979.

22. On the initial cool reaction to Barabba, see Judith I. DeNeufville, *Social Indicators and Public Policy* (New York: American Elsevier Publishing, 1975), p. 230. On Barabba's return to the bureau in 1979, see *New York Times*, Apr. 13, 18, 28, 1979.

riers to a complete count of hard-to-enumerate groups. Bureau officials concentrated on programs to reduce the undercount of minorities and inner city residents. They also confronted the new and difficult challenge of counting the illegal alien population.

The illegal alien population had been growing during the 1970s and had been increasingly at the center of discussions of immigration policy. As we have seen, there is a long tradition of debate about the appropriate level and character of immigration and the role that immigrants play in American life. Undocumented immigrants, those entering the country without official permission and therefore without being counted, present especially difficult questions to policymakers and statisticians alike. Such immigrants seek to remain anonymous to avoid deportation, yet they are of great interest to policymakers precisely because of the need to know how many undocumented immigrants there are, where they live, how they live, and so on. Congress began to consider immigration reform legislation in the late 1970s as it became clear that illegal immigration had as great an impact on the society as legal immigration.[23]

Thus the bureau very much wanted to count the alien population in 1980. And since most commentators agree that the bulk of illegal aliens are Hispanic, and that they live in the South, in the Southwest, and in the large cities of the Northeast and Midwest, city officials and representatives of these areas were also interested in an accurate count. One problem was convincing undocumented immigrants that the census results would not be given to the Immigration and Naturalization Service officials for use in deportation proceedings. The bureau sought to enlist the aid of the Roman Catholic church to convince people in the local community of the confidentiality of census records. The church refused. Hispanic leaders suggested that the federal government offer amnesty to aliens in the country and thus obviate the need for hiding from the census taker. This suggestion was not adopted. Local officials in areas thought to have high concentrations of illegal immigrants did organize local campaigns to convince people to fill out the census. They also pressed the Immigration and Naturalization Service to curtail its efforts to round up illegal aliens during the census period.[24]

23. Simply arriving at a reasonable estimate of the illegal alien population in the country is very difficult. The Immigration and Naturalization Service estimated 8 million illegal aliens in the country in 1976. The FAIR v. Klutznick suit, discussed below, estimated 5 million. Legal immigration was about 300,000 to 450,000 a year from the late 1960s to 1970s. The foreign-born population was about 10 million in 1970. For 1986 estimates of the illegal alien population, see Jeffrey S. Passel, "Undocumented Immigrants: How Many?" *Proceedings of the Social Statistics Session of the American Statistical Association* 28 (1985). The passage of immigration reform legislation in 1986 has added to these debates. The amnesty provisions of that legislation will allow several million undocumented immigrants to apply for legal residency.

24. *New York Times*, May 7, June 7, Aug. 16, Sept. 3, Oct. 3, Nov. 15, 18, Dec. 6, 1979.

Others thought that illegal aliens should not be part of the official census and that they should not be counted for reapportionment purposes or for distributing federal aid. In December 1979, the Federation for American Immigration Reform (FAIR) and several congressmen filed suit in federal court asking that the census separate legal and illegal aliens and exclude illegal aliens for apportionment. The court dismissed the case on the grounds, among others, that in the 1920s Congress had considered the question of whether to exclude aliens for the purpose of apportionment and had decided not to do so. Thus the alleged eight million illegal aliens in the country were to be counted for apportionment if they filled out their census forms.[25]

In late 1979 and 1980 statisticians in the bureau and around the nation also debated whether they should adjust the reported census figures to correct for an undercount. As the census day drew near, city officials and minority leaders feared that all the efforts to eliminate the differential undercount would still not produce an equitable count. These officials shifted their attention to proposals for adjusting the count in light of the known undercount. Such an adjustment seemed to many a reasonable solution to the intractable problems and huge expense of counting everyone. The bureau and private demographers began efforts to devise mechanisms to adjust the figures—not only nationally but also on the state and local level.

These efforts raised extraordinarily difficult technical, legal, and political issues. And they provoked a huge barrage of verbiage and argument on all sides. The Census Bureau and its critics had to decide if adjustment was necessary, practical or possible, legal, or politic. They had to decide if announcing that the results would be adjusted would detract from the actual enumeration and if an adjustment would have the effect of undermining the overall credibility of the census. These questions challenged some of the most deeply held beliefs about the objectivity and efficacy of quantitative analysis. If the numbers were to be tinkered with because they were flawed, what did it mean for the fairness of the entire apportionment system?[26]

25. FAIR v. Klutznick, 486 F. Supp. 564 (1980); *New York Times*, Dec. 21, 1979. The plaintiffs lost their appeals to higher courts.

26. The literature on the undercount is voluminous. For an annotated bibliography of many of the most important sources, see Barbara Ginsburg and Juliette Redding, *The U.S. Census: A Checklist of References on Census-Taking Procedures, Error Estimation, and Technical and Legal Aspects of Undercount Adjustment*, Working Papers in Employment and Training Policy (DeKalb, Ill.: Northern Illinois University Center for Governmental Studies, 1983). For the bureau's positions, see *Conference on Census Undercount*; Mitroff, Mason, and Barabba, *1980 Census*; Bureau of the Census, *Data User News*, June 1980, October 1980, December 1980, January 1981, February 1981, December 1981 issues. For some earlier studies that brought the issue to public attention, see David Heer, *Social Statistics and the City* (Cambridge, Mass.: Joint Center for Urban Studies, 1968); *Counting the Forgotten*; National Academy of Sci-

Sorting these issues out was no easy task, and the conflicting reports in the press probably confused the public as much as they informed them. But the Census Bureau did decide its institutional position on the matter. It announced in the fall of 1980 that they would not adjust the count. A potential challenge to this position exists in the lower federal court decisions that ordered the bureau to adjust. It is useful to describe the two positions in some detail, since it is doubtful that the issue is fully resolved.

Beginning in the spring of 1980, numerous lawsuits were filed in federal court charging that the census had undercounted the population. (The bureau's final count of such suits came to fifty-four.) The best known and most significant for law were those filed by the city of Detroit (Young v. Klutznick) and the state of New York (Carey v. Klutznick). In these cases, the federal district courts found for the plaintiffs in the fall of 1980 and ordered the Census Bureau to adjust the population figures for the 1980 census "at the national, state, and substate level to reflect the undercount, and to adjust the differential undercount to prevent the known undercount of Blacks and Hispanics, as well as whites." These orders were stayed by the Supreme Court pending appeal. Throughout the fall and winter of 1980 the cases worked their way through the courts.[27]

The plaintiffs in Young v. Klutznick argued that past experience in counting hard-to-enumerate groups indicated that there would be a differential undercount in 1980. They noted that the coverage improvements used in 1970 did not significantly reduce the size of the differential undercount. An undercount in 1980 would result in "hidden" malapportionment. Since the equal protection clause of the Fourteenth Amendment mandated the allocation of House seats such that each person would have an "equally weighted vote," it was incumbent on the Census Bureau to adjust the count. The plaintiffs further argued that the bureau had the capability to make such adjustments and had done so in 1970, when it added people during the National Vacancy Check. Former acting census director Philip Hauser and University of Wisconsin sociologist Karl Taeu-

---

ences, National Research Council, Advisory Committee on Problems of Census Enumeration, *America's Uncounted People* (Washington, D.C.: National Academy of Sciences, 1971); Charles H. Teller, ed., *Cuantos Somos? A Demographic Study of the Mexican American Population* (Austin, Tex.: Center for Mexican American Studies, University of Texas at Austin, 1977). For a discussion of the legal issues, see "Demography and Distrust: Constitutional Issues of the Federal Census," *Harvard Law Review* 94 (1981), pp. 843–63, and Michael V. McKay, "Constitutional Implications of a Population Undercount: Making Sense of the Census Clause," *Georgetown Law Journal* 69 (1981): 1427–63. For a key statistician's analysis of the issues, see Nathan Keyfitz, "Information and Allocation: Two Uses of the 1980 Census," *American Statistician* 33 (May 1979), pp. 45–50.

27. Young v. Klutznick, 497 F. Supp. 1318 (1980), quotation on pp. 133–39; Carey v. Klutznick, 508 F. Supp. 420 (1980).

ber, who testified as expert witnesses for the plaintiffs, substantiated many of these assertions. Judging from the court's use of Hauser and Taeuber's testimony, they played a major role in explaining the difficult statistical questions to the court and in assuring the court that an adjustment would not violate the accuracy or reputation of the census.

The Census Bureau responded to these arguments by citing their own efforts to improve coverage. They assured the court that coverage would improve in 1980. In their view, the plaintiffs had now shown that any injury or harm would necessarily befall them if the census were not adjusted. They suggested that it was inappropriate for the plaintiffs to sue for relief before the census results were known and analyzed. They further pointed out that there was no generally accepted method of adjustment for state and local civil divisions. Though it might be statistically possible to calculate a national undercount rate, it did not necessarily follow that it was statistically possible to distribute the undercount below the national level. The Census Bureau also argued that its constitutional requirement to conduct an "actual enumeration" of the population for apportionment meant that it could not legally adjust the census. And it argued that an adjustment could not be calculated within the time frame set up by Congress for reporting the count.[28]

Although it appealed the court orders to adjust, the bureau did not close off the possibility of an adjustment until late in 1980. The bureau developed its position on the undercount during 1979 and 1980 in a series of workshops and conferences. These forums provided the range of opinion necessary to sort out the legal, political, and statistical issues. As *The 1980 Census: Policymaking amid Turbulence*, by Ian Mitroff, Richard Mason, and Vincent Barabba attests, that effort itself was a fascinating story of institutional decision making. Since most discussion took place during the census enumeration itself, the day-to-day events of the count— especially the snafus, minor scandals, and mistakes—further complicated the picture. The bureau, for example, was forced to cancel one phase of the widely heralded "local review" process; the address lists were not available on time. Local officials were thus only given one chance to check the numbers before they went to Washington. The field office in Brooklyn burned; the enumeration had to be redone. Reports circulated of improperly filled out forms and mass dismissals of temporary census workers. By the summer of 1980 the bureau was falling behind schedule in completing the count. As early figures dribbled out to the press, headlines announced that the older cities in the Northeast and Midwest were experiencing dramatic population losses. The counts for the South and West were coming in higher than bureau estimates. New York City's population, for

28. Young v. Klutznick; Carey v. Klutznick.

example, was reported in September 1980 as off by almost 14 percent to 6.8 million. (The final count proved to be 7.1 million.)[29]

In December 1980 Vincent Barabba announced that the Census Bureau would not "adjust the 1980 census population totals to compensate for undercount unless directed by the courts." He further reported that "the Bureau will publish the entire series of decennial census reports without adjustment for undercount." Two factors informed his decision. First, the Census Bureau decided that the census enumeration itself was of sufficient quality to make an adjustment unnecessary. The bureau had reported over four million more people than expected. Second, they admitted that they had no means to measure the "number and distribution of illegal residents." Together "these two factors have the effect of negating the method currently available for estimating the undercount." In short, the bureau admitted that because it had covered the population more completely, its own methods of estimating coverage and undercount had been shown to be flawed.[30]

In late December 1980, the Supreme Court ruled that the bureau could release the unadjusted data to Congress. The lower court rulings were stayed pending appeal. In June 1981 the Second and Sixth Circuit Courts of Appeal upheld the bureau's positions in Carey v. Klutznick and Young v. Klutznick on the grounds, in effect, that the plaintiffs had not shown that a differential undercount would create an injury to the plaintiffs. There the issues stand. The Supreme Court refused to take the cases in 1982.[31]

Further legal challenges to the census may emerge, but future suits will probably take different forms. For example, the courts may shift their attention from the undercount as a question of principle to consider what magnitude of undercount would constitute malapportionment. The Supreme Court had considered congressional districts with population variances of 4.1 percent "malapportioned." Such rulings could provide a rule of thumb for evaluating census undercounts.[32]

After all the controversies, the 1980 census did, of course, proceed to

29. Mitroff, Mason, and Barabba trace the decisionmaking process in *1980 Census*. On the plans for the local reviews, see the GAO Report to the House Committee on Post Office and Civil Service, *Programs to Reduce the Decennial Census Undercount* (Washington, D.C.: GAO, 1976), pp. 16–17. On the cancellation of one phase, see House Committee on Government Operations, Commerce, Consumer, and Monetary Affairs Subcommittee, *Hearing on the Problems with the 1980 Census*, 96th Cong., 2d sess., Mar. 18, 1980. See also *New York Times*, June 14, July 18, Sept. 26, October 28, 29, 30, 1980, Sept. 20, 1982.

30. Data User News (January 1981).

31. Carey v. Klutznick, 653 F. 2d 732 (2d Cir. 1981), cert. denied Mar. 8, 1981; Young v. Klutznick, 652 F. 2d 617 (6th Cir. 1981), cert. denied Feb. 22, 1982, 455 U.S. 939.

32. See "Demography and Distrust," for a discussion of possible further avenues of litigation; *Data User News* discussed the estimates of 1980 census undercount (March 1982). The black rate reported is 4.8%.

count the population. Vincent Barabba reported the official count of 226.5 million people on December 31, 1980. As expected, the census confirmed some dramatic changes in the nature of the United States population. Seventeen seats were reapportioned in the House of Representatives. The losers were almost all in the Northeast and Midwest, the gainers in the South and West. The Census Bureau reported that the population grew at an overall rate of 11.4 percent between 1970 and 1980, the slowest growth rate in the nation's history except for the decade of the Great Depression.[33]

The census results also showed that the black population grew 17 percent and the Spanish population 61 percent during the decade. Clearly some of this increase was an artifact of the new questions and commitment to avoid a minority undercount. There were 14.6 million Hispanics and 26.6 million blacks in the United States in 1980.[34]

There were also some dramatic changes in the migration patterns and living arrangements of Americans. For the first time since 1820, the exurban regions of the country were population gainers. By contrast, highly urbanized New York State experienced an absolute population loss of almost 700,000 people, the largest in the history of the nation. The size of the average household shrunk to 2.75 people, and the number of households grew radically—up 27 percent during the 1970s. Nonfamily households grew by 72 percent; family households headed by women grew by 51 percent.[35]

In short, the 1980 census is proving to be a major demographic watershed. Future generations of Americans may use the 1980 census the way we use the 1890 census to mark the closing of the frontier or the 1920 census to mark the shift from a rural to an urban nation. During the 1970s, for example, the standard twentieth-century migration pattern for blacks reversed. The 1970s saw the Sunbelt come into its own. And the nation's old industrial cities lost population to their own suburbs and the nonmetropolitan areas of the nation.[36]

These demographic changes are in certain ways deeply ironic when considered in the context of the census controversies we have been discussing. In particular, many of the minority representatives and urban officials who pressed for improved coverage in the 1980 census argued that the improvements were necessary to make up for past inequities— the undercounts of the past, the malapportionments of the past. They asked that the census be returned to its historic role of providing an

33. *New York Times*, Jan. 1, 1981; *Data User News* (January 1981).

34. *New York Times*, Feb. 24, Mar. 1, 1981; *Data User News* (April 1981).

35. *New York Times*, Mar. 3, May 23, 1981; Bryant Robey and Cheryl Russell, "How America Is Changing: 1980 Census Trends Analyzed," *American Demographics* 4 (July/August 1982): 16–27.

36. Robey and Russell, "How America Is Changing"; *Data User News* (March 1982).

accurate measure of the demographic strength of a geographic area. In large measure, those pressing for better coverage won that battle, only to discover that their population base was eroding. And, unlike the rural interests who faced this dilemma in 1920, the big cities did not prevent reapportionment and redistricting in their own self-interest.

Nor would they necessarily prefer such an outcome. For the controversies surrounding the census have also led to other achievements that have made the 1980 census a statistical, as well as a demographic, watershed. The data on the Hispanic population are clearly an improvement. The data on the illegal alien population are improving. Minority groups who became involved in the census advisory committees saw their recommendations accepted and have grappled with the logistical problems of taking a national census in a large and ethnically diverse nation. Congress has raised its consciousness about its myriad allocation formulas. Complex formulas based on complex indicators can be brittle in operation. Indications are that in the future Congress will write its legislation with more sensitivity to the problems with the data. And the way the Census Bureau debated the undercount issues indicates that the bureau itself survived its ordeal by fire and developed new administrative techniques to cope with the increased demands on its data and expertise.[37]

The future is not completely promising. These data improvements proved very costly, and the grant programs that use census data have come under increasing attack. As the 1980 census was being completed, the election of Ronald Reagan signaled a major shift in federal spending and in the political priorities of the nation. During 1981 and 1982, the Census Bureau suffered from budget cuts and furloughs, a delay in the appointment of a new director, more retirements, and a further decline in agency morale. The General Accounting Office issued several reports urging the bureau to plan new procedures to cut costs in 1990. The Reagan administration disbanded the Office of Federal Statistical Policy and Standards and moved toward cutting the funds available for statistical programs generally. Observers of the statistical scene suggest that President Reagan considers the current elaborate census "an invasion of privacy and a waste of money." The Reagan Justice Department accepted the neoconservative critique of affirmative action quotas as unconstitutional reverse discrimination and sought to dismantle federal contract compliance systems. By the mid-1980s, the revenue sharing program was phased out under the pressure of budget cuts. Gramm-Rudman and the

37. Cheryl Russell, "The News about Hispanics," *American Demographics* 5 (March 1983): 14–25. "Demography and Distrust" discusses the new sensitivity of Congress to the census and the bills and resolutions introduced in Congress that would allow data adjustments to remedy and undercount. See nn. 12, 82, 145.

ballooning federal deficit placed severe restraints on statistical innovations and program planning.[38]

Given these developments, it is not at all clear how we will ultimately
evaluate the 1980 census. It may well mark the beginning of a truly new
concept of statistical service. In the future a variety of census users will
work closely with the bureau to develop data. Or perhaps the 1980 census
will be seen as an expensive white elephant, which did a better job of
"counting the forgotten," but at too great a public cost. The question is
open and, as we have seen from this census history, is inextricably tied to
the larger social trends of the nation.

38. New York Times, July 13, Nov. 25, 1981, Jan. 31, 1982; Washington Post, Aug. 2, 1982;
Wall Street Journal, Mar. 9, 1982; GAO Report to the Congress, A $4 Billion Census in 1990?
(Washington, D.C.: GAO, 1982); GAO Report to the Subcommittee on Census and Popula-
tion, Committee on Post Office and Civil Service, H. Rep., The Census Bureau Needs to Plan
Now for a More Automated 1990 Decennial Census (Washington, D.C.: GAO, 1983); James T.
Bonnen, "The Government Statistical Muddle," American Demographics 4 (July/August
1982): 28–31; Bryant Robey, "More Than One Bathtub," ibid. 5 (April 1983): 2; Bonnen,
"Federal Statistical Coordination Today: A Disaster or a Disgrace," Milbank Memorial Fund
Quarterly/Health and Society 62, no. 1 (1984): 1–41; and comments by Elliot L. Richardson
and John T. Dunlop, ibid., 42–52.

Conclusion

This story of census taking and the politics of population in the United States does not end. In 1990 the Census Bureau will take another decennial census—the bicentennial census, as a matter of fact. That census will again raise issues of the fairness and adequacy of our census apportionment systems, the accuracy of the count itself, and of what questions should and should not be asked. And, necessarily, the way we as a nation address those questions will be determined by both the historical record of how we have dealt with these issues in the past and where we think the country is and ought to be going in the future. The census is, in short, a Janus-faced instrument, simultaneously looking backward and forward. It is designed to provide continuity between past and future and to adjust periodically the relative shares of power and resources among the various constituent elements of the population.

That much the framers of the Constitution originally intended for the census. Population growth was already rapid in the eighteenth century. Americans knew from the outset that they were creating an experimental form of government that would have to handle social change systematically. What was not so clear at the outset was just how dynamic that population growth and change would be. Nineteenth-century Americans found out and in the process developed the new science of statistics to understand their rapidly changing world.

By the mid-nineteenth century, Americans had discovered that population growth patterns differed among the various races and regions of the nation. They also learned that the apportionment system they had created rewarded growth areas and punished those with stable or declining populations. At midcentury Americans also confronted the question of the politics of the numbers themselves—their relativity, their authenticity, and their objectivity. As major efforts were made to improve the census, Congress and the first generation of professional statisticians argued about which questions to ask and how to ask them. Census classifications became the very language of social discourse, and the chief categories defined races, sections, and the relative growth of both.

During the Civil War Americans confronted the inexorable logic of their apportionment system. Having counted slaves as three-fifths of a person for apportionment, they discovered that reversing the system was not easy. The South would reap a major political windfall from emancipation. Northern Republicans tried to fashion a negative apportionment system to penalize states that restricted the franchise. With the Fifteenth Amendment they conceded the right to vote to freed blacks to maintain their hold on the national government.

But the Republican will to create a new negative apportionment system to protect black voters died in the Gilded Age, as the census takers and Congress focused their attention on the emerging social issues of industrialization, urbanization, and the end of the frontier. Concern about race and region gave way to concern about labor conflict, immigrant communities, urban machine politics, agricultural distress, and the reach of the new industrial corporations. An expanded census became the instrument to monitor and describe the new phenomena. Technical innovations in data processing, administrative reforms in the census machinery, and the general development of the social sciences led to growth in the quantity and the quality of census data. Counting the population for legislative apportionment became merely one element of a much larger process of measuring and analyzing the trends in American society.

Nevertheless, the apportionment system, which was the ultimate justification of the census, continued to exert real influence on the character and scope of federal population statistics. In the early twentieth century, the grant-in-aid system, which used population measures for its apportionment formulas, followed the logic of distributing resources among the states "according to their respective numbers." And the periodic legislative reapportionments continued to draw attention to the areas of the country with rapidly growing populations or to those that were losing political power. In the 1920s, Congress restricted immigration in terms of the "national origins" of the population according to census data and refused to reapportion itself because to do so would, in its view, shift power to the cities, where unruly workers and immigrants lived.

Ironically, perhaps, this use of the census to preserve an idealized rural or small-town American way of life occurred just before the cataclysm of the Great Depression fundamentally changed both the nation's balance of political forces and the theories of the just distribution of the country's political and economic resources. The Census Bureau and its programs were restructured to meet the new realities. The expanded federal grant-in-aid system became the new apportionment system to foster equitable distribution of society's resources.

In the postwar era, statistical innovation has continued, as have new efforts in the field of civil rights to use statistics to guarantee a proper apportionment of jobs, educational opportunity, and voting rights among the constituent elements of the society. The Supreme Court reversed the decisions that upheld the constitutionality of the malapportioned legislatures of the first half of the twentieth century. Congress formally recanted the National Origins Act. The census has felt the increased burden of these apportionment decisions both in terms of creating new data and in guaranteeing that existing data are unbiased.

Now, in short, some census-based apportionments reward population growth while others cushion population decline. Many constituencies that clamor for data are well aware of the power of the numbers and are generally not naive about the politics of the statistics themselves. They will mobilize for the 1990 census, bring pressure on Congress and the Census Bureau, and may well change the shape of the census-taking process.

The decennial American population census is both a fundamental element of the political system and the major statistical baseline measure for American social science. This melding of social science and politics creates the peculiar logic that shapes the way we count the population and interpret the results. The Census Bureau is strictly a scientific agency, with authority only to collect and tabulate the statistics. Congress and federal agencies legislate and write rules using the numbers. There is a gray area of joint discretion for defining what is to be counted, tabulated, and analyzed. Such a separation of authority has been justified as crucial to guarantee general trust in the confidentiality of responses and the competency of the statisticians themselves. In general the system has worked, although changing political winds have periodically battered the agency.

As the social sciences have developed in their own right in the last century, the decennial census has played a relatively smaller role in overall production of empirical information on the American population. Until the twentieth century, even as a temporary agency, the Census Bureau collected the most sweeping and detailed data on the "progress of the population." In the first third of the twentieth century, university and foundation-based research began to rival census data in depth and detail, if not in scope. Since the development of accurate methods of taking sample surveys in the mid-twentieth century, a wide variety of public and private agencies are capable of producing national-level population information. These technical developments have in turn led to the growth of the new "demographics industry," which serves business with population projections, marketing segmentation strategies, and the like. Technical developments have also led the Census Bureau and other government agencies to rely increasingly on such current surveys as the Current

Population Survey or the new Survey of Income and Program Participation for complex questions and intercensal analysis.

Today, some statisticians are even suggesting that the complete house-to-house decennial census should be replaced by a totally new method of counting the population—for example, a sample survey or a phone census. Such a proposal would have been unthinkable a half-century ago and even now leads to major concern over the constitutionality and propriety of tinkering with the census method. But, as we have seen, many innovations in census taking were daring and dramatic when first used. It is highly unlikely that the process of change will stop.

Planning is already well underway for the 1990 census. The political and social issues that will shape the count are already fairly clear. The Census Bureau is still working on reducing the differential undercount of minorities and inner city residents. They are developing better geocoding systems to identify addresses and control the field enumeration. The network of advisory committees developed for the 1980 count continues to advise the bureau on policy, questionnaire design, and future needs.[1]

On the political front, several issues are likely to have an impact on the 1990 count. The 1986 immigration reform legislation promises to change the issues surrounding counting the alien population. Several million undocumented aliens who arrived before 1982 may be eligible for amnesty, legal residency, and eventually citizenship. The application process is underway. Undocumented immigrants who came in 1982 or after are still considered illegal residents of the country and are subject to deportation. The intent of the law was to encourage these more recent undocumented immigrants to leave the country voluntarily. It is not clear that they will. Employers must certify that all new employees are citizens or legal residents of the United States. It is too soon to tell if the law will function as intended or whether it will make it easier or harder for the bureau to fulfill its mandate to count all residents of the country in 1990—legal or illegal. The statisticians will have to monitor the situation closely.

Further, several Supreme Court rulings in the past two years will probably affect the political uses and perhaps the shape of the 1990 census. In 1986 the Supreme Court considered a gerrymandering case (Davis v. Bandemer) and ruled that, under certain circumstances, gerrymandered legislative districts might not be constitutional.[2] In 1987 the

1. For an overview of planning activities in the bureau, see *Data User News* and the *Proceedings* of the Annual Research Conferences held in 1985, 1986, and 1987 (Washington, D.C.: GPO, 1985–87).

2. 106 S. Ct. 2797 (1986). See also Karcher v. Daggett 462 U.S. 725 (1983). Gerrymandering is the practice of drawing legislative districts in such a way as to maximize one party's political advantage. For example, if two parties share 55% and 45% of the vote in a state, respectively, it is fairly easy for the majority party to draw legislative districts to reflect a

court ruled that carefully drawn voluntary affirmative action plans did not constitute reverse discrimination against white men. These cases have reinforced the use of numerical analyses of the elements of the population for policy purposes and thus will necessarily lead to pressure on the census to produce accurate and appropriate data.[3]

The census remains both an apportionment tool and a baseline measure for American social science. These dual functions have provided the impetus for technical innovation in the past and will continue to do so in the future. The census—however taken—is never irrelevant to current social policy debate. The introduction of machine tabulation, computers, sampling methods, or improved field administration has been the means to serve new constituencies or to identify social issues with new data collections. Whatever may be the future shape of the decennial population census, Americans will undoubtedly continue to conceive of social issues in terms of census categories and to redistribute the benefits and burdens among the people—"according to their respective numbers."

75% to 25% split in seats. Is such a weighting unconstitutional? Political theorists have debated the issue since legislators discovered how to draw districts to maximize party advantage in the early nineteenth century, but the courts have only recently been willing to consider it. For a recent in depth exploration of the issue see the special issue of the *UCLA Law Review* 33, no. 1 (October 1985), entitled "Symposium: Gerrymandering and the Courts."

3. See, e.g., Justice Brennan's recent opinion in Johnson v. Transportation Agency, Santa Clara County, California, et al., no. 85–1129, 107 S. Ct. 1442 (1987); see also Sheet Metal Workers' v. EEOC, 106 S. Ct. 3019 (1986), and Firefighters v. Cleveland, 106 S. Ct. 3063 (1986). These cases have clarified many of the ambiguities surrounding affirmative action plans. The Supreme Court has ruled that voluntary efforts of employers to improve the representation of women and minorities in underrepresented occupations do not necessarily constitute reverse discrimination against white men.

APPENDIX: CENSUS COSTS, POPULATION AND APPORTIONMENT DATA, 1790 TO 1980

Table 1. Population and Area: 1790 to 1980

| Census Date | Resident Population | | | | Area (sq. mi.) |
| | Number | Per square mile of land area | Increase over preceding census | | |
			Number	Percent	
Coterminous U.S.[a]					
1790 (Aug. 2)	3,929,214	4.5	(x)	(x)	891,364
1800 (Aug. 4)	5,308,483	6.1	1,379,269	35.1	891,364
1810 (Aug. 6)	7,239,881	4.3	1,931,398	36.4	1,722,685
1820 (Aug. 7)	9,638,453	5.5	2,398,572	33.1	1,792,552
1830 (June 1)	12,866,020	7.4	3,227,567	33.5	1,792,552
1840 (June 1)	17,069,453	9.8	4,203,433	32.7	1,792,552
1850 (June 1)	23,191,876	7.9	6,122,423	35.9	2,991,655
1860 (June 1)	31,443,321	10.6	8,251,445	35.6	3,021,295
1870 (June 1)	39,818,449[b]	13.4[b]	8,375,128	26.6	3,021,295
1880 (June 1)	50,155,783	16.9	10,337,334	26.0	3,021,295
1890 (June 1)	62,947,714	21.2	12,791,931	25.5	3,021,295
1900 (June 1)	75,994,575	25.6	13,046,861	20.7	3,021,295
1910 (Apr. 15)	91,972,266	31.0	15,977,691	21.0	3,021,295
1920 (Jan. 1)	105,710,620	35.6	13,738,354	14.9	3,021,295
1930 (Apr. 1)	122,775,046	41.2	17,064,426	16.1	3,021,295
1940 (Apr. 1)	131,669,275	44.2	8,894,229	7.2	3,021,295
1950 (Apr. 1)	150,697,361	50.7	19,028,086	14.5	3,021,295
1960 (Apr. 1)	178,464,236	60.1	27,766,875	18.4	3,021,295
United States					
1950 (Apr. 1)	151,325,798	42.6	19,161,229	14.5	3,618,770
1960 (Apr. 1)	179,323,175	50.6	27,997,377	18.5	3,618,770
1970 (Apr. 1)	203,302,031[c]	57.4[c]	23,978,856	13.4	3,618,770
1980 (Apr. 1)	226,545,805	64.0	23,243,774	11.4	3,618,770

(x) Not applicable.

[a]Excludes Alaska and Hawaii.

[b]Revised to include adjustments for underenumeration in southern states; unrevised number is 38,558,371 (13.0 per square mile).

[c]Figures corrected after 1970 final reports were issued.

Source: Adapted from U.S. Bureau of the Census, Statistical Abstract of the United States, 1985 (Washington, D.C.: GPO, 1984), p. 6.

Table 2. Growth of the Decennial Census, 1790 to 1980

Census Year	Total U.S. Population (*millions*)	Number of Enumerators[a]	Maximum Size of Office Force	Total Pages in Published Reports	Total Cost (*thousands of dollars*)	Cost Per Capita (*cents*)
1790	3.9	650[b]	[c]	56	44	1.1
1800	5.3	900[b]	[c]	74	66	1.2
1810	7.2	1,100[b]	[c]	469	178	2.4
1820	9.6	1,188	[d]	288	208	2.1
1830	12.9	1,519	43	214	378	2.9
1840	17.1	2,167	28	1,465	833	4.8
1850	23.2	3,231	160	2,165	1,423	6.1
1860	31.4	4,417	184	3,189	1,969	6.3
1870	38.6	6,530	438	3,473	3,421	8.8
1880	50.2	31,382	1,495	21,458	5,790	11.4
1890	63.0	46,804	3,143	26,408	11,547	18.3
1900	76.2	52,871	3,447	10,925	11,854	15.5
1910	92.2	70,286	3,738[e]	11,456	15,968	17.3
1920	106.0	87,234	6,301[e]	14,550	25,117	23.7
1930	123.2	87,756	6,825[e]	35,700	40,156	32.6
1940	132.2	123,069	9,987[e]	58,400	67,527	51.1
1950	151.3	142,962	9,233	61,700	91,462	60.4
1960	179.3	159,321	2,960	103,000	127,934	71.4
1970	203.2	166,406	4,571	200,000	247,653[f]	121.8
1980	226.5	[g]	[g]	n/a	$1.1 bill.	486.0

[a]Designated as assistants to the marshals, 1790–1870.
[b]Estimated; records destroyed by fire.
[c]None employed.
[d]Amount expended for clerk hire: $925.
[e]Includes all employees in years 1910–40. Most of the 700 to 900 in the permanent force were probably actually engaged in decennial operations at the peak period.
[f]At July 1969 pay rates; covers some additional expenditures for tests of new procedures introduced in 1970.
[g]Not applicable.

Source: Adapted from A. Ross Eckler, *The Bureau of the Census* (New York: Praeger, 1972), p. 24, with data from Lee-Jay Cho and Robert L. Hearn, eds., *Censuses of Asia and the Pacific: 1980 Round* (Honolulu, Hawaii: East-West Population Institute, 1984), chap. 19.

Table 3. Apportionment of Membership in House of Representatives by State: 1790 to 1980

Region, Division, and State	Membership Based on Census of—																		
	1790	1800	1810	1820	1830	1840	1850	1860	1870	1880	1890	1900	1910	1930	1940	1950	1960	1970	1980
U.S.	**106**	**142**	**186**	**213**	**242**	**232**	**237**	**243**	**293**	**332**	**357**	**391**	**435**	**435**	**435**	**437**	**435**	**435**	**435**
Regions:																			
Northeast	57	76	97	105	112	94	92	87	95	95	99	108	123	122	120	115	108	104	95
Midwest	(x)	1	8	19	32	50	59	75	98	117	128	136	143	137	131	129	125	121	113
South	49	65	81	89	98	86	83	76	93	107	112	126	136	133	135	134	133	134	142
West	(x)	(x)	(x)	(x)	(x)	2	3	5	7	13	18	21	33	43	49	59	69	76	85
N. Eng.	**29**	**35**	**41**	**39**	**38**	**31**	**29**	**27**	**28**	**26**	**27**	**29**	**32**	**29**	**28**	**28**	**25**	**25**	**24**
ME	(x)	(x)	(x)	7	8	7	6	5	5	4	4	4	4	3	3	3	2	2	2
NH	4	5	6	6	5	4	3	3	3	2	2	2	2	2	2	2	2	2	2
VT	2	4	6	5	5	4	3	3	3	2	2	2	2	1	1	1	1	1	1
MA	14	17	20	13	12	10	11	10	11	12	13	14	16	15	14	14	12	12	11
RI	2	2	2	2	2	2	2	2	2	2	2	2	3	2	2	2	2	2	2
CT	7	7	7	6	6	4	4	4	4	4	4	5	5	6	6	6	6	6	6
Mid. Atl.	**28**	**41**	**56**	**66**	**74**	**63**	**63**	**60**	**67**	**69**	**72**	**79**	**91**	**93**	**92**	**87**	**83**	**79**	**71**
NY	10	17	27	34	40	34	33	31	33	34	34	37	43	45	45	43	41	39	34
NJ	5	6	6	6	6	5	5	5	7	7	8	10	12	14	14	14	15	15	14
PA	13	18	23	26	28	24	25	24	27	28	30	32	36	34	33	30	27	25	23
E. No. Cent.	**(x)**	**1**	**8**	**18**	**30**	**43**	**48**	**56**	**69**	**74**	**78**	**82**	**86**	**90**	**87**	**87**	**88**	**86**	**80**
OH	(x)	1[a]	6	14	19	21	21	19	20	21	21	21	22	24	23	23	24	23	21
IN	(x)	(x)	1[a]	3	7	10	11	11	13	13	13	13	13	12	11	11	11	11	10
IL	(x)	(x)	1[a]	1	3	7	9	14	19	20	22	25	27	27	26	25	24	24	22
MI	(x)	(x)	(x)	(x)	1[a]	3	4	6	9	11	12	12	13	17	17	18	19	19	18
WI	(x)	(x)	(x)	(x)	(x)	2[a]	3	6	8	9	10	11	11	10	10	10	10	9	9

(continued)

Table 3. (Continued)

Region, Division, and State	Membership Based on Census of—																		
	1790	1800	1810	1820	1830	1840	1850	1860	1870	1880	1890	1900	1910	1930	1940	1950	1960	1970	1980
W. No. Cent.	(x)	(x)	(x)	**1**	**2**	**7**	**11**	**19**	**29**	**43**	**50**	**54**	**57**	**47**	**44**	**42**	**37**	**35**	**33**
MN	(x)	(x)	(x)	(x)	(x)	(x)	2[a]	2	3	5	7	9	10	9	9	9	8	8	8
IA	(x)	(x)	(x)	(x)	(x)	2[a]	2	6	9	11	11	11	11	9	8	8	7	6	6
MO	(x)	(x)	(x)	1	2	5	7	9	13	14	15	16	16	13	13	11	10	10	9
ND	(x)	(x)	(x)	(x)	(x)	(x)	(x)	(x)	(x)	1[a]	1	2	3	2	2	2	2	1	1
SD	(x)	(x)	(x)	(x)	(x)	(x)	(x)	(x)	(x)	2[a]	2	2	3	2	2	2	2	2	2
NE	(x)	(x)	(x)	(x)	(x)	(x)	(x)	1[a]	1	3	6	6	6	5	4	4	3	3	3
KS	(x)	(x)	(x)	(x)	(x)	(x)	(x)	1[a]	3	7	8	8	8	7	6	6	5	5	5
So. Atl.	**46**	**56**	**62**	**61**	**61**	**47**	**43**	**36**	**43**	**49**	**50**	**53**	**56**	**54**	**56**	**60**	**63**	**65**	**69**
DE	1	1	2	1	1	1	1	1	1	1	1	1	1	1	1	1	1	1	1
MD	8	9	9	9	8	6	6	5	6	6	6	6	6	6	6	7	8	8	8
VA	19	22	23	22	21	15	13	11	9	10	10	10	10	9	9	10	10	10	10
WV	(x)	(x)	(x)	(x)	(x)	(x)	(x)	(x)	3	4	4	5	6	6	6	6	5	4	4
NC	10	12	13	13	13	9	8	7	8	9	9	10	10	11	12	12	11	11	11
SC	6	8	9	9	9	7	6	4	5	7	7	7	7	6	6	6	6	6	6
GA	2	4	6	7	9	8	8	7	9	10	11	11	12	10	10	10	10	10	10
FL	(x)	(x)	(x)	(x)	(x)	1[a]	1	1	2	2	2	3	4	5	6	8	12	15	19
E. So. Cent.	**3**	**9**	**18**	**25**	**33**	**32**	**32**	**28**	**34**	**36**	**37**	**38**	**39**	**34**	**35**	**32**	**29**	**27**	**28**
KY	2	6	10	12	13	10	10	9	10	11	11	11	11	9	9	8	7	7	7
TN	1[a]	3	6	9	13	11	10	8	10	10	10	10	10	9	10	9	9	8	9
AL	(x)	(x)	1[a]	3	5	7	7	6	8	8	9	9	10	9	9	9	8	7	7
MS	(x)	(x)	1[a]	1	2	4	5	5	6	7	7	8	8	7	7	6	5	5	5

W. So. Cent.	45	42	41	42	44	45	41	35	25	22	16	12	8	7	4	3	1	(x)	(x)
AR	4	4	4	6	7	7	7	7	6	5	4	3	2	1	1[a]	(x)	(x)	(x)	(x)
LA	8	8	8	8	8	8	8	7	6	6	6	5	4	4	3	3	1[a]	(x)	(x)
OK	6	6	6	6	8	9	8	5[a]	(x)	(x)	(x)	(x)	(x)	(x)	(x)	(x)	(x)	(x)	(x)
TX	27	24	23	22	21	21	18	16	13	11	6	4	2	2[a]	(x)	(x)	(x)	(x)	(x)
Mt.	24	19	17	16	16	14	14	8	7	5	2	1	(x)	(x)	(x)	(x)	(x)	(x)	(x)
MT	2	2	2	2	2	2	2	1	1	1[a]	(x)	(x)	(x)	(x)	(x)	(x)	(x)	(x)	(x)
ID	2	2	2	2	2	2	2	1	1	1[a]	(x)	(x)	(x)	(x)	(x)	(x)	(x)	(x)	(x)
WY	1	1	1	1	1	1	1	1	1	1[a]	(x)	(x)	(x)	(x)	(x)	(x)	(x)	(x)	(x)
CO	6	5	4	4	4	4	4	3	2	1	1[a]	(x)	(x)	(x)	(x)	(x)	(x)	(x)	(x)
NM	3	2	2	2	2	1	1[b]	(x)	(x)	(x)	(x)	(x)	(x)	(x)	(x)	(x)	(x)	(x)	(x)
AZ	5	4	3	2	2	1	1[b]	(x)	(x)	(x)	(x)	(x)	(x)	(x)	(x)	(x)	(x)	(x)	(x)
UT	3	2	2	2	2	2	2	1	1[a]	(x)	(x)	(x)	(x)	(x)	(x)	(x)	(x)	(x)	(x)
NV	2	1	1	1	1	1	1	1	1	1	1	1[a]	(x)	(x)	(x)	(x)	(x)	(x)	(x)
Pac.	61	57	52	43	33	29	19	13	11	8	5	4	2	2	(x)	(x)	(x)	(x)	(x)
WA	8	7	7	7	6	6	5	3	2	1[a]	(x)	(x)	(x)	(x)	(x)	(x)	(x)	(x)	(x)
OR	5	4	4	4	4	3	3	2	2	1	1	1	1[a]	(x)	(x)	(x)	(x)	(x)	(x)
CA	45	43	38	30	23	20	11	8	7	6	4	3	2	2[a]	(x)	(x)	(x)	(x)	(x)
AK	1	1	1	1[a]	(x)	(x)	(x)	(x)	(x)	(x)	(x)	(x)	(x)	(x)	(x)	(x)	(x)	(x)	(x)
HI	2	2	2	1[a]	(x)	(x)	(x)	(x)	(x)	(x)	(x)	(x)	(x)	(x)	(x)	(x)	(x)	(x)	(x)

(x) Not applicable.

[a] Assigned after apportionment.

[b] Included in apportionment act in anticipation of statehood.

Source: U.S. Bureau of the Census, Statistical Abstract of the United States, 1985 (Washington, D.C.: Government Printing Office, 1984), p. 242.

Table 4. Chronology of the States of the Union

1. Delaware	7 Dec. 1787	26. Michigan	26 Jan. 1837
2. Pennsylvania	12 Dec. 1787	27. Florida	3 Mar. 1845
3. New Jersey	18 Dec. 1787	28. Texas	29 Dec. 1845
4. Georgia	2 Jan. 1788	29. Iowa	28 Dec. 1846
5. Connecticut	9 Jan. 1788	30. Wisconsin	29 May 1848
6. Massachusetts	6 Feb. 1788	31. California	9 Sept. 1850
7. Maryland	28 Apr. 1788	32. Minnesota	11 May 1858
8. South Carolina	23 May 1788	33. Oregon	14 Feb. 1859
9. New Hampshire	21 June 1788	34. Kansas	29 Jan. 1861
10. Virginia	25 June 1788	35. West Virginia	20 June 1863
11. New York	26 July 1788	36. Nevada	31 Oct. 1864
12. North Carolina	21 Nov. 1789	37. Nebraska	1 Mar. 1867
13. Rhode Island	29 May 1790	38. Colorado	1 Aug. 1876
14. Vermont	4 Mar. 1791	39. North Dakota	2 Nov. 1889
15. Kentucky	1 June 1792	40. South Dakota	2 Nov. 1889
16. Tennessee	1 June 1796	41. Montana	8 Nov. 1889
17. Ohio	1 Mar. 1803	42. Washington	11 Nov. 1889
18. Louisiana	30 Apr. 1812	43. Idaho	3 July 1890
19. Indiana	11 Dec. 1816	44. Wyoming	10 July 1890
20. Mississippi	10 Dec. 1817	45. Utah	4 Jan. 1896
21. Illinois	3 Dec. 1818	46. Oklahoma	16 Nov. 1907
22. Alabama	14 Dec. 1819	47. New Mexico	6 Jan. 1912
23. Maine	15 Mar. 1820	48. Arizona	14 Feb. 1912
24. Missouri	10 Aug. 1821	49. Alaska	3 Jan. 1959
25. Arkansas	15 June 1836	50. Hawaii	29 Aug. 1959

Source: Encyclopedia of American History: Bicentennial Edition (New York: Harper & Row, 1976), p. 616.

BIBLIOGRAPHIC ESSAY:
GOING FURTHER INTO CENSUS HISTORY

This short essay is designed to direct scholars or general researchers to key sources on the history of the census and the growth of the federal statistical system. Readers are generally interested in the history for two reasons: They may be working on the history of statistics per se and are tracing the origins of a particularly statistical series, methodological tradition, or administration structure, or they may be interested in using the historical census data to acquire an understanding of the context and assumptions that went into the collection of the data or to determine whether unpublished data on the subject exists. The references listed below should address both interests in a general sense. Those interested in more detailed information are directed to the references in the footnotes.

General Histories of the Census and the Census Bureau

The major histories of the census are Carroll Wright and William C. Hunt, *History and Growth of the U.S. Census* (Washington, D.C.: GPO, 1900); W. Stull Holt, *The Bureau of the Census: Its History, Activities and Organization* (Washington, D.C.: Brookings Institution, 1929); and A. Ross Eckler, *The Bureau of the Census* (New York: Praeger, 1972). See also Hyman Alterman, *Counting People: The Census in History* (New York: Harcourt, 1969), and Ann Scott, *Census U.S.A.* (New York: Seabury Press, 1968). Wright and Hunt list all the census questions through 1890, major census legislation, publications, and the instructions to the enumerators. Holt contains tables on the laws, finances, and publications of the census and an annotated twenty-three-page bibliography on census history. Holt's study was a volume in the Brookings series of monographs on agencies of the U.S. government; other statistical agencies or other agencies with statistical programs are treated in other monographs. See also Congressional Research Service, *The Decennial Census: An Analysis and Review* (Washington, D.C.: GPO, 1980).

The best sources for details of early census procedures are the technical documents that accompanied the census. Record Group 29 at the National Archives contains what is left of the official records. See Katherine H. Davidson and Charlotte M. Ashby, comps., *Records of the Bureau of the Census* (Preliminary Inventory no. 161) (Washington, D.C.: National Archives and Records Service, 1964);

James B. Rhoads and Charlotte M. Ashby, comps., *Cartographic Records of the Bureau of the Census* (Preliminary Inventory no. 103) (Washington, D.C.: National Archives and Records Service, 1958); and later accessions to the collection. Some correspondence is in RG 48, Records of the Interior Department. The archival material is uneven: for some years all the forms and instructions are available; for others they have been destroyed. The instructions to the enumerators for the early twentieth-century censuses were published in the main census volumes and were usually published separately by the bureau for census users. The Census Bureau Library in Suitland, Maryland, contains more recent material (primarily post-1940). Several professional historians serve on the Census Bureau's official history staff in Suitland (Data User Services Division). They generally work on the agency's recent history.

Procedural histories are available for the censuses taken since 1940. See Robert M. Jenkins, *Procedural History of the 1940 Census of Population and Housing* (Madison, Wis.: University of Wisconsin Press, 1985); U.S. Bureau of the Census, *The 1950 Censuses: How They Were Taken* (Washington, D.C.: GPO, 1955); U.S. Bureau of the Census, *1960 Censuses of Population and Housing: Procedural History* (Washington, D.C.: GPO, 1966); U.S. Bureau of the Census, *U.S. Census of Population and Housing: 1970 Procedural History* (Washington, D.C.: GPO, 1976); and U.S. Bureau of the Census, *Census of Population and Housing (1980): History, 1980 Census of Population and Housing,* Parts A, B, and C (Washington, D.C.: GPO, 1986). The 1980 history is not yet complete.

Description of Census Questions, Schedules, and Publications

See U.S. Bureau of the Census, *Twenty Censuses: Population and Housing Questions, 1790–1980* (Washington, D.C.: GPO, 1979), or the older U.S. Bureau of the Census, *Population and Housing Inquiries in U.S. Decennial Censuses, 1790–1970,* Working Paper no. 39 (Washington, D.C.: GPO, 1973). For publications, see U.S. Bureau of the Census, *The Catalog of United States Census Publications, 1790–1945* (Washington, D.C.: GPO, 1950); U.S. Bureau of the Census, *Bureau of the Census Catalog of Publications, 1946–72* (Washington, D.C.: GPO, 1974); and the annual *Bureau of the Census Catalog.* See also Suzanne Schulze, *Population Information in Nineteenth-Century Census Volumes,* and *Population Information in Twentieth-Century Census Volumes, 1900–1940* (Phoenix, Ariz.: Oryx Press, 1983, 1985).

The manuscript schedules of the population censuses are available for public use seventy-two years after the census has been taken. Currently the schedules from 1790 to 1910 are available in the National Archives and in numerous libraries around the country. Most the schedules from the 1890 census were destroyed in a fire in the early twentieth century. Public Use Samples or Public Use Microdata Samples (PUMS) are available for the censuses of 1900 and 1940 through 1980. These data files are available from the Inter-University Consortium for Political and Social Research (ICPSR); they contain individual level data. The sample sizes range from 1 percent to 1 per thousand; some files are household samples, others sample individuals. See ICPSR, *Guide to Resources and Services* (Ann Arbor, Mich.: ICPSR, published annually since 1973). Further information about using old census data is available from ICPSR or the Data User Services Division of the Census Bureau.

Other References:

Joseph Duncan and William Shelton, *Revolution in United States Government Statistics, 1926–1976* (Washington, D.C.: GPO, 1976), traces the general growth of the federal statistical system in the first three-quarters of the twentieth century. U.S. Bureau of the Census, *Historical Statistics of the United States: Colonial Times to 1970,* 2 vols. (Washington, D.C.: GPO, 1975), contains the major compilations of published historical statistics. The technical notes direct the reader to data sources. The annual *Statistical Abstract of the United States,* now in its 107th edition, updates many of these tables and is also published by the Census Bureau. The Congressional Information Service's *American Statistics Index* indexes, abstracts, and microfiches every statistical publication of the U.S. government (published since 1973). The Census Bureau's monthly newsletter, *Data User News,* published since 1965, describes current programs and data. Before 1975, this was called *Small-Area Data Notes;* before 1970, *Small-Area Data Activities.* See also the bureau's *Factfinder* publications, particularly U.S. Bureau of the Census, *Census '80: Continuing the Factfinder Tradition,* comp. Charles P. Kaplan and Thomas Van Valey and Associates (Washington, D.C.: GPO, 1980). See also *Review of Public Data Use,* available since 1969. *American Demographics,* published monthly since 1979, and the *Numbers News,* published monthly since 1982, are a good entrée into the new demographics industry and its services and publications.

INDEX

Bureau of Corporations, 118, 119, 122, 123
Bureau of Efficiency, 129
Bureau of Fisheries, 119
Bureau of Foreign Commerce, 118–19
Bureau of Home Economics, 184
Bureau of Labor, 101, 104–5, 109, 117, 119. *See also* Bureau of Labor Statistics
Bureau of Labor Statistics, 117, 163, 167–68, 190
Bureau of Navigation, 119
Bureau of Standards, 119
Bureau of Statistics (Treasury), 117, 118, 122
Bureau of the Budget, 129, 220
Burr, Clinton Stoddard, 145
Bushnell, Horace, 57
Business Cycles and Unemployment, 162
Butler, Andrew, 40

Calhoun, John C., 29, 32, 35
Capt, J. C., 193
Carey v. Klutznick, 230–32
Carnegie Endowment, 126
Carter, Jimmy, administration of, 226
Cartography. *See* Census maps
Census, military uses of, 63–64. *See also* Civil War; World War I; World War II
Census adjustment, 229–32
Census Advisory Committee (ASA-AEA), 128–29, 159–60, 164, 167, 176, 199, 225–26
Census Advisory Committee on the Black Population, 225
Census Board, 35–40
Census clause. *See* Constitution
Census errors, 28–31. *See also* Census undercounts; Census overcounts; Survey error
Census legislation: *1790,* 13–14; *1800,* 18; *1810,* 18–19; *1820,* 23; *1840,* 26; *1850,* 34–42; *1880,* 95, 98–99; *1900,* 111–12; *1902,* 118–19; *1929,* 159–60
Census maps, 64, 67–68, 83, 92
Census of Boston, 45
Census of population: *1790,* 13, 14; *1800,* 18; *1810,* 18–19; *1820,* 23–25; *1830,* 14, 25; *1840,* 26–31, 50, 52; *1850,* 34–57; *1860,* 50, 59–68; *1870,* 50–51, 76–77, 86–94; *1880,* 50–51, 95–102; *1890,* 2, 106–9; *1900,* 111–14; *1910,* 123–25; *1920,* 2, 131–34; *1930,* 159–66; *1940,*

186–89; *1950,* 197–201; *1960,* 201–2; *1970,* 210–12, 221–22, 224; *1980,* 221–22, 225–35
Census overcounts, 124. *See also* Census errors; Survey error; Census undercounts
Census tallying, 43, 44, 49–51. *See also* Machine tabulation; Computerization of census processing
Census undercounts, 78, 89, 106–8, 124, 151, 195, 201–2, 210–12, 221–23, 228–34, 239. *See also* Census errors; Census overcounts; Survey error
Central Bureau of Planning and Statistics, 128
Central Statistical Board, 172, 174–76, 178, 183
Chandler, Alfred, 48
Chase, Salmon P., 64
Checks and balances, 10. *See also* Constitution
Civil Rights, U.S. Commission on, 224
Civil rights, 82, 238
Civil Rights Act of *1964,* 207, 224
Civil service, 100, 104, 114, 123
Civil War, 32, 63–68
Civil Works Administration, 176
Clague, Ewan, 171
Class of *1940,* 194–95
Clay, Henry, 38
Clayton, John M., 37
Cleveland, Grover, 105–6
Coalition for a Black Count, 212
Coast and Geodetic Survey, 118
COGSIS. *See* Committee on Government Statistics and Information Services
Cohen, Patricia Cline, 16, 20, 29
Colegrove v. Green, 208
Collamer, Jacob, 37
Commerce, Department of, 115, 118–19, 170, 172
Commerce and Labor, Department of. *See* Commerce, Department of
Committee on Government Labor Statistics (CGLS), 166, 171
Committee on Government Statistics and Information Services (COGSIS), 170–71, 173
Committee on the Scientific Work in Government, 119
Commons, John R., 143
Compendium (*1850* Census), 52, 53, 55
Compromise of *1850,* 33, 38, 48